Chrétien de Troyes
and the Dawn of
Arthurian Romance

Chrétien de Troyes and the Dawn of Arthurian Romance

WILLIAM FARINA

McFarland & Company, Inc., Publishers
Jefferson, North Carolina, and London

William Farina is also the author of *Perpetua of Carthage: Portrait of a Third-Century Martyr* (2009), *Ulysses S. Grant, 1861–1864: His Rise from Obscurity to Military Greatness* (2007), and *De Vere as Shakespeare: An Oxfordian Reading of the Canon* (2006), all from McFarland.

LIBRARY OF CONGRESS CATALOGUING-IN-PUBLICATION DATA

Farina, William, 1955–
 Chrétien de Troyes and the dawn of Arthurian romance / William Farina.
   p.   cm.
 Includes bibliographical references and index.

  ISBN 978-0-7864-4866-1
  softcover : 50# alkaline paper

 1. Chrétien de Troyes, 12th cent.— Criticism and interpretation.   2. Chrétien de Troyes, 12th cent.— Influence.   3. Arthurian romances — History and criticism.   I. Title.
PQ1448.F36   2010
841'.1— dc22   2010024739

British Library cataloguing data are available

©2010 William Farina. All rights reserved

No part of this book may be reproduced or transmitted in any form or by any means, electronic or mechanical, including photocopying or recording, or by any information storage and retrieval system, without permission in writing from the publisher.

Cover image: Pantaleone, mosaicist, monk. King Arthur rides to seek the Grail. Floor mosaic, 1166, Cattedrale, Otranto, Italy (Erich Lessing/Art Resource, NY)

Manufactured in the United States of America

McFarland & Company, Inc., Publishers
 Box 611, Jefferson, North Carolina 28640
 www.mcfarlandpub.com

To Marion — two hearts became one.

Table of Contents

Acknowledgments ix

Introduction 1

PART I. LITERARY THEMES: THE POET

1. Everyone Knows Lancelot Was French 11
2. Arabic Roots 19
3. From Wales to Brittany and Beyond 28
4. Medieval Feminism 36
5. *Cligès*, the Anti-Tristan 44
6. A Melting Pot of Ideas 52
7. The Desecration of Aquitaine 60
8. An Arthurian Geography Lesson 67
9. Geoffrey of Monmouth Proves Reading Is Believing 76

PART II. HISTORICAL THEMES: THE KNIGHT

10. The Birth of Chivalry 87
11. Erec, Enide, and the Pitfalls of Happiness 95
12. The Achievement of Malory 103
13. Restless Second Sons 111
14. Legacy of the Crusader Kingdoms 118

15. Normans Gone Native 126
16. The Fragile and Hard-Won Sanity of Yvain 134
17. A Dreadful Foreboding 143

Part III. Religious Themes: The Clergyman

18. Good Guys, Bad Guys, and No In-Betweens 155
19. The Problem with Merlin 164
20. Triumph of the Gothic 171
21. Perceval Gets Religion in Spite of Himself 179
22. The Grail and the Lance 187
23. Ecclesia Versus Synagoga 195
24. Chrétien Who? 203

Conclusion 211
Timeline of the High Middle Ages, 1000–1300 217
Chapter Notes 219
Bibliography 237
Index 241

Acknowledgments

This book could not have been written without many who tolerate and indulge me. Thanks yet again to Philip and Kathleen Farina, as well as to Jerome Bloom, for your endless encouragement and support. Thanks to Nancy Seeger for your unequivocal friendship. Thanks to Richard and Marion Bories for your hospitality and kindness. Thanks again to Alexandra Parfitt and to David Deis of Dreamline Cartography for their professional assistance. Thanks to the International Arthurian Society for doing what they do year after year — helping to bring it all together. Lastly, thanks to a younger generation of Breton storytellers for their contagious inspiration. A new chapter is eagerly anticipated by all.

Introduction

Powerful forces had been at work between the eleventh and the thirteenth centuries to transform Arthur from an insular into an international figure, from the subject of a purely Welsh and Cornish legend into a king whose literary fame rivaled that of Charlemagne, even in France itself.
— Roger Sherman Loomis.[1]

Non-specialists in medieval literature may be surprised to learn that definitive elements of the King Arthur legends originated not in England but in France. While Thomas Malory's watershed *Le Morte d'Arthur* (1485) more or less set the stage for modern interpretation of these stories, the very title of Malory's book hinted at his drawing upon pre-existing French source material. Upon first encounter, the tremendous scope and quality of these continental works can come as quite a shock to the Arthurian neophyte. One can easily see how Malory was inspired. Among these medieval French romancers, one name towers above all the rest: Chrétien de Troyes. In fact, it was Chrétien who pretty much single-handedly invented the Arthurian romance genre during the late 12th century, producing no fewer than five full-fledged romances of undisputed authorship, the very first of their kind and all written in octosyllabic verse.[2] As one compares this earlier material to the work of Malory, it becomes apparent that the King Arthur literary tradition was far more French and international in spirit and attitude than it was Welsh or Anglo. The French inventions created or utilized by Chrétien include the knights of the Roundtable (along with the pivotal figures of Lancelot and Perceval), emphasis on the unwritten code of chivalry and precepts of *amour courtois*, and the important symbolic designations of Camelot and the Holy Grail. On a strictly historical level, it is now generally agreed that these tales were the product of a dramatic cultural cross-fertilization, facilitated in part by the French-speaking Norman military machine that swept across western civilization during the first half of the High Middle Ages.

Praise for Chrétien's poetic legacy among modern critics has ranged from grudging, deep respect to fervent, unabashed adulation. During the 19th century, before the poet had been fully rediscovered by Arthurian enthusiasts, even French-biased commentators such as Gaston Paris only felt inclined to pay Chrétien a kind of backhanded compliment as a mere stylist: "Chrétien's great merit lay in his form: never before was the language handled with such ease and facile grace."[3] During the 20th century, however, the poet's reputation came into its own. Ruth Harwood Cline, the leading English translator of his work, pointedly summed up the near-universal current opinion: "Chrétien de Troyes was the creator of the Arthurian romance as a literary genre...." She specifies: "[H]e was the first known writer in Western Europe to put the Celtic legends of King Arthur and his knights into the long romance form in order to illustrate themes from the twelfth-century codes of love and chivalry."[4] Cline does not stop there, however: "[H]e dominates French literature of the twelfth century as Shakespeare did English literature of the sixteenth century."[5] This is not an isolated view. The imminent critic Leslie Topsfield writes, "Chrétien de Troyes has a Shakespearean talent for absorbing and refurbishing the ideas he inherits, and for responding to and refashioning courtly taste."[6] Robert Hanning and Joan Ferrante (students of Chrétien's pioneering contemporary, Marie de France) acknowledge that Chrétien was "the creator of the Arthurian romance," one who "dominates the age."[7] Julian Harris said, "[I]t is generally agreed that Chrétien was the best French writer of his time, that he wrote the first-known Arthurian romance, and that he created the genre." Harris adds that Chrétien was "the most sophisticated writer of a very sophisticated period."[8] Other modern commentators have expressed similar admiration. D.D.R. Owen maintains that "[Chrétien] has a rightful place among the greatest and most influential figures of world literature. Yet he is also one of the most enigmatic."[9] W.W. Comfort puts the poet's stature more into perspective: "[H]is significance as a literary artist and as the founder of a precious literary tradition distinguishes him from all other poets of the Latin races between the close of the Empire and the arrival of Dante."[10] Joseph Duggan, allowing that Chrétien's innovations may have been borrowed from unpreserved sources, still asserts that the poet was a central figure in world literature: "He is the inventor of the quest as a grand subject for romance, and if he did not invent the Grail and the adulterous liaison between Lancelot and Arthur's queen, he certainly made them popular topics to a degree that later writers of romance could not ignore, for he created an audience demand for them."[11]

Claude Luttrell simply called Chrétien the "father of Arthurian romance."[12] Among this chorus of contemporary praise, the only thing resembling dissent comes from staunch defenders of the Anglo-Arthurian tradition such as Roger Sherman Loomis, who nonetheless admits that "the influence of his five poems was prodigious."[13] Amazingly, however, and in spite of the very real "prodigious" influence to which Loomis referred, many modern readers of the King Arthur legends have never heard of Chrétien de Troyes — thus, the impetus behind this book.

In planning this project, I have been impressed with the seemingly never-ending proliferation of books, films and documentaries on Arthurian subject matter. Most of these works attempt to discover the "historical" King Arthur, as opposed to the one passed down to us in popular literature and tradition. Few have concerned themselves with the origins of the tradition itself, or the "make-believe" Arthur that has so thoroughly captured the imagination of the reading and non-reading public over the last millennium. There is room to fill in this latter niche. It is impossible to truly know the historical Arthur, since verifiable data is almost non-existent. By contrast, the literary trail of the fictional Arthur is right before our eyes (in several languages), allowing us to trace its development and embellishment from the very beginning. This genuine beginning of the Arthurian romance was firmly rooted in the 12th-century poetic genius of Chrétien de Troyes. Chrétien's unique contribution is a good example of a basic truth widely accepted among specialists, but less familiar to those who read or watch the tales strictly for pleasure or edification.

As the Roman Empire unraveled during the fifth century, Britain — unlike other Roman provinces — put up a stout and prolonged resistance to barbarian invasions that seemed to suddenly come from everywhere at once. In the end, Britain succumbed to these invasions like everyone else. By the time it did so during the sixth century, however, the name of Arthur had become immortalized as a symbol of this resistance, and by the High Middle Ages, it was synonymous with chivalry itself. In spite of this fame, the documented historical record is far less impressive. As the famed English scholar Edmund Chambers ruefully notes, "History, asked to determine how much of veritable fact may underlie the imposing structure of the Arthurian legend, can only give a cold response."[14] The greatest historian of the English Enlightenment, Edward Gibbon, pronounced that "[t]he severity of the present age is inclined to question the very *existence* of Arthur."[15] Gibbon's most telling comment underscores the aim of our study by admitting that even if Arthur did in fact exist, the myth is still more fascinating: "The events of his life are less interesting than the singular revolutions of his fame."[16] In a somewhat narrow sense, this book is a historiography (i.e., a history of a history), in which Arthur's literary embellishment, especially via the poetry of Chrétien de Troyes, is traced from its obscure Celtic origins to the mass media of the present day. The historical Arthur — if in fact there was one — would no doubt have been startled and perhaps amused by his modern portrayal in films such as the 1953 camp classic *Knights of the Roundtable*, or, for that matter, the 1960 hit musical *Camelot*.[17]

None of this is to say that the French romance writers did not need the original Celtic lore to create the international blockbuster which Arthur later became; on the other hand, without the skills of the French writers, it is likely that there would never have been a King Arthur in the conventional modern sense. Moreover, among the French, it was Chrétien who by far achieved the most in this regard. Loomis, in his classic work, *Celtic Myth and Arthurian Romance*, laments that the initial surge in Chrétien's prestige almost overshadowed the original Celtic source material:

> An influential body of them [modern scholars] consider the vast literature of the Round Table cycle as mainly springing from the imaginations of French authors of the twelfth and thirteenth centuries. The old practice of claiming as authority the tales of the "Bretons" they consider mere convention; the romances, broadly speaking, a late invention.[18]

Writing in opposition to Loomis, Luttrell tried to argue that some Welsh "sources" were either really using Chrétien or that both were using common sources so different from the later Norman-French versions in terms of manners and outlook as to be (not surprisingly) displaced in popularity as a result.[19] Luttrell accused Loomis of attempting to characterize Chrétien as a "literary hack" not worthy of his recent ascendancy in reputation.[20] This may be an overstatement of Chrétien's case; few scholars have done more than Loomis to sharpen our understanding of the Arthurian tradition. His work reminds us from whence came the raw materials used by the poet to transform Arthur and his knights into the stuff of timeless, borderless fame.

Virtually nothing is known of Chrétien as a man (see Chapter 24). The details of his life are impossible to pin down beyond a few general points outlined by Urban Holmes: that he belonged to the minor church orders, that he was somehow associated with the city of Troyes and possibly composed most of his works there, that Marie of Champagne and Philip of Flanders were among his patrons, that he possibly visited England, and that he was active during the late 12th century.[21] In relation to his works, more meaningful data can be gleaned from the times in which he lived.[22] Owen notes that Chrétien's romances, after over eight centuries, still present an astonishingly vivid image of the poet's environment:

> We are left with the impression of a strikingly superior and many-sided talent. Chrétien has bequeathed to us a brilliant portrait of the society that gave him his livelihood. Much of his detail is drawn from life; yet there is much too that represents the ideal of chivalric and courtly ethic. It was an ideal which, I believe, held for him a great sentimental attraction: this was society as he would like to see it, a society of delicate manners, impeccably courteous, generous, honourable. But at the same time he was a man of sound sense and clear vision, aware of things as they were. So he flaunted the high ideal, while constantly hinting that this was but a poet's dream. We can take it or leave it: it is up to us. But for himself, he remains at heart the realist, a quizzical spectator of life, more observer than moralist.[23]

This "spectator" over "moralist" aspect is crucial, especially if coming from a poet trained as a clergyman. Chrétien rarely passes overt judgment; instead, he paints a detailed portrait in words and lets his readers do the judging. Like all great writers, Chrétien makes readers feel as if they are close collaborators with the artist in the process of bringing old material back to life.

During the High Middle Ages, particularly during the 12th century, Europe finally began to pull itself out of the Dark Ages following the collapse of the Roman Empire. This collapse, which occurred during the fifth century, also precipitated events in England during the sixth century, which — incredibly enough — would in turn help to inspire a "12th century Renaissance" some 600 years later. The historical, political-military event setting the stage for this development more than any other — certainly more than any historical truth to Arthur's legend — was the French-Norman diaspora of the late 11th century. By the time Chrétien picked up his pen during the mid–12th century, the entire Mediterranean world, including the Middle East, had felt the weight of their marauding arms. In terms of long-term impact, however, it was the ruthless Norman conquest of England in 1066 that helped to eventually create a new English language and lay the groundwork for an obscure Celtic myth to be celebrated all the way from Spain and Italy to Germany and Scandinavia (see Chapter 13). Things came full circle. The Saxons of Germany and Scandinavia, who were originally the mortal adversaries of Britain during the era of Arthur's supposed existence, eventually embraced his romantic legend with perhaps more enthusiasm than anyone else. Three operas of Richard Wagner represent only the tip of the iceberg in this regard.[24] Gibbon, in his inimitable style, gives a concise description of this literary evolution in which the legend "was enriched with the various, though incoherent, ornaments which were familiar to the experience, the learning, or the fancy, of the twelfth century." Gibbon explains how the Celtic fable was first blended with ancient classics such as the *Aeneid* (beginning with Geoffrey of Monmouth), then combined with "the reigning manners of chivalry" and embellished with miracles and magic. These latter ingredients had poured into Europe after numerous pilgrimages to and holy wars against the then more civilized and literary-cultivated Arab civilization of Spain and the Middle East (see Chapter 2).[25]

As is often the case with pre-modern literature, there are no "original" manuscripts for Chrétien's works, only medieval copies dating from long after the poet's death. While some modern scholars have proposed — at first glance, not unreasonably — that this corpus of staggering size and scope was produced over the course of half a century, some very recent and convincing research to the contrary has been put forth.[26] Many distinguished modern authorities, beginning with Jean Frappier, have saluted the 1950s work of Anthime Fourrier, who persuasively argued for a much narrower time frame of composition, specifically from 1170 to 1181.[27] If correct, this means that one of the most influential bodies of poetry ever written by a single individual, one comprising over 30,000 lines of highly-disciplined, eight-syllable rhymed couplets, was composed over the course of approximately 11 years. Such an achievement would be comparable, if not superior to, the famed Ring cycle of four operas by Wagner, which took 26 years to complete, while Chrétien's Arthurian cycle of five romances may have taken less than 11. The prodigious impact of both on future generations has certainly been similar.

As in my previous study (on the Latin prison diary of Saint Perpetua), no attempt has been made to differentiate between variant, medieval manuscript sources. Even if I possessed the specialized language skills necessary to do this, it would deflect from my main point: namely, that translations from any language, particularly old ones into new, involve many objective and subjective choices made by the translator. In addition to word choice, source materials must be selected based on whatever is available at a particular time and place, and, more importantly, whatever is most congenial to the translator. Since there are no "original" manuscripts for Chrétien's work — the oldest extant date from the 13th century — variant readings in the Old French are, predictably, quite frequent. Thus what we, 21st-century English readers, ultimately behold depends not only on the style and vocabulary of the translator, but upon the evolution of the source material by medieval scribes — perhaps even more so the latter. To drive home this point, we shall periodically compare modern English translations of the same Old French text, not to judge between them, but rather to emphasize the difficulties and hurdles typically faced by modern translators of old books. Unless otherwise indicated, quoted line references from Chrétien are drawn from the magnificent series of translations made by Professor Cline, to which this reader is admittedly partial (see Bibliography). This is not to say, however, that other English translations are not worth seeking out, or that additional translations should not be made in the future; on the contrary, I would argue the more the merrier.

From this vantage point, it seems that today's interest in the *imaginary* Arthur is somewhat waning in favor of the *historical* Arthur, even though (as Gibbon pointed out long ago) the latter may well have never existed. This is doubly unfortunate because modern civilization seems to be descending into some sort of new, high-tech version of *Le Moyen Âge*, with an ever smaller percentage of the world's population exclusively controlling its once vast but now dwindling resources. As for my immediate aim to heighten awareness of Arthur's "Frenchness" among readers, one may well view this objective as a Quixotic endeavor. It is highly unlikely to take hold among those determined to glorify him as supposed proof of Anglo-American superiority, cultural and otherwise. If nothing else, this study may steer readers towards some very fine books on the subject. Above all, my intention is not to sound close-mindedly expert on this topic, but rather to impart my own learning process for the benefit of readers capable of forming their own opinions. Chrétien himself appears to have been a writer with formal education and rigid indoctrination, yet he also lived in times of tremendous change that would have challenged daily his reflexive preconceptions and long-held opinions. It would not be surprising if a person of this caliber of genius found himself occasionally changing his mind. The greatest literature — indeed, the greatest deeds in life — often result from such a dynamic, one might well argue. Could the fictional King Arthur himself be another outstanding product of western civilization's ongoing intellectual re-evaluation? If so, it would be a bonus, because as things presently stand, there can be no question that these stories are still well capable of engaging our collective attention.

PART I.
LITERARY THEMES: THE POET

Chapter 1

Everyone Knows Lancelot Was French

The irreligion of the religion of love could hardly go further. —C.S. Lewis.[1]

Modern misconceptions of the Arthurian legends usually begin with the famous knight who starts out as the king's most loyal subject but ends up being the unwitting instrument of his downfall. In the picturesque English landscape of this contemporary version, there can be no doubt from which country hails the very symbol of human weakness and socio-political discordance. The public image of Lancelot is French, thanks in part to the musical *Camelot* and Robert Goulet.[2] The Anglo-centric literary and dramatic persona of Lancelot the home-wrecker must of course be Gallic. And indeed, Lancelot has been French from the moment that Chrétien de Troyes first introduced him as a central Arthurian character during the late 12th century. In the interim, long forgotten is the early tradition that King Arthur himself was a symbol of human frailty, particularly with respect to lechery. This specific weakness would eventually prove his own undoing when he married Guinevere against the advice of Merlin. Moreover, the entire Arthurian cast (including its namesake) was, in the beginning at least, French in manners to varying degrees — not surprisingly, since they were almost exclusively the imaginary products of medieval French romancers.[3]

One thing most readers can agree upon is that Chrétien's character Lancelot has lived on powerfully in the popular imagination for over 800+ years. At a minimum, *Lancelot* or *Le Chevalier de la Charette* ("The Knight of the Cart") was, in the words of scholar Joseph Duggan, "one of the most influential works of the Middle Ages."[4] Leading English translator Ruth Harwood Cline chimes in, "The importance of *Lancelot* in literature cannot be exaggerated...."[5] Noting the work's springboard-like effect on other writers, Urban Holmes observed that "the combined poem was very popular. It was at the base of the great prose *Lancelot* of the thirteenth-century."[6] Holmes makes reference to the anonymous Lancelot-Grail cycle that later served as primary inspiration for Thomas Malory (see Chapter 12). This sprawling magnum-opus which followed in the wake of Chrétien's *Lancelot* was notable for, among many innovations, combining the Lancelot-Guinevere adultery thread with the Holy Grail motif into a single, unified tale. The timeless themes of worldly ambition frustrated by human frailty and the subsequent pursuit of heavenly perfection — themes impressively amplified in the Arthurian world by Chrétien — within a generation became one continuous narrative. It all appears to have begun, during the mid–1170s, with a seemingly distasteful commission to the poet by his noble patroness for him to expound upon the adulterous relationship between Queen Guinevere and one of Arthur's leading knights. No one knows exactly where the tale originated; all we know for certain is that Chrétien was the first to write it down.

Anyone with any life experience knows what it is to be forced to do something distasteful in order to earn a living. In effect, this is what Chrétien, as a *trouvère* in the Champagnois court, was compelled to do when he created his original *Lancelot*. As a religious cleric, Chrétien took a very dim view of marital infidelity; and yet, this was a subject he was required to glorify by the command of his patroness. Perhaps she was having fun by provoking him. Perhaps Chrétien had boasted once too often that he could outdo the scurrilous romances of the southern troubadours who were lacking in gravitas or true taste. In any event, he proceeded to turn a lemon into lemonade, as the saying goes.[7] This was accomplished first and foremost by injecting heavy doses of exaggeration into the work for the sake of maintaining a lighthearted tone. Roger Sherman Loomis classified *Lancelot* as a burlesque with "obvious humour," and the characterization is apt.[8] The work was produced in the genuine, tongue-in-cheek spirit of Ovid, viewing the more disreputable aspects of love through an ironic, over-the-top lens.[9] This attitude would in short order be erased or downplayed by later continuators, and the tale continues today to be told in a serious, cautionary light; nevertheless, Chrétien's initial Ovidian impulse was key to the work's world premiere.[10] Now, it seems odd to think that what started out as a parody eventually became a favorite tragic theme for world literature over the next millennium.

Like many of the world's greatest literary masterpieces, the sources and influences of *Lancelot* are as diverse as they are unlikely. In addition to Ovid (and rather obviously), the eponymous Tristan legend provided, if nothing else, a disreputable precedent to be avoided. Then the poet's classical training, courtesy of the cathedral schools, came into play, as did the conventions of courtly love from southern France, of which his patroness was a living embodiment and representative.[11] Numerous commentators have observed a thematic overlap between material in *Lancelot* and *The Art of Courtly Love* by Andreas Capellanus (see Chapter 4), including the controversial assertion that marital affection and arduous passion are mutually exclusive.[12] It may well be, however, that Andreas was influenced by Chrétien, rather than vice-versa, since *The Art of Courtly Love* is now, more often than not, dated to the following decade.[13] The most traceable source for Chrétien's version of the tale — specifically, the Guinevere abduction theme — probably comes from the 12th-century *Life of St. Gildas* by Caradoc of Llancarfan.[14] This was the same motif depicted in stone on the Cathedral of Modena during the early part of that same century (see Chapter 14). Neither Lancelot nor the adultery aspect of the legend, however, are mentioned in *Gildas*. It appears that Chrétien was the first to integrate these. Strictly speaking, the name Lancelot du Lac ("Lancelot of the Lake") first appears in Chrétien's Arthurian debut, *Erec and Enide* (line 1674), as a member of the Roundtable. This earlier, passing mention reinforces the impression that Chrétien was drawing upon some form of pre-existing and established oral tradition.[15]

The historical backdrop behind Chrétien's innovative work is no less complex or nuanced. Written (as the poet informs readers) at the express command of Marie de Champagne, the first 29 lines of the romance are in praise of his patroness, from whom he took "material and theme" (line 26). Holmes observes that "it is quite clear that Courtly Love is the principal theme in Lancelot," and that "Marie of Champagne had a Courtly Love fable in mind which she proposed to Chrétien for his elaboration."[16] The most likely range for dating is 1177 to 1181, during which time the poet also composed his *Yvain*.[17] During this approximate same period (1179–1181), Marie's husband, Count Henry the Liberal, was off crusading in the Holy Land. There are several allusions in the work to the Crusades, even though these are anachronisms since the historical epoch of King Arthur preceded the Crusades by several centuries, as well as the advent of Islam.[18] Within the story's chronology of events, the Christian feast days of Pentecost and St. John occur unusually close together, which was in fact the case in the year 1177.[19] Adding to this suggestive scenario is the fact that Marie was married to an absent husband nearly twice her age, to whom she had been engaged at age 13 and wed at age 19.[20] From all appearances, it was precisely the kind of marriage that possessed mutual friendship and affection, but not necessarily mutual passion; in short, not unlike the marriage between Arthur and Guinevere.

As all of this would suggest, the greatest influences for Chrétien's

Lancelot may have come from real life rather than from books or fables. This may also partially account for the poem's comparative uniqueness among the poet's Arthurian romances. While Chrétien used the opportunity to repeat and develop many of the same themes from his previous romance, *Cligès*, these concerns also seem to have flowed from his surrounding environment.[21] Duggan correctly asserts that the entire project probably fell under the spell of not only the Countess Marie, but also of Marie's mother, Queen Eleanor of Aquitaine, as did most other innovative literary ventures of the time. By the mid–1170s, Eleanor had been imprisoned for supporting her sons in their rebellion against their father and her husband, King Henry II; however, she was still the living symbol of Angevin culture and, as many have plausibly asserted, was possibly Chretien's original model for the character of Queen Guinevere herself.[22]

The purpose of this study is not to give detailed plot summaries; in brief, however, *Lancelot* consists of an episodic series of rapidly-paced vignettes in which the hero, in succession, rescues the queen from her abductors, makes love to her, and then successfully defends her honor. Notably, as the poet himself informs readers, he stopped writing nine-tenths of the way through the story and farmed out the rest for completion to another cleric, one Godefroy de Leigny.[23] It has been rationally surmised by critics that Chrétien most likely lost interest in what he perceived to be immoral subject matter and wanted to focus his remaining energies on completing *Yvain*. As Duggan explains, "*Lancelot* is in essential ways unlike his other romances. This is true above all on the thematic level. The love that Lancelot and Guinevere share is consummated in a scene of adultery that is out of keeping with the depiction of love in Chrétien's other works...."[24] Exploiting medieval poetic convention to its fullest, Chrétien does not identify Queen Guinevere by name until line 1098; as for the hero, he does not physically appear until line 271, and is not himself named (rather amazingly) until line 3660.[25] Before this sudden revelation, as the poet explains, Lancelot does not know "if he existed" let alone "his own name" (lines 716–717). The Countess Marie and her ladies-in-waiting surely smiled.

Transcending his censorious attitude towards the material, Chrétien found himself offering insights on human psychology and sexual attraction that appear to have been among the first of their kind in world literature — and have hardly been equaled since. Physical love, the proverbial schoolboy-schoolgirl crush — the Romeo and Juliet syndrome, if you will — is presented as an overpowering, irresistible force over which no one has any real control, a force sometimes triggered in mature and otherwise straight-laced adults (as modern psychology informs us) by sudden traumas in life. Lancelot and

Guinevere are not schoolchildren, and no one would mistake them for teenagers, yet they both find themselves, before they hardly realize what is happening, acting irrationally. Chrétien softens the blow by making the hero anything but promiscuous. Lancelot is constantly surrounded by beautiful women offering their favors to him, but his mind is set on one love and one love only. In an extraordinary sequence, Lancelot is given shelter by a sexual temptress in return for his promise to sleep with her; this promise he keeps by going to bed with his clothes on and then turning his back to her. After witnessing the hero's remarkable resolve and single-mindedness, the amorous hostess abandons her efforts. Later versions of the legend underscore the severity of Lancelot's eventual transgression with Guinevere by assigning him a pre-existing wife (Elaine) back in France, who dies of grief upon learning of her husband's affair with the queen. Their young son Galahad, however, grows up to become the traditional hero of the Holy Grail quest, displacing Chrétien's more fallible (and human) character in that same role, Perceval (see Chapter 21).

Lancelot's encounter with the amorous hostess serves as a cue for the poet to digress from the story with a stunning meditation on the nature of true romantic love. The beautiful Cline translation, written in octosyllabic verse (like Chrétien's French), captures the original inspiration:

> Those whom Love deigns to rule on earth
> should think themselves of greater worth.
> His heart has left Love so impressed,
> Love rules it over all the rest,
> and Love has filled it with such pride
> that I have no desire to chide
> if he rejects the one Love banned
> while he obeys Love's least command
>   [lines 1235–1242].[26]

To be in Lancelot's near-crazed state of mind is viewed by the poet almost as a privilege and sign of divine favor, rather than a curse or tragedy. Unrhymed English translations of the same verses frame the commentary in terms of a dramatic rhetorical question. Thus writes Burton Raffel:

> ... Love, which rules
> All hearts, allows them only
> One home. "All hearts?" No:
> All that Love finds worthy,
> Love's approval being worth
> A great deal. And Love valued
> Our knight higher than any,

> Creating such pride in his heart
> That I cannot blame him, and will not,
> For renouncing what Love denied him
> And striving for the love Love meant him
> To have...
>
> [lines 1237–1242].[27]

The power of love is seen as selecting of only the best and most worthy of human hearts. English prose translators W.W. Comfort, D.D.R. Owen, and David Staines are nearly identical in this respect. Like Raffel, they all have Chrétien asking "All hearts?" and then responding in the negative; only those hearts which Love "esteems" (Comfort) or "values" (Owen / Staines) are deemed worthy of the honor.[28] These are not words condemning adulterers to hellfire; rather it is a new way of looking at a complex situation — the poet may have even surprised himself by coming up with it.

Of the numerous trials and dangers Lancelot must pass through to prove his devotion to Guinevere, two in particular stand out. The first occurs early in the narrative when the hero is forced to temporarily mount a drawn executioner's cart, thus totally disregarding his personal honor as a knight — no small gesture to be sure. Lancelot agrees to the humiliation only after two steps' worth of hesitation. When he finally reaches Guinevere, she, instead of acting grateful, gives him the cold shoulder, later chastising Lancelot for slowness in casting aside honor for her sake. In this stunning passage, English translators are remarkably in sync with each other. Cline has Guinevere accusing Lancelot of being much "ashamed and afraid" as he "delayed" and "showed great reluctance."[29] In fact, Comfort, Owen, and Staines all use the word "ashamed," while Raffel opts for the ever-so-slight variant "shame."[30] In place of the word "delayed," other translators use verbs like "hesitated" and "lingered" or both (Raffel).[31] The power and clarity of this passage is such that five English interpreters working eight centuries later and several generations apart are all in near-agreement. The inspired poet was definitely on a roll, not unlike *la charrette* in the story.

After overcoming the mental anguish and public disgrace of the cart, the hero must endure intense physical pain. This he does to the nth degree while crossing a literal sword bridge, seriously lacerating himself in the process. This episode, which verges on the sadomasochistic, has provided modern English translators with a field day. Cline provides readers with a deliberate but concise snapshot:

> With greatest agony in store
> he crossed the bridge. His pain was sore;
> hands, knees, and feet were cut and bleeding,

> but Love, while guiding him and leading,
> consoled him, so his pains were sweet.
> He used his hands and knees and feet,
> and crawled across the narrow plank
> until he reached the other bank
>   [lines 3111–3118].[32]

Raffel, using free-form verse, memorably postulates that the power of romantic love can directly transform suffering into joy:

> ... accepting the immense
> Pain and suffering, he crossed,
> Hands and knees and feet
> Bleeding. But Love, who had led him
> There, helped him as he went,
> And turned his pain to pleasure.
> When he came to the other side
> None of his wounds were hurting
>   [lines 3115–3122].[33]

Other English prose writers add their own variations. For Comfort, Lancelot's "suffering is sweet" while love "assuages and relieves the pain."[34] Owen has Lancelot given "complete comfort and relief so that all his suffering is pleasant to him."[35] In a similar (and for the medieval convention, quite appropriate) medical vein, Staines has love offering Lancelot "relief and medication; for this reason his suffering was sweet."[36] For the hero, any pain can become pleasurable if endured in the name of true romantic love. The notion is simultaneously serious and comic, which was likely the poet's intent.

In a long work relentlessly packed with hyperbole and irony, the near-absurd middle finale comes in the aftermath of Lancelot and Guinevere consummating their passion. As an unnoticed Lancelot leaves the queen by secret necessity, he genuflects towards her bedroom in a gesture of humble piety. Duggan observes, "The religion of secular love has taken precedence over what can only be characterized as superficial Christianity, just as love service has triumphed over the vassal's fidelity to his lord."[37] Translators have Lancelot variously describing the bedroom (in the eyes of Lancelot) as a "shrine" (Comfort), "altar" (Raffel / Owen / Staines) or "altarstone" (Cline).[38] Raffel specifies that Lancelot "bowed and crossed himself" while Staines characterizes Lancelot as a "suppliant."[39] Rather than being elated at the success of their undetected tryst, Lancelot departs "sadly" (Raffel), "dejected" (Cline), "with a heavy heart" (Comfort) and in "deep anguish" (Owen / Staines).[40] Loneliness at being parted from his beloved — rather than guilt or shame — overrules all other emotions. Once again, the poet opts to ennoble the hero's sentiments rather than to condemn, thus making the hero more sympathetic despite what has transpired. This is not the kind of dramatized adultery that modern audiences are used to seeing.

It is nearly impossible to read Chrétien's *Lancelot* with any understanding and not come away amazed at the poet's high-mindedness. He was determined not to let a potentially sordid tale become prurient or smutty, perhaps out of necessity to earn a living, but also perhaps because his genius just happened to stumble onto something new. What started out as soap-opera entertainment ended as something completely new in the guise of the old, as C.S. Lewis put it rather perceptively (see Chapter 6). Rather than play to the lowest common denominator, the romance instead attempted to glorify all that is good, refined, and admirable in humankind. During the historical interim with the present, however, these attractive qualities in the story of Lancelot and Guinevere have somehow been lost or become submerged. Everyone knows Lancelot was French. What most do not seem to know is that Lancelot, at least in his original incarnation, is a universal figure who crosses international borders more easily than King Arthur does in his legendary military exploits. What the French cannot take credit for, on the other hand, is the invention or poetic expression of these finer sentiments. While Chrétien appears to have been the first western writer to give them an articulate voice, a growing number of scholars seem to agree that the courtly love ethos appears itself to have originated outside France, if not outside Europe entirely.

Chapter 2

Arabic Roots

> *If we compare, at the æra of the crusades, the Latins of Europe with the Greeks and Arabians, their respective degrees of knowledge, industry and art, our rude ancestors [the Latins] must be content with the third rank in the scale of nations* — Edward Gibbon.[1]

Where did Lancelot come from? To be more precise, where did the *idea* for him originate? Obviously, Chrétien was the first writer to record the name and legend of Lancelot, and may have been, for all practical purposes, the poet who created the story exclusively from his own imagination, although this seems rather unlikely. As a very great artist once quipped, good artists borrow and great artists steal.[2] Although Chrétien certainly imposed a powerful stamp of originality upon the tale, he was likely working with some kind of oral tradition and in fact says as much in the text by crediting his patroness, Marie de Champagne, as a main source. The most plausible scenario for the creation of this landmark text is that the poet took a pre-existing, popular story and embellished it, both consciously and subconsciously, with a host of influences to which he had been exposed throughout his career. These influences in turn extended back to ancient times and beyond Europe. Like most other worthwhile human achievements, Chrétien's *Lancelot* was a collaborative effort in the broadest sense, one in which the lasting public presentation of the work was crystallized by the genius of someone who happened to be in the right place at the right time.

Although the exact details of this extraordinary event are forever lost to the obscurities of time, a few good surmises can be made by anyone possessing a rudimentary knowledge of world literature. At this point, a brief restatement of some basic, generally agreed-upon-facts may prove useful. First, the classics of ancient Greek and Latin authors were being rediscovered by European writers during the 12th century, via the cathedral schools, and it is likely that Chrétien was trained in this manner, given the repeated classical points of reference in his writing. Second, these classical works had to be "rediscovered" because they were, for the most part, completely lost during the European Dark Ages after the fifth century A.D. Third, and worth constant repetition because of its stubborn lack of acceptance in western circles, is that classical learning was preserved largely through the efforts of non-western, Islamic scholars just as it was being lost and forgotten in Europe. Moreover, it was through the process of Islamic scholarship coming into contact with revived European learning and curiosity that these ancient treasures were re-introduced into the western canon. In this specific sense, the roots of Chrétien's *Lancelot* were Arabic. For example, the all-pervasive influence of the courtly love ethos in the creation of the Arthurian legend probably originated from the multi-cultural pressure cooker of Muslim Spain, where it had been inspired in part by the respected traditions of classical poetry and philosophy. These attitudes were in turn reinterpreted by the troubadours and *trouvère* of neighboring medieval France.

For those with any familiarity with western history and geography, one question naturally poses itself regarding the relationship between classical traditions and the Arthurian legends; namely, why did it seem to come through Muslim Spain and not the Byzantine Empire? The Greeks of Constantinople were, after all, Christians like the Latins of Europe. They also shared the western classical tradition, as well as geographic boundaries with Latins and Muslims, both of whom they were constantly at war with (though more so the latter). Why did ancient Greek and Latin traditions have to make a circuitous route through North Africa and Spain to France, as opposed to directly from eastern Europe to France, especially since French crusaders were traveling these routes regularly from the 11th century onwards? A definitive answer to this question must remain indeterminate, devilishly complex, and, in any event, well beyond the scope of this investigation. A few conjectures, however, may prove useful at this early stage. For one, the direct land route from Damascus to Troyes over eastern Europe may have been somewhat shorter in distance, but was in many ways more difficult in that multiple cultural divides had to be crossed instead of just one. Apart from language differences and a devastating religious schism that occurred between Catholic Rome and Orthodox Constantinople during that epoch, the hostility of eastern versus western culture was an ancient one and, for that matter, was far more entrenched than any hostility either had with followers of the Prophet. This deep divide found frequent expression in the numerous Latin-Greek wars of the period, which were in many ways more savage and destructive than any conducted against their Islamic neighbors.

For reasons such as these, the Byzantine Greeks may have been more a barrier than transmitter of classical learning to the French, as opposed to the Arabs of 11th-century Andalusia. By the second half of the 12th century, Spanish Muslims were merely trying to hold on to what they had. Although the Byzantine Greeks were in much the same position — they would spend the next three centuries fighting a losing war of survival against the Ottoman Empire — it must have not seemed that way at the time.[3]

A close read of Chrétien's Arthurian romances reveals indirect Arabic influences at every turn. The only reason these are not completely self-evident is that, like most other Arabic influences in western society, they are so omnipresent as to be forgotten or nearly taken for granted. We tend to forget that something so innocuous as the game of chess, conspicuously mentioned in several of Chrétien's romances (*Erec and Enide*, *Perceval*), originated in the Middle East long before becoming fashionable in medieval Europe. Instead, the easy tendency is often to conveniently reinvent history as it suits our whims, or worse, to reinvent the past in a condescending manner. Eminent Crusades historian Christopher Tyerman has recently highlighted the problem:

> A familiar but baneful response to history is to configure the past as comfortingly different from the present day. Previous societies are caricatured as less sophisticated, more primitive, cruder, alien. Such attitudes reveal nothing so much as a collective desire to reassure the modern observer by demeaning the experience of the past.[4]

A more useful approach, especially for any accurate contextualization of the Arthurian legends, is to identify that which we think belongs exclusively to our own society, and then to examine more closely where these things really come from, or at least how they have traveled through the past. The Arabic origins of European love poetry are only one small example of how this method can be applied. When the total dismissiveness of scholars towards this idea a century ago, or even a quarter century ago, is compared to its current widespread acceptance, one is reminded of similar sudden and dramatic shifts in modern academic thinking — say, the tectonic plate theory in geological science.

Today, it is easy to find respectable endorsement for the proposition that modern European love poetry originated in Islamic Spain, though the average western man on the street may still take umbrage at the suggestion. A respected religious historian like Karen Armstrong may state with unimpeachable matter-of-factness that "the cult of Courtly Love was probably inspired by Arab love poetry which Christians encountered in Spain and southern Europe," and yet such a statement makes an impression only on those who are open to the idea in the first place.[5] Referring to the brief period in which the Byzantine Empire was ruled by western interests and to how the works of Aristotle arrived in western Europe via Spain, Edward Gibbon, one of the most admired historians of all time, and a specialist in this particular field, spelled out the truth of the process for anyone willing to listen:

> Yet in a reign of sixty years, the Latins of Constantinople disdained the speech and learning of their subjects; and the manuscripts were the only treasures which the natives might enjoy without rapine or envy. Aristotle was indeed the oracle of the Western universities; but it was a barbarous Aristotle; and, instead of ascending to the fountain-head, his Latin votaries humbly accepted a corrupt and remote version from the Jews and Moors of Andalusia.[6]

Thus the "backdoor" theory of intellectual influence on France from Spain cannot even be classified as a new idea — it was being advocated by Gibbon and probably others as well during the 1700s, if not before that. During the 1800s, a translator of no less the caliber of Sir Richard Francis Burton maintained that medieval love poetry was more Arabic than Christian in its origins.[7] In more recent times, medieval specialist John Parry has written:

> The matter is still in dispute, but of the various possibilities that have been suggested the most reasonable seems to be that the troubadours were influenced by the writers of Moslem Spain, where many of the elements can be found before they appear among the Christians.[8]

This commentator does not intend to dwell much further on the matter, except to state that he unequivocally accepts the notion, but admittedly was not much aware of it before coming into contact with the French inventors of the Arthurian legend. Chrétien himself may not have been aware of it, although another possibility is that he knew quite well and was trying to improve upon a perceived heathen tradition.

Foremost among the surviving works of Andalusian Arabic poetry from that period, and often held up as a forerunner of the western courtly love style (as well as a transmitter of its style), is the early 11th-century masterwork, *Tawq al-Hamāma*, or *The Neck-Ring of the Dove*, by Ibn Hazm of Cordova. American historian David Levering Lewis, typical of a growing academic trend, recently pronounced this landmark of world literature a "masterpiece of courtly love" which "Europe's troubadours imbibed ... like fine wine."[9] Pioneering western scholars such as Roger Boase and Lois A. Giffen began to tout the importance of this poem during the last quarter of the preceding century, noting that Ibn Hazm's psychological insights on sensual love represented a major advance beyond the highly ironic and often bawdy love lyrics of Ovid and other Roman poets.[10] Boase forcefully stated a theme that is increasingly resonating among those who study this topic:

> In view of the long history of cultural contacts and sharing, including even marriage alliances in several instances between Christian and Muslim rulers, and patronage of Arab Muslim scholars, Arabized Jewish scholars and musicians by Christian rulers, it would seem quite incredible, in truth, if no ideas about love were discussed in these circumstances, when the influence in other areas of the arts, language, learning and material culture are well documented.[11]

None of this is to say that the French troubadours and *trouvère* had nothing new to add to the Arabic tradition. Parry, while definitely acknowledging the influence of works such as *The Dove* on western poetry, also points to significant differences. For one, the idealized woman in *The Dove* must be unmarried in the Arabic tradition (as opposed to married in the European one), while the French poets, at least in the north, were careful to add a spiritual or Platonic dimension to the sensual love glorified by Ibn Hazm.[12] This goes well beyond mere technical devices such as metrical similarities between troubadour and Moorish poetry, and well beyond stylistic jargon, such as the poet addressing his mistress in masculine, feudal terms such as "my lord" (see Chapter Four).[13]

Recent chroniclers of that time and place such as Levering Lewis and Maria Rosa Menocal have used, rather appropriately, the 1064 siege of Barbastro as a microcosm of how Arabic ideas and values were quickly transmitted to France via Spain (see Chapter 15). As Lewis reminds his mostly western readership:

> The Christians who besieged Barbastro under the pope's standard for forty days in 1064 were the unbathed, larcenous forerunners of a hundred thousand holy warriors whose sins would be forgiven in advance and salvation certified by Christ's vicar.... The Normans assimilated the culture of the conquered with a zest that their Muslim contemporaries reported with aggrieved curiosity. The Christian knights were entranced by the lyrics of the *qiyan* (singing girls) and seduced by the manners of their wealthy hostages.[14]

In nominal command of these "unbathed, larcenous forerunners" was Duke William VIII of Aquitaine, the great-great grandfather of Chrétien's patron who commissioned *Lancelot*, Marie de Champagne.[15] Nor was this an isolated and distant connection; Duke William's son and grandson (Marie's great grandfather and grandfather, respectively) also spent a lot of time in Spain during the *Reconquista*.[16] As Muslim rule began to permanently lose its foothold in the Iberian Peninsula after the fall of Toledo in 1085, unique Islamic contributions to world literature were simultaneously beginning a much different kind of conquest in France and western Europe. The family line that would produce key figures such as the first troubadour poet (William IX) and key supporters of courtly love literature (Marie and her mother, Eleanor of Aquitaine), thus became promoters for what later became the defining style of Arthurian romance.

A new poetic style was not the only intellectual property being transmitted from Spain to France, though (curiously enough) it has proven to be among the most controversial. As eminent Arthurian commentator Roger Sherman Loomis accurately observed over a generation ago:

> Every medieval scholar recognizes the great debt which the West owed to Arabic science and philosophy, and it is increasingly realized how prosperous and refined was the society of Moorish Spain in the eleventh and twelfth centuries. And in spite of intermittent wars, and partly because of them, there was a flow of cultural influences to the north.[17]

Ancient Greek scientific and philosophic traditions came to medieval France not, surprisingly enough, from the Greek Byzantine Empire, but roundabout from Arabia through Spain. Today, historians such as Levering Lewis agree that science, medical knowledge, astronomy, and philosophy — like the poetic arts — first came to France and the West via Islamic Spain:

> In the polarized twelfth century, the flow of knowledge gave way to a virtual flood. Muslim learning, having seeped into the Christian West for decades from Andalusia, commenced a torrential outflow. It was a process mimicking osmosis at first and, later, a conveyor belt.[18]

This process would prove highly significant for the Arthurian romances of Chrétien, since his poetry was often set apart by its newfangled use of physiology in relation to human love, particularly in making explicit connection between the senses (especially eyesight) and feelings of the heart. To be exact, this trend had begun somewhat earlier in France during the 12th century with works directly inspiring Chrétien such as the *Roman d'Enéas*.[19] It was Chrétien, however, who first made poeticizing about love in this precise manner *de rigueur*, a standard which continues to the present day.

Given these historical circumstances, it is important to view Chrétien's Arthurian innovations as part of a larger trend within the sphere of European learning. Since it was likely that the poet was trained as a cleric, he would have been ideally placed to have acutely felt and taken advantage of this revolutionary development. Armstrong, writing with respect to the religion and philosophy of the time, makes the pointed observation that during the twelfth century, European scholars had flocked to Spain, where they encountered Muslim scholarship. With the help of Muslim and Jewish intellectuals they undertook a vast translation project to bring this intellectual wealth to the West. Arabic translations of Plato, Aristotle and the other philosophers of the ancient world were now translated into Latin and became available to the people of Northern Europe for the first time. The translators also worked on more recent Muslim scholarship, including the work of Ibn Rushd as well as the discoveries of Arab scientists and physicians.[20]

Armstrong makes reference to the seminal work of the Andalusian philosopher Abu al-Walid ibn Ahmad ibn Rushd of Cordova (1126–1198), better known in the West as Ibn Rushd or Averroës, and widely admired by both Christian and Jewish thinkers of the era. Later, during the 13th century, his extensive commentaries on Aristotle were translated into Latin and these heavily influenced the Catholic theologian Thomas Aquinas.[21] The great Jewish disciple of Averroës was Rabbi Moses ibn Maimon (1135–1204), better known as Maimonides, and like Averroës, hailed originally from Cordova.[22] Maimonides later produced his *Guide for the Perplexed* (1190), which Levering Lewis declared to be "the highest triumph of Arabic Aristotelian scholarship."[23] While Chrétien probably never heard of Maimonides or his work, it is hard to imagine the poet's Arthurian corpus, so imbued with scientific and psychological causal connections, without the same broader trend that led to these parallel, contemporary syntheses.

Back in Spanish Toledo during this same period, perhaps the most remarkable of all Arabic poetry translations was then taking shape. In the year 1143, an English-born, French-educated clergyman by the name of Robert of Ketton, assisted by Herman of Carinthia and at least one unidentified Muslim scholar, translated the *Qur'an* into Latin. This stunning commission had been given to Ketton by none other than Peter the Venerable (1092?–1156), Abbot of Cluny (see Chapter 20). Unlike his more xenophobic (and more influential) contemporary, Saint Bernard of Clairvaux (see Chapter 18), Peter believed that Christendom could benefit from studying Islamic texts. The result was a highly flawed but important watershed event in world literature, in some ways demarking the true initiation of ancient learning being re-introduced into western universities. As Levering Lewis summed up, "Another hundred years of such rarified Judeo-Christian-Muslim collaboration as that at Toledo would produce the entire corpus of the recovered ancient learning known today."[24] If the *Qur'an* itself was now being translated and disseminated, then the flow of information from Islamic Spain to Christian France must have indeed been irresistible.

No one will ever know precisely how Chrétien was impacted by these intellectual currents, except to the extent these are reflected in the text. It would be quite extreme, on the other hand, to insist that the greatest poet of the 12th century was completely oblivious to the foremost literary trend of his time. As for the text itself, even surface traits are indicative. Spain is overtly mentioned or alluded to in all five of Chrétien's Arthurian romances, a distinction not held even by Wales, the traditional homeland of Arthur.[25] Part of this was due to Chrétien's sources being under the same influence. For example, Geoffrey of Monmouth has the enemies of King Arthur (upon his second invasion of France) muster from all over the Muslim world, even though Islam did not begin until long after the alleged historical epoch of Arthur. Some of these enemies include King Ali Fatima of Spain, kings of Africa (read: North Africa), plus kings or dukes of the Parthia, Persia, Libya, Egypt, Babylon, Phrygia, and Syria — all geographic areas that later became Muslim.[26] More important than these surface characteristics are similarities in style and attitude, which were eventually transformed into the European concept of courtly love, as epitomized in works such as Chrétien's *Lancelot*. As C.S. Lewis observed, "Every one has heard of courtly love, and every one knows that it appears quite suddenly at the end of the eleventh century in Languedoc [southern France]." Lewis gives a good, short definition of courtly love as "Humility, Courtesy, Adultery, and the Religion of Love"— Lancelot's character in a nutshell. He then adds that "the whole attitude has been rightly described as 'a feudalisation of love.'"[27] Putting it all into perspective, Lewis concluded:

> French poets in the eleventh century, discovered or invented, or were the first to express, that romantic species of passion which English poets were still writing about in the nineteenth. They effected a change which has left no corner of our ethics, our imagination, or our daily life untouched, and they erected impassable barriers between us and the classical past or the Oriental present. Compared with this revolution the Renaissance is a mere ripple on the surface of literature.[28]

So much for Shakespeare! Although no troubadour or *trouvère* was ever known to have said, "Yes, I stole this from the Andalusians" (and even that would not satisfy many doubters), it makes perfect, intuitive, common sense that the entire process occurred pretty much in this manner.

Arabic origins in feeling and style, however, were only one part of a very complex process, as we shall presently see. During the 12th century, this new literary aesthetic would collide head-on in France with another irresistible force coming down from the British Isles, the "matter of Britain," as it has been sometimes mislabeled. This collision was in turn shaped and configured by a host of myriad influences that, after 800 plus years, is still only barely understood by specialists in the field. The truly amazing aspect of the event is that, like many a great recipe, the individual ingredients were so unlikely a combination and yet so fabulous when blended together in precise proportions. No mere mortal could have planned it that way. It surely happened by means of some happy accident, and rather suddenly at that. Chrétien de Troyes then proved to be the talented fountainhead of its poetic expression for all of posterity.

Chapter 3

From Wales to Brittany and Beyond

> *A class of wandering minstrels, with histrionic talents, found that this novel material captivated barons and their ladies, not only in Brittany but wherever French was understood. More and more they adapted fantastic tales to French tastes, manners, and standards of rationality, costumed their characters according to the latest mode, and introduced all the pageantry of chivalry. Their audiences, somewhat bored by a monotonous diet of epics dealing with the quarrels and wars of Charlemagne and his paladins, were fascinated by the new and various tales of love and marvel and adventure, and were easily persuaded to accept the Breton image of Arthur as the nonpareil of kings—* Roger Sherman Loomis.[1]

Not long ago, a German-American friend of the author, upon learning of the Breton roots of the King Arthur legends, declared: "I knew it. The whole Lady of the Lake thing smacks of Frenchness." This remark elicited hearty laughter from all standing within earshot; nevertheless, the thought was not intended to be ironic or sarcastic. The Lady of the Lake *was* French, as was Lancelot, and, arguably, King Arthur himself. In point of fact, many broad and specific aspects of the legends today normally associated with Arthur originated in the imaginations of poets and storytellers hailing from French-speaking areas of the European continent. Yes, certain details had their beginnings in the British Isles, but it was the French—Chrétien de Troyes in particular—who amplified this primitive and provincial Celtic lore into an international phenomenon. The subsequent propagation and dissemination of Chrétien's work represented the first and perhaps greatest literary diaspora of the High Middle Ages in western culture. Within a generation, the triumphs and tragedies of King

Brittany and Wales
C. 1170

Arthurian lore from the Dark Ages first traveled from English Wales to French Brittany, where it found favor and imaginative embellishment at the hands of professional storytellers and entertainers. The boundaries between these two regions were so fluid that Chrétien's arch-hero Yvain travels from one to another within the span of two days, with no mention of the "English" Channel.

Arthur would be on the lips of everyone throughout Europe and, in some cases, well beyond Europe.

One must of course begin in Great Britain and Wales to discover the first literal references to the name of Arthur during the Dark Ages. These sources were comprehensively identified during the previous century by British and American scholars, not least among whom was the late, great Roger Sherman Loomis. From a strictly mythical and poetic standpoint (the focus of this study), the Arthurian tradition may date back as far as the 6th century to the Welsh bard Taliesin, although this is impossible to prove and factually improbable, though still a remote possibility.[2] The name Arthur is itself Welsh in origin.[3] More important to the romance tradition which later started and flourished under the pen of Chrétien was Celtic source material for the stories that he developed. For example, the Welsh *Mabinogion*, a collection of ancient prose tales, the earliest surviving version of which was written down a century after Chrétien's death, contains the rough outlines for no fewer than three of his major works: *Erec and Enide* (adapted from *Gereint, Son of Erbin*), *Yvain* (taken from *Owein* or *The Lady of the Fountain*), and *Perceval* (based on *Peredur*).[4] The main thing to keep in mind, however, is that these older stories bear only the faintest resemblance to ones later versified by the poet and other French romancers who came after him. As Edmund Chambers cautioned, "One must beware of exaggerating the Celtic element in the *matière de Bretagne*."[5] The Welsh originals provided Chrétien with raw material and basic outlines as a mere starting point for something which later became epics that the Welsh bards would hardly have recognized, if at all. A major factor behind this transformation was that various intellectual influences were coming into France from a number of distinctive, simultaneous directions, and Wales happened to be only a single component of this (see Chapter 6). The poet also happened to be in the right place at the right time, and with the right training and background, to take full advantage of this convergence. The final result represented one of the great literary syntheses of all time.

As suggested elsewhere in this book, King Arthur would have likely remained an obscure local legend (or possibly even faded completely from memory) had not an important world event occurred during the 11th century. In the year 1066, England, admittedly after putting up a good fight, was decisively and forever conquered by a close coalition of Norman cavalry and Breton infantry fighting under the banner of Duke William at the battle of Hastings. To paraphrase Loomis, when the Normans conquered England, Arthur returned with them to re-conquer England, especially in transplanted English-Breton households, as well as those of the Anglo-Normans.[6] This is a slightly different take than that of historian Edward Gibbon, who suggested that the Norman fondness for Arthur came mainly into being after the conquest (see the opening quote to Chapter 9). During this same period, it was Breton *jongleurs* who embellished and couriered the legends — in other words, made them popular. They succeeded in turning their fabrications into a deeper truth. They were most likely the key players in the preliminary process leading to Chrétien's later achievement. The first written manifestation of this burgeoning popularity came early in the 12th century with *The History of the Kings of Britain* by Geoffrey of Monmouth (see Chapter 9), himself of probable Breton origin. With the temporary unification of the Anglo-Norman kingdom on both sides of the channel, the fame of King Arthur began to fan out across the European continent. Even by the end of the 11th century, hundreds of male children in the Breton-speaking portions of France were being named Arthur.[7] Loomis reminds us, "We can safely conclude, therefore, that the Matter of Britain originated in the blending of historic reminiscences of a British battle-leader with a highly fanciful mythological tradition going back to pagan times."[8] He then goes on, however, to specify that this "blending" should be primarily credited to Breton storytellers or *conteurs*, along with their most famous exponent, Geoffrey of Monmouth.[9] It is sometimes said that the Irish are the world's greatest liars, but the Bretons would probably give them a good run for their money.[10] Fortunately for the western tradition, one result of this propensity was the attractive projection of the Arthurian legend far beyond the British Isles.

By the end of the 12th century, thanks to the Bretons, Normans, and French, the legacy of Arthur had spread across Europe to Spain, Italy, Germany, and Scandinavia. Loomis, who believed that the personage of Arthur had some sort of factual basis, summarized: "The probabilities are that Arthur began his career in history, extended his conquests into the realm of Welsh, Dumnonian and Breton myth, and completed his triumph by achieving the sovereignty of European romance."[11] As this was the era of the Crusades, Arthur may have served as a convenient symbol of supposed European invincibility. Period artwork can still be seen portraying a legendary 6th-century English king riding a camel.[12] In pondering how garbled Celtic folklore of dubious historicity from the Dark Ages found itself transported to the desert sands of Arabia or Africa within a few generations, one must give credit where credit is due. In an illiterate age of oral tradition — one in which the printed word was unknown — the power of reading and writing could still be substantial, especially during the High Middle Ages. Thanks to the French language (the European predecessor to English as the contemporary language of all nations), and thanks to Norman military aggression which concentrated staggering amounts of wealth into a few hands (see Chapter 13), book learning began to make a serious comeback in the 11th century and was in full flower by the time of Chrétien. This revival was, in many respects, the engine that propelled King Arthur from Glastonbury to Aleppo as fast as word of mouth could travel.

The first Breton reverberations that manifested themselves in literature came not from within Brittany but from Marie de France, a Frenchwoman writing in England, and Chrétien de Troyes, a Frenchman writing in France. While Marie may or may not have been the first poet to inject Arthurian material with a refined and romantic spirit, it was most certainly Chrétien who first did so on a massive, influential scale. As W.W. Comfort perceptively observed, "Chrétien belonged to a generation of French poets who took over a great mass of Celtic folk-lore which they imperfectly understood, and made of it what, of course, it had never been before: the vehicle to carry a rich freight of chivalric customs and ideals."[13] In short, it was Chrétien who gave absolute clarity to Dark Ages folk tales that can often seem like childlike gibberish to the modern reader, even after sympathetic translation. Although the personal identification of the poet will likely forever remain an enigma (perhaps for the better), and even though his tombstone cannot be seen anywhere, let alone at the Cimetière Montparnasse in Paris, it was he, more than anyone, who first took the Arthurian vehicle and forged it into great romantic poetry for all future generations to enjoy.[14]

Arthur's international image and usefulness for propaganda purposes are perhaps no better demonstrated than in a bizarre series of incidents leading to the alleged discovery of his tomb at Glastonbury in 1190 or 1191. This was probably about a decade after the death of Chrétien and immediately after the death of Henry II, who ruled the Angevin Empire during most of the latter part of the poet's lifetime.[15] About the same time that Chrétien was creating his first full-fledged Arthurian romance, *Erec and Enide* (circa 1170, see Chapter 11), a French-Norman writer, probably by the name of Étienne de Rouen, was producing a largely forgotten but highly interesting work titled *Draco Normannicus* (*Standard of the Normans*). One of the more unusual features in a very unusual piece of writing was its inclusion of a letter, allegedly written in the name of King Arthur. The author could sound credible with this conceit because of a longstanding and widespread belief that Arthur never died and would one day return to re-establish his rightful sovereignty. Geoffrey of Monmouth, it should be remembered, was among those who prominently helped to preserve this tradition of an Arthurian second coming. The message of this forged letter, addressed to none other than

King Henry, was simple and blunt: Henry should stop harassing his Breton subjects or Arthur would return to chastise him and set things right. How Étienne managed to escape punishment for this impudence is unclear, but Henry seems to have been more agitated by the letter itself than any actual rebellious activities of the Bretons. Years later, after a conspiracy by his wife and sons had been put down with relative ease, Henry's hold on Brittany again seemed to weaken, thanks in large part to the scheming of his son Geoffrey, whom he had earlier made Duke of Brittany and married to Constance, a Breton heiress. Geoffrey then died unexpectedly in 1186, but his posthumous son, provocatively named Arthur, was born the following year.[16] This, combined with an alliance forged earlier between Geoffrey and his close friend, King Philip Augustus of France, seemed yet again to threaten the very backyard of Henry's vast kingdom.

With only a short time left to live, Henry reacted to this crisis, it appears, by ordering a post mortem of sorts on King Arthur in order to prove conclusively that the formidable battle leader from distant days of yore was indeed dead, and in fact would not return again to Brittany for a punitive second coming. Regarding Arthur's hoped-for return, Chambers asserted that "the balance of evidence is in favor of treating it as in origin a Breton rather than a Welsh belief."[17] Chambers, tongue barely in cheek, relates how this propaganda war played out in Henry's efforts to maintain the Breton unity of his empire.[18] An official search for Arthur's tomb was initiated. Before any firm discoveries were made, however, Henry died in 1189 and the fragility of his unwieldy kingdom manifested itself, with his two most prominent surviving sons, Richard (*Coeur de Lion*) and John, vying for supremacy.[19] To possibly help counter this instability, at least among the Bretons and Welsh, it was soon announced to the world that Arthur's tomb had finally been discovered at Glastonbury. Unfortunately, the tombstone itself could not be produced, only a drawing of it ("Here lies King Arthur," etc.) made by a monk before it too allegedly disappeared.[20] The Glastonbury site remains popular to the present day as a speculative site for Arthur's final resting place, as well as the Isle of Avalon, having once been surrounded by marshes (see Chapter 8). It should be added that Breton rumors of Arthur's resurrection or second coming seemed to have waned after this revelation. Nevertheless, the episode reflected the power of Arthur's name among the Bretons, Welsh, Normans, and French, only a few years after Chrétien's death.

Arthur's international appeal has not diminished since the 12th century. This author saw for himself firsthand proof as he attended the 22nd triennial congress of the International Arthurian Society in 2008, quite appropriately hosted by the University of Rennes in Brittany, France. Scholarly representation at the conference was, in a word, global. Delegates were sent from almost everywhere that English is spoken as a first or second language. Daytrips to numerous landmarks and institutions located in the heart of the Breton countryside reinforced and underscored the local belief that the King Arthur tradition is more firmly rooted in the genius of human storytelling and art, rather than any physical place or documented historical grounding. Perhaps the most telling moment witnessed by this observer came when a paper was delivered to a large audience by a German-Dutch presenter speaking in perfect English, then questions in French were responded to by the same presenter in French. At that moment, it was clearly apparent that King Arthur has transcended all languages, at least within western culture. A more surprising moment occurred when a visiting Welsh professor mournfully declared at the beginning of his presentation, "The Welsh don't really care about King Arthur." This sad fact has probably been true for a long time. It may have become a reality from the moment that the Bretons marched into England alongside the Normans. It may have been true ever since Breton storytellers appropriated—or rather hijacked—the tradition from their Welsh cousins. The reason the Welsh do not seem particularly interested in Arthur may be because the original Welsh version of him is not very interesting compared to the later Breton and French updates!

Whether one attends scholarly conferences in Brittany or simply is an observant tourist in the same region, it is difficult to miss or not be profoundly struck by this unlikely amalgamation of French-Celtic heritage. Bastille Day in Rennes on July 14, 2008, was a perfect example of this. A military marching band entered the city square proudly flying the French *tricolore*, but with the distinctive sound of bagpipes droning beneath the other instruments. The band played the obligatory "La Marseillaise," followed in short order by an interlude with the Celtic folk tune "Wild Mountain Thyme" on solo bagpipe (Breton pipes, not English). To these ears, the effect was surprising and incongruous, but not to the local audience, who listened with pleasure as if to say, "Yes, this is who we are." Prior to this, the author had heard distant rumors to the effect that the Bretons, traditionally jealous of their regional independence, were lukewarm in celebrating Bastille Day, but this was not so. It would be more accurate to say that French independence day in Brittany becomes a celebration of unique, cross-cultural identity. Foreign preconceptions and stereotypes are quickly shattered. The overall effect is exhilarating. This is the same dynamic that helped to create the Arthurian romance and inspired the poetic genius of Chrétien de Troyes. It took someone like Chrétien to effectively tap into the tradition, however—someone standing from slightly outside of Brittany (in Champagne), rather than immediately within — to immortalize Arthur's wayward knights with his imaginative art.

The rapid and remarkable spread of the Arthurian saga across and beyond Europe in the Chrétien's wake must cause anyone with a healthy curiosity to ask two questions: how and why? Obviously, the Norman conquest of England and other large sections of the western world, plus the temporary establishment of the Angevin Empire under Henry II and Eleanor of Aquitaine, provided the means by which these tales were transmitted with astounding alacrity. One must go further, however, and ask why. What made the stories so popular to begin with? Without basic, widespread appeal, good lines of communication alone would not have made much of a difference. Moreover, the theory that King Arthur made an effective and useful symbol for Crusader propaganda in the Middle East does not by itself offer a satisfying explanation. European footholds in the Holy Land were already eroding and permanently on the wane by the time that Chrétien wrote, and in any event, most of these fanatical crusaders were illiterate, however much they may have appreciated a good yarn. A more persuasive reasons had to do with the new economic prosperity being enjoyed throughout Europe during the second millennium. This prosperity, among other things, enabled patronage of literature to flourish, especially by French noblewomen when their crusading husband-knights left them behind, beginning with Queen Eleanor herself.[21] These powerful ladies wanted to hear about something besides tales of war and juvenile magic from their court poets and entertainers. For this task, another new trend making its way up from the south of France had to be adopted by French poets in order to earn a livelihood. It also required a whole new way of viewing relations between the two sexes, one that has stayed with us to the present, thanks in part to tales of King Arthur and his knights.

Chapter 4

Medieval Feminism

Real changes in human sentiment are very rare — there are perhaps three or four on record — but I believe that they occur, and that this is one of them — C.S. Lewis.[1]

The great medieval scholar C.S. Lewis may or may not have objected to the title of this chapter, but he most likely would have agreed that something quite extraordinary happened in the poetry of 12th-century France. When the swaggering, super-manly tales of King Arthur burst out of Wales onto the French mainland via Geoffrey of Monmouth, these traditions collided head-on with another irresistible literary trend making its way up from the south. While Islam had failed in its earlier bid to conquer Europe (and by then was in a defensive military posture on the Iberian Peninsula), its rich secular culture asserted influence over the European mind, even as its force of arms were being contained in the field. The spark supplied by 11th-century Andalusian poets such as Ibn Hazm had profoundly touched the troubadours of Aquitaine at the very same moment in time that an Aquitainian princess was assuming the crown, first of France, then later of the Anglo-Norman Angevin Empire. Moreover, it was this latter dominion which acted as a direct conduit for ideas traveling between Great Britain and the continent. This great confluence of poetic sentiment, along with other various factors (see Chapter 6), resulted in one of the benchmark ideological shifts referred to by Lewis with a mixture of awe and admiration. And C.S. Lewis was not one to be easily impressed.

What had existed before this "real change" took place? In short, Europe before the advent of romantic chivalry was not a very good time and place to be a woman. Even if a woman happened to be a member of the nobility — one of the very lucky and infinitesimally small group of people enjoying wealth, status, and relative comfort — to be a noblewoman was still to be relegated, for all intents and purposes, to the status of chattel. As Lewis himself put it, "We are back in a world where women are merely the mute objects of gift or barter, not only in the eyes of their fathers, but even in the eyes of their lovers."[2] Urban Holmes chimed in that "[m]ediaeval warriors had a distressing habit of appropriating the women of their adversaries."[3] This is not to say that the introduction of Arthurian literature substantially liberated women of *Le Moyen Âge* from these ills. Any positive effect of the new, more civilized values conveyed by these works was limited to the literate ranks of medieval society (again, a very small group), and this effect was, at least in the short term, extremely gradual. But it was nevertheless real, tangible, and above all, revolutionary. Even as late as the 16th century, one can clearly view the shocking residuals of feudal male chauvinism in works such as Shakespeare's *Two Gentlemen of Verona*, in which the protagonist generously offers his fiancée to his best friend as a gift.

Before the time of Chrétien, as observed by Emanuel Mickle, King Arthur and his knights (as fancifully embellished in Geoffrey's *histoire*) were still not particularly concerned with love. Instead, Mickle notes, "one finds in Geoffrey's text the fully developed story of an ancient legendary king whose extant historical reality is little more than that of a warrior chieftain named Arthur."[4] Geoffrey related in passing that Arthur's knights competed more enthusiastically in tournaments when their ladies were watching, and that personal morals improved overall, but he makes no reference to the precepts of courtly love. After the time of Chrétien, however, the tone of Arthurian literature moves into completely new territory. Roger Sherman Loomis summed up the change: "It was largely these same love stories which raised the aristocratic woman from the inferior position imposed on her by society and the Church, and gave her at least the illusion and sometimes the reality of equality in love and marriage."[5] Chrétien de Troyes stood in the vanguard of this new poetic trend.

With male-female equality came controversy. Equality in love meant freedom of choice, including freedom to choose love outside the bounds of marriage. Audiences ever since have been shocked to varying degrees by Guinevere's adultery with Lancelot. Loomis, with his usual dispassion, put things into proper perspective. First, he reminds us that "adultery cannot be condemned too severely in a society where typical marriage in the propertied classes was almost always determined by property or politics, and was often forced on the couple in childhood."[6] As a predictable result, it was more typical for medieval lovers to seek marriage in tales than in reality (this remains true with modern lovers to some extent as well). Second, as Loomis explained, Arthurian heroes and heroines even in their worst moments usually behave better than do people in real life:

> It may be fairly said that, in general, the standards of sexual morality in Arthurian literature, though varying enormously from one work to another, were higher than those of contemporary society. It is principally due to these romances that what we may call the 'romantic' conception of love, as something spontaneous, lasting, all-absorbing, ennobling, woman-honouring — though seldom realized in life — has long been and still is a dominant theme of literature.[7]

Loomis concludes by quoting the American sage Benjamin Franklin, who had firsthand knowledge in these things: "Where there is marriage without love, there will be love without marriage." The primary residual of Arthurian courtly love was not adultery, but rather the revolutionary *fin amor* or woman-worship that defied the Church by rejecting arranged marriages and substituting free-choice. Accordingly, it placed women, not merely equal to, but above men in terms of worth and status.[8]

With respect to the French poetry of courtly love as stylized by Chrétien, C.S. Lewis once again pretty much said it all and said it better than anyone:

> Chrétien de Troyes is its greatest representative. His *Lancelot* is the flower of the courtly tradition in France, as it was in its early maturity. And yet this poet is not wholly the product of the new conceptions: when he began to write he seems scarcely to have accepted them.... He was among the first to welcome the Arthurian stories; and to him, as much as to any single writer, we owe the colouring with which the "matter of Britain" has come down to us. He was among the first (in northern France) to choose love as the central theme of a serious poem: such a poem he wrote in his *Erec*, even before he had undergone the influence of the fully developed Provençal formula. And when that influence reached him, he was not only the first, but perhaps the greatest, exponent of it to his fellow countrymen; and, combining this element with the Arthurian legend, he stamped upon men's minds indelibly the conception of Arthur's court as the home *par excellence* of true and noble love.[9]

Lewis then went on to make another important observation: "What was theory for his own age had been practice for the knights of Britain. For it is interesting to notice that he places his ideal in the past. For him already 'the age of chivalry' is dead."[10] During the 12th century, nostalgia for an imaginary past was used to sell new ideas — in this case, the idea of female equality through the ideals of courtly love. By inventing an imaginary past, a new reality was thus created for the future, and Chrétien was neither the first nor the last poet to use this highly effective technique.

The tension between the sacred and profane in 12th-century European literature is well represented by the oft-competing rival cults of *fin amor* and religious worship of the Virgin Mary — the latter being a relative newcomer to the cultural scene of the time. It appears that the Virgin's newfound prestige as the Queen of Heaven came in response to the explosion in popularity of the courtly love ethos. As Lewis emphasized, "[T]here is no evidence that the quasi-religious tone of medieval love poetry has been transferred from the worship of the Blessed Virgin: it is just as likely — it is even more likely — that the colouring of certain hymns to the Virgin has been borrowed from love poetry."[11] In a similar vein, Loomis dismissed the possibility of influence flowing in the opposite direction because "religious influence on troubadour poetry is singularly lacking" and because southern France was "a hotbed of heresy."[12] Associating (like Loomis) the courtly love movement with the Cathar heresy of southern France (see Chapter 7), Karen Armstrong writes that the Virgin "was the Church's answer to Catharism and its pure and powerful women. She was also the religious answer to the secular Courtly Love ideal."[13] During that time, *fin amor* was having a noticeable impact on European aristocratic society. The establishment church sensibly adopted a strategy to the effect that if one cannot beat an insurgent new idea, one should at least try and adapt that same idea to one's own agenda.

This new prestige for the female sex exerted itself in Chrétien's work both directly through the precepts of courtly love, as well as indirectly through the cult of the Virgin. In *Cligès*, when Fenice cries out "Saint Mary!" (line 4055) in a moment of deep concern, she is repeating the fashionable lingo of her time. Another example occurs in *Yvain* when the younger daughter of the Black Thorn Lord calls "on God, His Mother, then on all the saints" (lines 4630–4631) in a prayer for help while she is alone in the forest. Admittedly, such examples represent women calling to the Virgin as an intercessor; it may be that the poet, despite his progressive attitudes for the time, felt the Queen of Heaven to be a more appropriate object of prayer for women than for men. Minor episodes like these are far overshadowed by those such as in *Lancelot*, in which the hero physically bows before the bedroom of Queen Guinevere as if it were a holy shrine (line 4717). To what extent the poet was burlesquing, in scenes such as these, the quasi-religious overtones inherent in the secular courtly ethos of his time is difficult to say; more likely than not, there is an element of humor. Chrétien's patroness, the Countess Marie, would no doubt have smiled at it.[14]

No individual better represented the modern notion of women's liberation during the High Middle Ages than Marie's mother, Eleanor of Aquitaine (1124–1204). Not surprisingly, Eleanor probably did more than any single patron to encourage the creation and promulgation of the Arthurian romance as we know it today. Although there is no evidence that she ever directly commissioned Chrétien, we know that one of her daughters (Marie) and one of her nieces (Elisabeth) belonged to powerful households that did. Furthermore, during her entire life Eleanor stood at the center of the literary movement that influenced and was influenced by Chrétien, beginning with her own grandfather, William IX of Aquitaine, the first documented troubadour poet.[15] More than one commentator has made the obvious surmise that she may have served as the original model for Queen Guinevere, as least as modern audiences tend to think of her.[16] Even the simultaneous beginnings of gothic church architecture in the *Ile-de-France* during the mid–12th century (see Chapter 20) probably owe something to her initiative.[17] When Karen Armstrong described Eleanor as "the most powerful woman of her time," this characterization certainly included (among many other important aspects) her omnipresent influence on literary trends of the period.[18] Moshé Lazar perhaps put it most forcefully when he asserted that "Eleanor of Aquitaine was soon to become the first woman to orient the spirit and the ideals of a new society in which love songs and romances of love progressively superceded warriors' epics, Crusaders' and pilgrims' chronicles."[19] The central role played by Eleanor as both a patron and role model for troubadour poets provided a direct and prominent impetus to Chrétien's later presentation of the adulterous love affair between Guinevere and Lancelot.[20]

Not to be confused with Marie de Champagne but also crucial in the development of 12th-century literature was the gifted and groundbreaking poet, Marie de France. Marie, as aptly described by Mickle, "probably ranks second only to Chrétien de Troyes among the best-known writers of mediaeval French literature in the twelfth and thirteenth centuries."[21] Robert Hanning and Joan Ferrante begin their study on Marie by stating that Marie was "perhaps the greatest woman author of the Middle Ages and certainly the creator of the finest medieval short fiction before Boccaccio and Chaucer."[22] Given the uncertainty of dating for most 12th-century literature, she may well have been the first to address Arthurian themes in French verse, although she does not compare to Chrétien in terms of sheer quantity of output, range of material, and universal influence. Her short poems or *lais* include three (*Lanval, Chevrefoil,* and *Guigemar*) that make explicit reference to Arthurian material. *Lanval* mentions Arthur, his queen, and the Roundtable, as well as Avalon ("Avalun") and the knights Gawain and Yvain. *Chevrefoil* deals with an episode from the Tristan legend. *Guigemar* is set in the Brittany of King Hoel (an Arthurian backdrop) and includes the killing of a white stag, similar to the opening section of Chrétien's *Erec and Enide*. As for Marie, most critics agree that she was a French writer working out of Angevin England under royal patronage, probably from Queen Eleanor herself.[23] In her poems, Marie repeatedly cites her source material as being French Breton in origin, as opposed to Welsh.

Another British critic, Edmund Chambers, gives as good an overview as anyone of the poetic style for both Marie and Chrétien. He notes that the key aspect of their art concerned their audience, which was overwhelmingly aristocratic, female, and lacking freedom in marriage choices.[24] Accordingly, themes of love (and its perils) are given prominence. In *Lanval* (a Breton name, according to Marie), the hero rejects the amorous advances of Arthur's queen, who then publicly accuses him of being gay. King Arthur is portrayed unfavorably as being clueless and credulous. Assuming that Marie wrote first, these themes foreshadow those emphasized later by Chrétien, especially in his *Lancelot*. In Marie's *Chevrefoil*, the adulterous lover Tristan is portrayed in the French courtly tradition as a sensitive, harp-playing knight, similar to the one found in Thomas of Britain (who wrote in French), as opposed to the non-courtly tradition of the same story found in Béroul.[25] It may well have been that Chrétien drew inspiration from Marie's poetic treatment of the Tristan adultery theme (then in the process of being amalgamated into the Arthurian corpus), although he proceeded to either criticize it in his other works or create his own version of the same theme in *Lancelot*.

After the massive achievement of Chrétien in his French Arthurian romances, and in the immediate aftermath of his death, the precepts of the new sensibility in relations between the sexes were codified by one of his French contemporaries.[26] Andreas Capellanus, writing in Latin, produced his famous treatise, *De Amore* (popularly known today as *The Art of Courtly Love*), written at the request of Countess Marie, Chrétien's former patron in Troyes.[27] Lewis referred to *De Amore* as the first work of "theory" on courtly love in wake of Chrétien, although this theory is often presented in a humorous, facetious, or even cynical tone.[28] This is especially true in the first of its three sections, which includes chapter titles such as "The Love of Clergy," "The Love of Nuns," "Love Got with Money," "The Easy Attainment of One's Object," "The Love of Peasants," and "The Love of Prostitutes" (chapters 7–12). Books II and III deal only somewhat more seriously with "love" themes. Perhaps the work's most memorable passages occur in Book II, Chapter 7, when the Countess Marie, her mother Eleanor, and other noblewoman are portrayed as court judges and arbiters in "real-life" cases of love disputes. Whether such things actually transpired or were done merely for amusement is beside the point; what matters is that the women in these scenes are the ones who are calling the shots, not the men. In its lighter or ironic vein, the treatise of Andreas ultimately comes across as a kind of self-conscious (and crudely joking), medieval update on Ovid's *The Art of Love* (see Chapter 6).[29]

Although Andreas has little to say about King Arthur, Book II, Chapter 8, of *De Amore* includes a variant of the same Sparrow-Hawk incident found in the opening passages of Chrétien's *Erec and Enide*. In Chrétien's version of the tale, the hero Erec wins honor and acclaim for himself and his bride by defeating an arrogant rival knight for the right of his lady to claim and publicly display a prize Sparrow-Hawk. Joseph Duggan correctly pointed out that the use of a similar device by Andreas did not necessarily represent a direct copy of Chrétien and that both authors could have been drawing from a common source, an observation shared by Lewis.[30] Similarities such as these, however, underscore an important reminder that Chrétien and Andreas were both writing in approximately the same time and place, for the same patrons, and using a similar vocabulary. On the other hand, each wrote with a completely different style and purpose, as well as in a different language — Chrétien in French and Andreas in Latin. Moreover, the Sparrow-Hawk contest portrays the knights not fighting *over* a woman, but rather fighting *for* their respective ladies and their proper competitive standing in society. This represented something relatively new in literature at the time and no doubt in medieval sensibilities as well.

As noted by almost every modern medieval scholar, Chrétien did not share the widespread misogyny of his contemporaries; the poet appears to have genuinely liked his benefactors.[31] As Ruth Harwood Cline observed, "Chrétien draws particular fine portraits of women, the natural audience for vernacular literature. The character of Guinevere is so finely drawn that the image Chrétien created of that queen has come down to us unchanged over eight centuries."[32] Even if Chrétien's Guinevere did not in fact portray Eleanor of Aquitaine (and more likely it did), Karen Armstrong asserts that Eleanor had an indirect influence on Chrétien's romances in terms of presenting the knight as a courtly lover, in addition to being a crusader. Under this influence, the knightly quest becomes a sojourn rather than a crusade, and the mystical influence of Saint Bernard is strongly felt during this sojourn, particularly in the story of Perceval.[33] Jean Frappier appreciated that "Chrétien is at his delightful best in slow-motion scenes of lovers, startled or troubled by thoughts of love, who seek self-understanding."[34] The apotheosis of this introspective, mutual respect between lovers occurs in Chrétien's *Yvain* as the trappings of courtly love are portrayed strictly within the bounds of marriage. Cline remarked that this combination was "an interesting idea since the prevailing opinion was that the legal obligations and enforced proximity of marriage accorded ill with a freely given, inspirational emotion, particularly one which made the lover submit to his lady's commands."[35] All in all, by the time Chrétien had laid down his pen, the archetypical, medieval knight (in poetic literature, at least) thought and acted quite differently than his brutish counterpart from only a generation previous.

While Chrétien de Troyes was indisputably far advanced for his time in terms of developing thematic content especially appealing to female audiences, by today's standards many of his heroines might appear constrained and inhibited. Nevertheless, for the late 12th century, these characters represented a great quantum leap forward when it came to their independence, vivaciousness, and determination. Several of these heroines, Guinevere being the most famous example, are often imperious and strong-willed to a fault. Some, such as Enide, while (usually) subservient to the will of their lovers, are also physically hardy to a startling degree, sharing in all dangers and hardships with the men — sometimes even fighting enemies alongside of them. In terms of supporting free choice in love, however, Chrétien's progressiveness went only so far. Most prominently, he repeatedly recoiled from praise of the adulterous love between Tristan and Isolde then so popular in literature of the time. Before, however, creating a more complex and nuanced portrait of adulterous love in *Lancelot* at the specific behest of his patroness, the Countess Marie, Chrétien first felt a need to lash out against the Tristan legend in the second of his great Arthurian romances, *Cligès*.

Chapter 5

Cligès, the Anti-Tristan

Women often have the final say over men, especially in matters of love. This was another important aspect of "medieval feminism" which deserves separate and extensive treatment. While the hero of Chrétien's *Erec and Enide* could certainly make no claims to the title of Mr. Sensitive, both Cligès and his father Alexander do more than offset this limitation in the poet's second great Arthurian romance. Unlike Erec, both heroes in *Cligès* take plenty of time to court their lady-loves, and in fact are hesitant to do so initially. Once they begin their courtships (only after receiving assurance that attraction is mutual), there are numerous and rather long love-monologues to be soulfully recited, in addition to the normal dramatic obstacles posed by the outside world.[1] There also seems to be a political dimension to all of this. It was as if the poet suddenly realized who was putting bread into his mouth; most likely, it was Marie, daughter of Eleanor, along with the other noblewomen at the Champagnois court. The important lesson to this new style was that true love must be reciprocated and nurtured, rather than won at a competition or taken for granted as it would be, say, by a male adolescent. In this respect, *Cligès* represented a great leap forward from *Erec and Enide*. Emotionally, it was a much more advanced, cultivated, and mature work, one that surely solidified the poet's reputation. To emphasize the main theme even more, the action in *Cligès* begins on the French side of the channel in Brittany as Arthur's retinue travels there. This is the same geographic location in which *Erec and Enide* had come to a close.[2]

The sources for *Cligès* are so diverse and varied that it is impossible to do full justice in a short space. Ruth Harwood Cline provided the best quick summary when she wrote, "*Cligès* has multiple sources. It is a fusion of classical and medieval stories."[3] Regarding the poet's citation of his mysterious source book from the church of Saint Pierre in Beauvais (lines 18–21), she added, "There is no immediate reason to disbelieve him." Some have contrarily argued that this kind of alleged credit was more likely a fictional device which medieval writers were fond of using to obfuscate their own imaginative inventions. If Chrétien had such a motive it is no longer discernable to us. What exactly the book at Saint Pierre (if real) contained is anyone's guess, but a good bet is that it included elements forming the main plot nucleus in *Cligès*. Prominent among these was the heroine feigning death in order to avoid sleeping with the antagonist, and then later reuniting with her hero-lover. The documented sources for this aspect of the drama are ancient and have always been popular. Most obvious among these is one cited by Chrétien himself (lines 5802–5806), the tale of King Solomon's reluctant wife.[4] The most famous example of the same conceit occurs in Shakespeare's *Romeo and Juliet*, a play written at least 400 years after Chrétien's first Arthurian romances.[5]

Among ancient sources, the most prevalent used in *Cligès* was Ovid. This, in fact, is true for all of Chrétien's works (see Chapter 6), with the notable exception of his first romance, *Erec and Enide*. The affair between hero and heroine in *Cligès* reflects elements from, or allusions to, several of Ovid's tragic lovers in the *Metamorphoses*, especially Books VI and VII. Some of these doomed couples include Myrrha and Cintras (line 2966), Narcissus and Echo (line 2727), Medea and Jason (line 4365), and in a more general way, Pyramus and Thisbe, since Cligès (like Pyramus) contemplates suicide when uncertain if his lover still lives (lines 6059–6063).[6] Paris and Helen from Ovid's *Heriodes* are also evoked.[7] Unlike these many unfortunates, those in *Cligès* experience a happy ending. More importantly, the synthesis achieved by the inventive French *trouvère* of Troyes represented far more than any slavish imitation of Latin models. Above all, it seems clear that Chrétien, by the time he wrote his second Arthurian romance, had obviously immersed himself in the styles and attitudes of the ancient world's premiere love poet.

The name of the heroine, Fenice, is partially traceable to the *Metamorphoses* as well, since it is derived from the legendary phoenix bird, used as a symbol by Ovid in the climactic chapter of his masterpiece while expounding on the immortality of the soul. Chrétien adopts the image in the following passage, and his brilliant simplicity shines through even in modern translation:

> Fenice was this fair maiden's name,
> and hardly chosen without aim,
> for as the phoenix is more fair
> than other birds, so very rare
> there's only one at any time,
> I think Fenice was as sublime;

> her beauty peerless, lyrical,
> a marvel and a miracle,
> and Nature never could create
> a replica or duplicate
>   [lines 2685–2694].

Chrétien's Fenice, as a female, human emblem of the phoenix, is further suggestive of Shakespeare's Juliet in that she seems to resurrect from death near the end of the story. In the case of Fenice, the parallel is strengthened by her being an eastern, Byzantine princess by birth, while the legendary phoenix, according to Ovid, was only to be found in the East (Assyria, to be exact).[8]

Among the medieval sources that impacted Chrétien's work, one prominently stands above all the rest. This is the legend of Tristan and Isolde, which could have reached the poet from any number of places, given its boundless popularity at the time. This same popularity, however, appears to have irked Chrétien, mainly because the tale had no moral redeeming value in the conventional sense. It merely conveyed the valuable lesson that pure sexual attraction is sometimes an overwhelming force of nature, no matter how at odds it may be with orthodox church teachings on marriage and monogamy. The origins of the Tristan story are murky and controversial. Urban Holmes conceded, "No one can write with complete assurance on this matter.... Most scholars agree that the first suggestion of the Tristan plot came from southwest Scotland...."[9] He noted that the tale came from the north, spread south through Wales and Cornwall, then, like other Arthurian stories, across the channel to Brittany and Normandy.[10] Loomis, among other notables, concurred with this scenario.[11] Loomis also noticed that there was a prominent historical personage named Tristan documented near Rennes in 1030, and that the name itself had become popular throughout Brittany by the beginning of the second millennium.[12] One of the earliest known redactors of the tradition was the Anglo-Norman poet, Thomas of England, whose *Tristan and Iseult* was written in Old French. The date of the Thomas poem, however, is heavily disputed and may or may not predate Chrétien's Arthurian romances.[13] The same holds true for a surviving fragment of lesser quality written by the Norman poet Béroul.[14]

Chrétien's relationship as a writer with the Tristan legend was clearly both close and turbulent. All critics agree that its influence upon the poet was tremendous.[15] While reciting his credentials with previous French translations of Ovid in the prologue to *Cligès*, Chrétien notes that he had also translated his own version of "King Mark and fair Isolde" (line 5). King Mark, those familiar with the tale will recall, was the husband of Isolde and the uncle of Tristan. Unfortunately, the work is lost. It is possible that Chrétien's poem predated that of Thomas, or was written at about the same time; if before, this would make it the very first surviving written reference to the Tristan legend. Moreover, one of Chrétien's two credited songs (or *chansons courtoises*) mentions Tristan as well.[16] Perhaps most notable of all, Chrétien had earlier named Tristan as a member of the Arthurian Roundtable in *Erec and Enide* (line 1687)—the very first poet to do so, thus directly connecting Tristan with Arthurian legend. Was Chrétien in fact the first storyteller to link Tristan with King Arthur? If so, it was a bold innovation, and has firmly stuck in the public imagination ever since.

In *Cligès*, Chrétien's intense interest in (and disapproval of) the adultery of Tristan and Isolde borders on obsession. The poet makes direct, negative reference to Tristan four times (lines 2751, 3107, 5200, and 5253), Isolde four times (lines 3107, 3110, 5201, and 5253), and King Mark once (line 2751). Professor Cline reminds us that "*Cligès* has been termed an anti–Tristan," and the poem, like *Tristan and Iseult*, begins with a prologue telling the story of the hero's parents.[17] Taking this idea further, all of Chrétien's Arthurian heroes are, in a very real sense, anti–Tristans. This is even applicable to Lancelot, whose adulterous story in many ways represents a burlesque on the theme of courtly love.[18] All of these heroes do things and behave in ways that depart considerably from the normal Tristan template. If Chrétien's lost "King Mark and fair Isolde" was really the first written King Arthur saga, one could argue that the poet's Arthurian romances were themselves reactions to the Tristan adultery theme, which in turn subsequently produced the great Lancelot and Grail motifs. Moreover, this same assertion would hold true even if the first connections between Tristan and Arthur were not made by Chrétien until later in his *Erec and Enide* and *Cligès*.

In the opening prologue to *Cligès*, the poet gives a brief pseudo-history for the concept of chivalry, placing its beginnings in ancient Greece and Rome and then currently residing (not surprisingly) in medieval France (lines 28–42).[19] This residence has, in many respects, become permanent since French history will be forever associated with the birth of chivalry (see Chapter 10). The term, as has been previously noted, was by then much more than a military concept—now it linked proper knightly behavior in both matters of love and war. Unlike Chrétien's last three romances that followed (*Lancelot*, *Yvain*, and *Perceval*), the theme of *Cligès* is not concerned with a knightly quest.[20] Instead, concerns of love predominate, with war and adventure provided as backdrops. In addition to the story, and the pervasive influence of *Tristan* and Ovid throughout, the work is sprinkled with conceits relating to matters of the heart. One example of this includes an allusion to the fictional "courts of love" (line 3821), later portrayed by Andreas Capellanus in *The Art of Courtly Love* (see Chapter 4).[21] Another is the poet's play on the word "will" four times over the course of nine lines.[22] Still others are the spontaneous yet slowly-paced romantic relationships. This style too had precedent in recent popular works such as the *Roman d'Eneas*, which gave an extensive treatment to the romance between Eneas and Lavinia, one not to be found in the ancient original of Virgil.[23] In the back story, Cligès' Greek father, Alexander, whose name suggests Alexander the Great, must come to Arthur's court in Brittany to learn true chivalry — because the medieval Byzantine Greeks had apparently forgotten, it is strongly implied. All in all, the romance presents the poet's early thesis on the chivalric aspects of courtly love, later to be further developed in his revolutionary work, *Lancelot*.

The back story of the romance between Cligès' parents is itself interesting on several levels. His mother is Soredamors, sister of Arthur's nephew Gawain and hence Arthur's niece, which makes her son Cligès the grandnephew of Arthur. This is yet another amazing innovation by Chrètien.[24] Her courtship by Alexander is a case of mutual attraction paralyzed into speechless inactivity, until Queen Guinevere (portrayed as the presiding arbiter of love at Arthur's court), figures things out and more or less pushes the two of them together. Chrétien describes in detail the moment of Guinevere's realization in this humorous passage, as (again) translated by Cline:

> The queen, astonished at the sight,
> watched Soredamors turn red and white
> and pondered in her heart the air
> and countenance shown by the pair,
> first separately, then both combined.
> The truth seemed certain to her mind:
> the changing colors of complexion
> had love as cause and as connection
>   [lines 1573–1580].

The phrase "love as cause and as connection" has a nice ring, and is useful for the clever construction of rhymed octosyllabic couplets, but other English translators have opted for completely different word choices. Burton Raffel, utilizing free form verse, employs the somewhat more precise "signs of love," but still pretty much conveys the same meaning.[25] Earlier prose translators were just as diverse. W.W. Comfort imaginatively chose "fruit of love,"[26] while D.D.R. Owen inserted a more plaintive "effects of love."[27] David Staines appropriately maintained the repetitive medical imagery of the Old French original with "symptoms of love."[28] With so many choices for the modern English reader, it is safe to say that none of these various interpretations are definitive and all have various merits, depending on individual taste. Perhaps one gets the best sense of the poet's original intention by reading all of these interpretations and comparing them.

The storyline of *Cligès* offers some thick tangles as well. The basic problem is how far can one go outside the bounds of legal matrimony without committing adultery as did, say, Tristan and Isolde? Fenice is forced to marry the Greek emperor, Cligès' uncle Alis, against her will after she and the hero have fallen for each other. Later, Cligès and Fenice consummate their love while her husband is still alive. Their similarity with Tristan and Isolde ends there. Rather than dying tragic (and cautionary) deaths, Cligès and Fenice live happily ever after. Chrétien must pull out all the stops to prevent his audience from morally condemning the lovers. First, Fenice never consents to marry Cligès' uncle and is forced to participate in the wedding ceremony, while the uncle, by marrying her, breaks an earlier oath he had made to Cligés' father to remain single in return for the throne. Then Fenice, thanks to various magical potions, never has to sleep with Alis and is later able to feign death, after which she and Cligès become lovers. When Alis discovers the truth, he first goes ballistic, then insane when he cannot wreak vengeance, and finally dies of self-inflicted grief. Some have pointed out quite correctly that none of this changes the fact that Cligès and Fenice have still, strictly speaking, committed adultery.[29] Perhaps Chrétien, as he would later do in *Lancelot*, was making the theme as unobjectionable, and the characters as sympathetic, as possible.

Among all the characters who are sympathetic, the most surprising is John the serf, who custom-builds a special tower for Fenice and Cligès that doubles as a fake tomb and secret love nest. That John has the status of a feudal serf or slave is never stated overtly, but given other aspects of his situation there can be little doubt; for example, he and his heirs are "freed" by the hero in return for his services (line 5572). His function is similar to that of the nurse Thessala, whose concocted potions help to protect Fenice's chastity after she is forcibly married to Alis. As for John, not only does he play a Figaro-like role of enabler for the clandestine affair, he also holds up with admirable courage and dignity under harsh interrogation by the emperor when the ploy is eventually brought to light. As noted by Professor Cline, the sympathetic portrayal of John the serf is unique in Chrétien in that the lower classes are normally presented by the poet as cowardly, greedy, and ignorant.[30] Urban Holmes saw John as another example of the poet's social concerns, which was very unusual during those feudal times and was otherwise unprecedented in Chrétien's oeuvre.[31] The episodes with John also help to bolster the aristocratic hero's standing as a benevolent and more worthy ruler than his uncle.

Before the reader might become too carried away with this theme of proletariat solidarity, however, a little perspective is in order. Chrétien de Troyes cannot be categorized as a political friend of the masses, in spite of this isolated interlude in one of his romances. Within *Cligès* itself— near the outset of the tale, in fact — the father of the hero, Alexander, delivers a speech to his father in justification of his risky pilgrimage to Arthur's court in search of knighthood and honor:

> So valor weighs upon a knave
> as cowardice upon the brave.
> Acclaim and rest do not accord.
> So any man whose sole reward
> is gaining wealth without digressions
> becomes a slave to his possessions
> [lines 158a–162].

This from the inventor of Arthurian romance, and so much for the "poor-boy-makes-good" capitalist ethos. Pursuit of wealth alone is considered moral baseness and, in effect, another form of slavery; in any event, the common man is typically not capable of doing much else. This cynical sentiment is very feudal, and yes, even Shakespearean in attitude. If someone like John the serf happens to make himself worthy of freedom and honor in one of Chrétien's romances, then it is more likely because those noble qualities were already inherent in his character, or so it would seem.

Nevertheless, the role of John the serf in *Cligés* anticipates the increased social concerns of the poet, general though these may be, as later expressed in his final three Arthurian romances, *Lancelot*, *Yvain*, and *Perceval*. Protection of the weak (however undeserving), after all, remained one of the central principles of feudal knighthood. As for the rising merchant class, they were deemed necessary but were still despised for the things they did. This latter item was probably a major factor in the rising anti–Semitism of the age (see Chapter 23). The non–Arthurian romance, *Guillaume d'Angleterre*, if the work of Chrétien (see Chapter 18), would be another example of such ambivalence. Chrétien, like Shakespeare long after him, had an essentially aristocratic outlook on feudal society, but one that was well-informed and slightly tempered by education and experience. Thus the nobility of Cligès, though certainly portrayed as inborn, must also be tested and proven with various trials and tribulations.

As for unsympathetic characters in *Cligès*, apart from Alis, the villainous Duke of Saxony, who literally tries to steal the bride, is memorable and probably based on a historical personage. Henry the Lion of Saxony was an insubordinate and rebellious subject of the German Holy Roman emperor Frederick Barbarossa during the latter's negotiations with Byzantine emperor Manuel Comnenus in the early 1170s. These talks included the possibility of a marriage alliance between Frederick and Manuel's daughter. Count Henry of Champagne (as well as his court) would have been familiar with all of these players, since Henry himself had recently negotiated with Barbarossa on behalf of the French King Louis VII, and also had been earlier knighted by the emperor Manuel while visiting Constantinople as a crusader. Based on these multiple associations, Henry the Lion of Saxony may well have been Chrétien's bad-guy prototype.[32] They also help to date the work to around 1176.[33] Another parallel with the story is the fact that Count Henry's mother had been a German-Austrian princess.[34] Like Cligès, Henry the Liberal had multi-cultural parentage, which probably contributed to his enlightened attitudes. When Cligès travels to King Arthur's English court at Wallingford for a great tournament, he takes care to dress "with elegance, his wardrobe in the style of France," though he is himself a native of Greek Constantinople (lines 4933–4934). This passage, we should remember, was written by a biased French author, but probably was also a true reflection of Count Henry's international background and style. These were the values — unusual both then and today — that attractively imposed themselves on the first Arthurian romances.

Henry the Liberal's enlightened, globetrotting outlook, which played such a central role in influencing the poetry of Chrétien and hence the imaginative Arthurian world, was more than simply the result of personal wanderlust or restlessness. Chrétien, Henry, and his wife Marie all lived in a European world that was changing rapidly as new ideas coming from completely opposite worlds collided with each other in medieval France. To be an effective leader or thinker or doer of any sort in this environment now required absolutely more than the outdated, insular, and narrow vision that had been the norm only a few generations before. Thanks to the Crusades, thanks to Norman adventurousness, and thanks to Plantagenet ambition, an entirely new kind of cross-cultural mobility had appeared, one that aided the exchange of ideas, as well as marriage diplomacy. Armies, trade, and intellectual property were moving together further and faster than at any time since antiquity. By the 12th century in France, its impact was being felt by nobleman and commoner alike.

Chapter 6

A Melting Pot of Ideas

What is new usually wins its way by disguising itself as the old—C.S. Lewis.[1]

In a memorable episode from Chrétien's *Cligès*, the knight Bertrand, after accidentally discovering that Fenice is not only still alive, but is also the hero's lover, has his leg chopped off by Cligès as he tries to escape. Surviving this trauma, Bertrand then informs everyone in town of what he has witnessed, but is accused by the townspeople of being a "troubadour"—that is, a liar and a teller of tales (line 6424). The incident serves as a convenient reminder to future readers that troubadour poets, whatever their merits as entertainers, were generally held in low esteem for lack of veracity. We should also keep in mind that Chrétien himself was not, strictly speaking, a troubadour, but rather a *trouvère*—that is, a northern French poet (a troubadour was typically from the south). The distinction is significant because, not only was a different French dialect used in the north, but *trouvères* tended to be associated with a more formal, classical education found in the cathedral schools of those regions, and no doubt thought of themselves as being more cultivated and sophisticated. Even lower on the social rung were the Breton *jongleurs*, who had their own unique associations with northwestern France and the Arthurian tradition imported directly from Wales. If patient readers are by now becoming confused by these fine and often debatable distinctions in medieval French poetry, then they should not be too concerned. Even the greatest poet of the Middle Ages before Dante felt comfortable blurring the lines, and in his case there was probably an element of frustration with the shiftless, untrustworthy troubadours of southern France, whose work was often hackneyed and heavy-handed besides. The more important point, however, is that Chrétien de Troyes was at the time being influenced, whether he liked it or not, from more than one direction. Only a complete blockhead would insist that the multi-dimensional complexity of Chrétien's romances came from one source and one source alone.

Because of the universal truth that not all foreign innovations are immediately welcomed into our hearts and homes with open arms, alien sources of good ideas often must be masqueraded. Another example of this is when longstanding local tradition is intentionally given mistaken credit for completely newfangled ideas. This is what C.S. Lewis was referring to when he wrote about disguising new ideas as old ones. As Europe finally began to look beyond its own insular borders at the beginning of the second millennium, ancient learning lost for centuries began to gradually resurface and was duly imitated by growing numbers of admirers. The process included epic poetry. *La Chanson de Roland* (*The Song of Roland*) in France and *El Cantar de mio Cid* (*The Song of my Cid*) in Spain were early examples of the *chanson de geste* or *cantar de gesta*, glorifying the respective national heroes of each language. Works such as these represented the great prelude to the Arthurian romances first appearing in the latter half of the same century. In effect, the so-called "Matter of Britain" would quickly supercede in popularity the "matters of Rome, France, Spain," or whatever one prefers to call these earlier predecessors.[2] Moreover, part of this triumph would involve the new Arthurian poetic concoctions disguising themselves as much older traditions.

Like most perceptive critics who saw fit to dig below surface appearances, Urban Holmes recognized that the creation of the Arthurian romance represented a new brew of many diverse and unlikely ingredients. Specifically, Holmes named three main factors: 1) the tremendous expansion of the Anglo-Norman empire under Henry II; 2) the "look" by western poets towards eastern sources and motifs coming from places like Germany, Sicily, and Byzantium; and 3) the new and dramatic rise of the cathedral schools as educational institutions. Holmes also emphasized that the most important of these factors (the first one) was crucially aided by the marriage of Henry II to Eleanor of Aquitaine in 1152, which led to the massive unification of Celtic peoples within the Angevin kingdom, including (most critically), the Welsh and the Bretons.[3] This unification was the engine that propelled the *matière de Bretagne* past its secular rivals, and whose vernacular forms of romance and *conte* were quickly adapted by Chrétien de Troyes and Marie de France (see Chapter 4) to great effect.[4] The second factor was the result of Norman mobility and adaptability (see Chapter 15). The third factor was also greatly facilitated by the Normans, who did everything they could to encourage learning, if for no other reason than to promote their own exploits and political agenda. In this respect, Holmes drew an apt comparison between the Normans and the Americans of recent centuries, since the Normans were an "enterprising people" and, in a sense, were the "Yankees" of their own time.[5] It was this enterprising spirit that allowed or forced cultural influences from diverse geographic sources such as Muslim Spain, English Wales, and Greek Byzantium to coalesce in northern France during the 12th century.

The increased international awareness that characterized the High Middle Ages was well-embodied in the persons of Chrétien's two exceptional early patrons, Count Henry the Liberal and his wife, Marie of Champagne. Henry, a Norman great grandson of William the Conqueror, was also a German on his mother's side. Marie, who was the daughter of Eleanor of Aquitaine (and hence great granddaughter of the first troubadour poet, Duke William IX), was also the daughter of King Louis VII of France and half-brother of his successor, King Philip Augustus, and was thus a prominent member of the royal House of Capet. In effect, Henry and Marie, between the two of them, were related to just about everyone who ruled Europe. This kinship also applied to the church. For example, Henry's uncle was Henry of Blois, bishop of Winchester and abbot of Glastonbury, both places in England with close traditional associations with the Arthurian legends.[6] He also was the brother of Guillaume aux Blanche Mains, the famous "Whitehands" bishop of Reims and Sens who played an important role as European power broker and negotiator during this era. Henry had another half-brother, Hugh of Lagny, abbot of St. Benet of Holme, located in the Norfolk-Suffolk region of England, a region closely tied with the alleged source of *Guillaume d'Angleterre*, possibly written by Chrétien early in his literary career (see Chapters 8 and 18). The inevitable result of such an extensive family network would have been an international and multi-cultural outlook for anyone who was prominently placed in the court of Champagne, as the poet Chrétien de Troyes most certainly would have been.[7]

As previously noted, however, it was in 11th-century Spain that some kind of humanist spark ignited, setting off a fire of creative activity eventually spreading across western Europe. As observed by C.S. Lewis, it was in Spain that European pagan roots, which had continued to dominate Christian societies during this era, finally met (or rather collided) with all forms of Islamic sophistication, learning, and refinement.[8] The very idea that neighboring Muslims, Jews, and Christians could interact and cooperate in producing new intellectual and artistic endeavors appears to have a been a new one (at least in this part of the world), and far from everyone in each of the three camps approved of it. Despite opposition from various reactionary corners, however, this is exactly what transpired, and its influence on Christian Europe was both enormous and permanent. The chain reaction had begun, and one of its many, many literary offshoots would be the creation of the Arthurian romance. For example, the very symbol of the Arthurian legends, the Holy Grail, may well have had its origins south of the Pyrenees Mountains in Spain (see Chapter 22). There is an old saying that all people must ultimately choose between being cultured or sub-cultured, and in France at that time, many chose the former path, largely because of the pioneering efforts of their multi-cultural Spanish neighbors. Along the route from Cordova to Troyes, other influences would assert themselves, leaving their mark as well.

From Iberia, the new intellectual force of the High Middle Ages invaded Aquitaine and southern France, where the first troubadour love poetry appeared, then it spread to northern France, and finally to the Champagne of Chrétien de Troyes.[9] This is not merely the personal opinion of this writer. Literary critics, including some of the very best, have strongly asserted it long before this observer was born. C.S. Lewis, among others, traced its geographic progress: "Another stream found its way northward to mingle with the Ovidian tradition which already existed there, and so to produce the French poetry of the twelfth century."[10] Specifically in regard to the Arthurian legends, Lewis elaborated on the literary mix:

> We have seen how social conditions gave the new feeling its bent towards humility and adultery; how literary conditions entangled it with the pre-existing Ovidian tradition though it was forced to modify and even misunderstand that tradition; how the Arthurian stories supplied it with matter; and how, in the hands of a great poet [Chrétien], the Arthurian story, treated in terms of courtly love, produced the first notable examples of psychological or sentimental fiction.[11]

Few have ever taken serious issue with Lewis' view of the process, and with good reason. Contemporary Arthurian scholar Joseph Duggan observed, "Chrétien is the earliest known *trouvère* to have composed in the troubadour manner...."[12] As to how and why such a transformation occurred, Duggan, like Lewis before him, saw the court of Henry and Marie in Troyes as a likely meeting place between north and south:

> Marie's court was certainly a key point of contact between troubadours composing in Occitan and *trouvères* composing in French, and since Chrétien is the earliest author of chansons written in the troubadour manner, he may have absorbed elements of the troubadour ethic at the court of Champagne.[13]

It was in the lengthy works of Chrétien, most likely composed at Troyes or under the patronage of its nobility, the interior, psychological concerns of the southern love poets met up and fused with the epic romance form based on imitations of classical antiquity. This was something new, and it clearly created a sensation.

Just as Geoffrey of Monmouth had earlier tried to create an English national epic by casting (and no doubt expanding) older Arthurian material into a classical epic form (see Chapter 9), Chrétien strove to do the same, but added to it the emotional power and range of Provençal love poetry. By that time, a growing number of French writers were becoming familiar with Virgil's *Aeneid* (particularly Book IV) and were creating their own various imitations such as the *Roman d'Alexandre*, the *Roman de Thèbes*, the *Roman de Troie*, and, above all, the *Roman d'Enéas*, collectively sometimes included under the misleading category, "Matter of Rome."[14] Benoît de Sainte-Maure was the author of the important last work, and possibly parts of the others as well. These epics also display some of the earliest and most extensive uses of the rhymed octosyllabic couplet in French, which Chrétien later adopted for his own highly effective usage.[15] Chrétien, based on many other internal similarities with his Arthurian romances, was well acquainted with this earlier body of work.[16] It is curious that both the style and the framework of these longer literary forms were pioneered and established by poets such as Benoît and Wace, both of whom were affiliated with the southern court at Poitiers under Eleanor of Aquitaine, and that these presumably coexisted with the new courtly love poetry of the troubadours. In spite of this, these various innovations were not blended together into a cohesive entity in the south; instead, this was accomplished a few years later in the northern court at Troyes under the patronage of Eleanor's daughter Marie. All of this suggests that there were still some crucial missing elements of Chrétien's Arthurian romance formula, as indeed there were.

One such crucial element was a thorough familiarity with the Latin poet Ovid, which Chrétien seems to have possessed, possibly courtesy of a formal cathedral school education. Some Arthurian scholars such as Urban Holmes have opined that, ultimately, the so-called Romantic "spirit" of Chrétien had its roots in scholastics such as Anselm and Bernard, as well as the mysticism of Hildegard von Bingen (see Chapter 20).[17] This may well be; however, the more obvious, direct choice for this honor seems to be Andalusia via Aquitaine. It is entirely possible, of course, that the "new feeling" noted by Lewis gained access to southern Europe after receiving a sympathetic passport, if not endorsement, from in-tune Christian scholastics such as Peter Abelard (see Chapter 20). As for the technical jargon of love (as opposed to the courtly attitude), the main source, by general consensus, was the ancient pagan Ovid, whose poetry was taught and revered in the progressive cathedral schools of northern France. This terminology was in turn injected into the octosyllabic epic French romance invented by Chrétien's predecessors in Aquitaine during the 12th century, while being simultaneously fused with the progressive and psychological subjectivity of courtly love.

Chrétien's intense interest in Ovid and the classics is self-evident.[18] In the opening verses of *Cligès*, he recites as his calling-card credentials prior French translations of Ovid, beginning with the *Commandments* (line 2), a sure reference to *The Cures for Love*, and *The Art of Love* (line 3), the latter perhaps Ovid's most notorious work, since it was the poem that resulted in his life-banishment from Rome. The sentence was personally pronounced upon the poet by Caesar Augustus, who was offended both in his capacity as a public arbiter of taste, as well as on some obscure, personal level that has never been conclusively established. In line 4, Chrétien credits himself with a French translation of Ovid's "the shoulder bite," an allusion to the Pelops legend from Book VI of the *Metamorphoses*. In lines 6–7, he additionally lists the tale of the "hoopoe, swallow, nightingale," to be associated with the tale of Philomena, which immediately follows that of Pelops in the *Metamorphoses*.[19] As Duggan concluded, Chrétien "clearly considered himself a legitimate successor to writers of classical antiquity such as Ovid."[20] Like many of his French contemporaries, and like Shakespeare four centuries later, Chrétien was enthralled by the premier Latin poet of love, and his work is suffused with the influence of the ancient master. Moreover, unlike many of the troubadour poets, who often took the ironic and mischievous Ovid at his literal word (sometimes with unintentionally humorous results), Chrétien seems to have understood perfectly well that the game of love is often just that — a game. For example, in his groundbreaking *Lancelot*, the poet fills the romance with references to Ovid's "love" poems, both serious and unserious, thus achieving a similar overall effect, one of heartfelt introspection combined with lighthearted burlesque. The same is true in his masterpiece *Yvain*, where the influence of Ovid's *The Art of Love* is strongly felt in the semi-ludicrous courtship scenes between the hero and Laudine. Specifically, reference is made to the possible excessive grief shown by Laudine at the funeral of her first husband, who was killed by Yvain in the heat of combat. According to Ovid, such situations represented a good opportunity to begin a new courtship.[21]

Lancelot deserves some additional commentary on this point because it has been such an incredibly influential work over the last 800 or more years. Even today, the romance is often taken by readers and critics alike too literally and too seriously. In both *Lancelot* and *The Art of Love*, the god of love is personified as one who gives commands to helpless, obeying mortals,[22] while love itself is portrayed as an illness needing to be treated by a physician (i.e., the poet). In both *Lancelot* and *The Cures for Love*, the poet-physician then offers very tangible remedies, such as dietary restrictions.[23] Also similar to *The Cures for Love*, love in *Lancelot* is compared to a sea journey, one that is both long and unpleasant.[24] In both *Lancelot* and *The Art of Love*, any male attempt to guard women against unfaithfulness is viewed as a totally futile endeavor.[25] And so forth. It is very hard to read passages like these and keep a straight face, and yet, to repeat, many readers of both Chrétien and Ovid still seem determined to do this, clearly against the original intent of both authors. This crucial element of irony and humor appears to be comparatively lacking in the more unrefined love poetry that came out of the south. In the hands of Chrétien it became an essential and unique element in the Arthurian romance, placing the concerns of the human heart front and center, and on equal if not superior footing to the concurrent, favorite themes of war, courage, and feudal knightly honor.

Lest we forget the obvious, the final ingredient thrown into the mix by the genius of Chrétien was the Arthurian tradition itself, or, to oversimplify once again, the "matter of Britain." As outlined in Chapter 3, this tradition began with Welsh bards and Anglo-Saxon chroniclers of the Dark Ages, but did not really gain international momentum or take full shape until the 12th century when Geoffrey of Monmouth, Wace, Marie de France, and Chrétien de Troyes began to adopt it as poetic material. It is entirely possible that Chrétien, who did more than anyone to popularize the genre as we tend to think of it, received *la matière de Bretagne* directly from England and writers such as Geoffrey, especially if he traveled there himself at some point. It is also nearly certain that he was immersed in the poets (both homegrown and Norman) who were patronized in Aquitaine and southern France, such as Wace. Above all, however, he likely gathered some of the more distinctive elements of his romances from the *jongleurs* of Brittany, even though these were oral and, if written down before Chrétien's versions, have mostly been since lost. Urban Holmes acknowledged this possibility when he wrote:

> The greatest contribution made by Chrétien (or possibly by an obscure predecessor) was to put into the new romance form a body of legends which were later referred to as the *matière de Bretagne*. This is the setting of King Arthur's court and the knights of the Round Table.[26]

The most likely "obscure predecessor" hypothesized by Holmes was a Breton *jongleur*. Yes, Chrétien had read Wace and possibly Geoffrey as well; yes, he had a genius for pure, unprecedented invention; nevertheless, there was oral tradition as well, and this was possibly more important than any other factor. Just as the troubadours were the great transmitters of courtly love to the north, so were the Celtic jongleurs of Brittany the conduit for and harbingers of Arthuriana on a very elemental, popular level not to be found in the polished writings of French or Latin poets of the age.

Finally, it should be re-emphasized that none of this innovation would have been possible for Chrétien or anyone else, were it not for the short-lived unification of the Angevin empire under Henry II of England. It cannot be overstated that the Plantagenet realm spread over a vast domain, unprecedented in western Europe since the time of the Caesars. This shattering of political borders, however uneasy and temporary it may have been, facilitated writers in absorbing multiple influences from Aquitaine, Brittany, Normandy, Wales, and England, as well as adjacent or nearby foreign powers such as Spain and the German Holy Roman Empire. Had the various French and English provinces been politically separate or at war with each other (the normal state of affairs), such an interflow of ideas would have been, at best, highly difficult. The advantage of unrestricted exchange was enhanced by a long-standing policy of literary subsidy, both in Normandy and in Aquitaine.[27] Above all, the unique position of Troyes and Champagne as a region formally aligned with the French crown but in reality quite independent and probably more in sympathy with the Norman-Anglo kingdom, provided a culturally interactive environment quite unlike anything before or since. One modest thesis of this study (and one that is hardly original) is that the greatest literary creativity often needs this kind of environment in order to flourish. The suddenness with which Chrétien found himself in such a unique time and place is partially reflected by his synthesis, which, although extraordinary in scope, is not complete. As noted by critics such as Lewis, the themes of romances reflect many dichotomies that are often found side-by-side rather than seamlessly fused together.[28] The latter development would take more time and great writers of future generations.

The unrestricted confluence of thought that represented 12th-century Champagne is something that all future readers can be grateful for, especially aficionados of King Arthur. Without it, safe to say, there would have been no King Arthur as we now know him, simply because that particular King Arthur was not a historical personage but rather a product of the French poetic imagination. Whether one speaks of profane courtly love à la *Lancelot* or the impenetrable mysteries of the Grail Quest, it is necessary to trace their development back to the remarkable ethnic pressure cooker in which Chrétien lived and wrote. Sadly, the land that had in many ways been the pipeline for that cooker (Aquitaine) had by the early 13th century also seen its best days. After Chrétien's death, southern France was on the cusp of a major disaster (a holocaust, in fact) that would eventually make repetition or reconstruction of this influential love poet's world difficult, if not impossible.

Chapter 7

The Desecration of Aquitaine

Honour and love combined to engage the attention of this society: these were its religion in a far more real sense than was that of the Church—
W. W. Comfort.[1]

Eleanor of Aquitaine died in 1204, age 82, at Fontevraud Abbey in France, surviving her younger second husband, King Henry II of England, by 15 years. She had outlasted her first husband, Louis VII of France, by 24 years. In 1199, five years prior to her death, her most famous son, King Richard I of England (*Coeur de Lion*), had died in her arms after suffering a battle wound in their own figurative backyard. Having survived for his entire adult life the worst that the Saracens, Germans, and English (as well as his own Norman cousins) could throw at him, Richard was finally dispatched by a teenage French crossbowman while supervising an otherwise insignificant, mopping-up operation near the city of Limoges in southern France.[2] Thus fate plays its tricks on the great and small alike. As for Richard's mother, Eleanor had for over half a century presided over, more than any other individual, the first great cultural renaissance in western Europe—exemplified in many ways by the genius of Chrétien de Troyes. She probably would have been thankful to have not lived long enough to witness the savage pillaging and oppression of her homeland by jealous and covetous neighbors during the early 13th century.

What made the French kingdom of Aquitaine (or "Occitan," as it is often called) so special?[3] Although precise geographic boundaries could be quite elastic depending on whom was fighting whom at any given moment, most historians would agree that the area always centered around Eleanor's native district of Poitou, with its seat of government at Poitiers. This was the very same ground on which, four centuries earlier, Charles Martel had successfully (and miraculously, it seemed at the time) defended Christendom against a determined Saracen onslaught directed from Spain. For the French, Poitiers had been hallowed ground for a long time leading up to this period. By the 12th century, it was the cultural capital of western Europe. Before that, Aquitaine had given rise to the troubadours and, as result, the birth of modern love poetry. It would in turn, through Eleanor's marriage to Henry II, serve to civilize the warlike Normans (particularly those who had conquered England), leading directly to the translation of Arthurian folklore into the French vernacular (see Chapter 10), and ultimately, its full flowering under the pen of Chrétien de Troyes and his continuators. These were its literary achievements in relation to the King Arthur legend. Other beneficial and long-term contributions to western civilization made by the unique society that was once 12th-century Aquitaine are far too numerous to list within this confined space, let alone to analyze in any depth or detail.

As suggested in the previous chapter, the reasons for the uniqueness of this place and time were due mainly to a great confluence of otherwise conflicting ideas, religions, and cultures, for which Aquitaine, more than any place in Christendom, was ideally suited. Tragically, it was this same uniqueness and independence that would lead to its utter destruction within a few years after Eleanor's death. Also contributing to the catastrophe was the weakening and disintegration of Henry II's unwieldy Angevin empire after his death (see Chapter 8). It simply became much more vulnerable. Eleanor, her forefathers, consorts, and children, were all living embodiments of this strange and enticing melting pot—a world that both fanatically and militantly embraced Christianity, but at the same time threw aside its more reactionary superstitions and stodgy social constraints. This was a land in which the stern preaching of Saint Bernard and Saint Dominic could make little headway (see Chapter 18). Traits such as these, taken in isolation, made Aquitaine different from its neighbors. Taken in tandem with a steady stream of refinement and scientific knowledge pouring in over the mountains from Spain and Andalusia, the social terrain was ripe for a cultural revolution.

The lure of a new intellectual freedom, combined with much higher economic standards of living, was too great to be resisted by any person of intelligence or depth of feeling.[4] Nine hundred years later, medieval Aquitaine can still seem like a land of startling contradictions to those who revisit its legacy; and yet it is from such places that truly great innovations often come. The dominant courtly love aspect of the King Arthur legends—perhaps the most essential and distinctive Arthurian ingredient—was only one small example of this phenomenon. Although there are no documented connections between Chrétien and Eleanor (or southern France, for that matter), that some kind of connection surely existed is almost taken for granted by scholars and rightfully so. After all, it was Eleanor's daughter Marie of Champagne who, in the 1170s, directed Chrétien to change the course of Arthurian (and world) literature with his invention of Lancelot as the lover of Guinevere. Moreover, it was Eleanor's grandfather, Duke William IX, who popularized the troubadour style adopted by Chrétien and countless other *trouvères* in northern France.

While its bracing intellectual freedom (as well as its unusual emphasis on education for its political leaders) may have attracted only a small, literate portion of society, the burgeoning economic prosperity of southern France gradually became the envy of all Europe. After a century of fomenting resentment (and some petty provocation), the lengthy human tragedy known to historians as the Albigensian Crusades unfolded over a 20-year period between 1209 and 1229. By the time it was over, the troubadours, at least as they had been known in their original incarnation, were no more. This was the least of it, however; no one really knows how many people died or how many towns were destroyed.[5] Various accounts, though wildly at odds with each other, all suggest that no one at the time had ever seen anything like it in terms of devastation and atrocities. It gives one pause to think that the Crusades, even with all of the negative press handed out by modern historians, are still rarely associated with this type of uninhibited, Christian-on-Christian warfare. Random violence that characterized the Albigensian venture, as well as a number of other, lesser-known episodes from the era, remain an obscure, lesser-known chapter of history. One cannot help but wonder how Chrétien and his circle of cultivated patrons, had they lived to see it, would have reacted. They probably all would have been horrified, and would have seen right through its sanctimonious, religious pretense.

In essence, and with surprisingly little effort at or concern over cover-up by its perpetrators, the Albigensian Crusades of the early 13th century were the biggest and most brazen land grab in the history of medieval France. We leave it to specialized scholars to tell the full story of this dismal chapter in human history, but a few general observations are relevant for purposes of the King Arthur legends and the northern French poet who did so much to popularize them. This was, after all, the same land that had introduced courtly love to western civilization. Without it, there would never have been any Roundtable or *Lancelot*, and probably no Holy Grail either (see Chapter 22). The long, bloody conflict that engulfed Aquitaine transpired over four interconnected time periods: 1209–1211; 1211–1215; 1216–1225; and 1226–1229.[6] Some historians have additionally postulated that the outrageously manipulative "Children's Crusade" of 1212 may have been an outgrowth of the Albigensian enterprise; that is, an excuse to levy troops for the holy war in southern France.[7] The name itself somehow came (again, no one knows exactly how) from the obscure town of Albi, which was only one small place within a very large territory involved in the conflict.[8] Modern scholars such as Maria Rosa Menocal eloquently blame the Albigensian Crusade for effectively wiping out the culture that had previously given rise to and supported the troubadours. While there has been some debate over this point, there can be no question that medieval Aquitanian society was soon replaced by one far less tolerant and assimilating.[9]

To summarize events, the arch-conservative Pope Innocent III in 1208 authorized the mobilization of armies in Germany, Italy, and northern France for the purpose of crushing non-conformist groups prevalent in the south, generally labeled as "Cathars." As historian Christopher Tyerman explained: "The novelty of the Albigensian crusades lay in the church's recruitment of an international force rather than rely[ing] on local secular Christian rulers to combat heresy, and the application to the campaigns of the privileges of Holy Land penitential warfare."[10] In effect, Pope Innocent III was not so innocent; by most modern standards he would be considered a common war criminal for authorizing and encouraging the massacres. The Cathar "heretics" who were the targets and victims of the crusade comprised an enormously diverse group whose main uniting feature was probably their material wealth. It is true that many of them were non–Christians or conventional Christians in only the loosest sense of the term, while many others were no more than what nowadays would be called Protestants.[11] Many, many victims were simply orthodox neighbors who did not feel as threatened by non-conformist beliefs as did the official church hierarchy in Rome.

An instructive sidebar to this mass persecution is that, while the war succeeded in destroying diversity and tolerance in southern France, heresy remained long after the crusade had subsided. As Tyerman emphasized: "The Albigensian crusades settled the fate of nations more readily than it did the destiny of souls or faith."[12] It finally took secret police within the church itself to root out heresy in Catholicism during the aftermath of the war. The Inquisition, which had its roots in these events, later became institutionalized for that specific purpose.[13] What had been a holy war in Chrétien's day to secure Jerusalem against Islam had become, less than two generations later, a holy war to stamp out all dissent within the church itself. As Christians gradually lost political and religious control of the Middle East, they attempted and often succeeded in exerting more political and religious control over each other. This trend also no doubt contributed to the increasingly heavy-handed Christianization of the Arthurian legends by poets and writers during this same time period. As a result, the light and subtle touch originally applied by Chrétien in this regard would be subsequently lost forever.

The legend of the Holy Grail and its quest is perhaps the best known example of this process. Although more fully explored in Chapter 22, it deserves some mention within this context. The Grail legend originally unveiled by Chrétien became forever linked with the Cathar heresy during this era, much to the delight of modern readers and writers of fictional mystery and adventure.[14] Whether or not one is a fan of *The Da Vinci Code* (this writer is not) it must be honestly conceded that the dubious Grail connection to the Albigensian Crusades has probably done more to introduce its legend to readers and movie goers than all other Arthurian literature combined. Thanks to Dan Brown, everyone has heard of the Holy Grail, while virtually no one has heard of Chrétien de Troyes, the great poet who, for all practical purposes, invented the conceit. Like the Shakespeare authorship question, the literary quest for the true meaning of the Grail has the potential to lead the reader straight into an endless universe of often bizarre and sometimes extravagant theories. Nevertheless, many of these can be instructive in that they demonstrate how small bits and pieces of information can first be gradually embellished, then interconnected as if they were, always and by necessity, causally related to one another. After all, this is how all Arthurian romance has developed from its very inception. Chrétien, if he were alive, would probably criticize it for being mediocre storytelling, rather than for being made up or misconstrued.

One example of this process can be used for illustrative purposes. In his tenacious, down-loading treatise, *Holy Blood, Holy Grail*, Michael Baigent authoritatively wrote that "during the Albigensian Crusade ecclesiastics fulminated against the Grail romances, declaring them to be pernicious if not heretical."[15] Presumably, this view is partially founded on a theory advanced during the 1930s in two cult classics written by the doomed German adventurer, Otto Rahn — *Crusade Against the Grail* and *Lucifer's Court*.[16] Reading these works, one would think that the crusade had been primarily motivated by literary criticism rather than economic plunder. A closer look at the assertion reveals that, while certainly real to some extent, orthodox church suspicion towards the Grail legends tended to be a more a matter of personal opinion rather than concerted and coordinated effort. In one work, *Chronicon*, written by Hélinand of Froidmont between 1211 and 1223 at the height of the Albigensian atrocities, the author expressed a desire to write a proper "Latin" version of the Grail legend that would be more plausible and edifying than the ones then in circulation.[17] Hélinand was also representative of a larger school of thought within the Catholic church (and among the Cistercian followers of Bernard) who were generally hostile towards all troubadour poetry because it glorified adulterous relationships. They also firmly believed that any moral laxity tended to foster religious heresy. It was during this same period in European history that the exalted praise of women in secular literature gradually shifted towards a sacred praise of the Virgin Mary (see Chapter 4).[18] All of this, though, is a far cry from asserting that the Arthurian Grail legends were the driving force behind the unhinged fury of the Albigensian Crusades.

Far more important than any individual obsession over the Grail legend was the crusade's unequivocal abolishment of the very same melting pot that precipitated and subsidized the King Arthur tradition to begin with. The desecration of a cultural attitude — one of openness and curiosity — is the big picture that we all should be mindful of. The Albigensian Crusade was a proverbial Sword of Damocles which destroyed both the good and bad — heresy and creativity — in one fell swoop. Medieval Aquitaine was an incubator for both activities simultaneously, it would seem. Admittedly, one cannot completely disassociate the Holy Grail from this region, given that the very origin of the word *graal* is in Provençal, according to most investigators of the sources.[19] To be more precise, it probably came to southern France from Catalonia in northeastern Spain.[20] It likely crossed the Pyrenees from its Muslim source and was hospitably received into Aquitaine because its inhabitants had a receptive, open-minded attitude, at least by comparative standards for their time. External influences (of which there were an endless number) were not automatically banned or feared; they were adapted without hesitation whenever useful or pleasurable. This outlook, however, came to a temporary halt, or rather was suppressed, during the early 1200s. To repeat, one of the many casualties of the crusade was the creative impetus and sparkplug that originally lay behind the creation of the Arthurian romance genre.

There is yet another paradox here, perhaps one even more difficult to untangle than the intertwined good and bad elements wiped out by the Albigensian Crusade. The struggle represented the climax of an irreconcilable conflict between the orthodox Catholic church and its countless and varied unorthodox offshoots residing in the Occitan; yet, in apparent contradiction, it was orthodox churchmen who probably helped to invent the King Arthur legend as much as (if not more than) the troubadours of the south. Chrétien was himself likely a clergyman, as were Geoffey of Monmouth, Wace, and many others who came before and after him. For some critics, such as Urban Holmes, the "Romantic spirit" itself had its true literary and spiritual roots in northern scholastic churchmen such as Saint Anselm, Saint Bernard, and possibly even 12th century mystics such as the famed German abbess, Hildegard von Bingen (see Chapter 20).[21] This view probably overstates their contribution; however, there can be little question that without monasticism and the Catholic church, there would be no King Arthur legends as we think of them today. There can also be no denying that Chrétien and many of his fellow Arthurian romancers were indelibly influenced by the sermons of Bernard, as were many writers at the time. Most can agree that Chrétien and other innovators took material that had originally been pagan lore and gave it, to varying degrees, a sacred veneer. This was done out of piety and/or necessity. As for the troubadours of Aquitaine and those who nurtured them, the quote by W.W. Comfort at the heading of this chapter probably comes closest to hitting the truth in terms of the secular religion that was the main focus of worship in that society.

In the end, the Albigensian Crusade proved to be another painful step in the ultimate remapping of western Europe, eventually leading to the creation of modern nation-states which included the territorial redefinition of France itself. Another victim of this process would be the once autonomous French dukedoms such as Champagne, which originally fostered the genius of Chrétien. His Arthurian romances, in retrospect, were the direct product of a very specific time and place. Had these been written at all sooner or later than they actually were, the results would have surely been much different and probably a lot less desirable. It should never be forgotten, however, that the geographic map of Europe during the time of Chrétien — the same European map that witnessed the dawn of the Arthurian romance — was quite different than the one we are used to thinking of today. This 12th-century historical atlas represented an ever-shifting political landscape that influenced the genesis of the fictional King Arthur as much as the imaginations of the poets from whom his legends sprang. Not surprisingly, when one attempts to study or reconstruct a map of the fictional Arthurian world, its precise boundaries, distances, directions, and place names seem to become more and more difficult to pin down.

Chapter 8

An Arthurian Geography Lesson

Try to imagine a map with no England or France as we think of these countries today; in fact, try to imagine no countries at all in the modern sense. Instead, picture one enormous kingdom united under a single monarch (Henry II), encompassing both sides of the English Channel, stretching from the highlands of Scotland to the Pyrenees of Spain. Such an empire would by definition encompass many languages, cultures, and conflicting shades of religious belief.[1] Next door, picture a French king (Louis VII) whose effective political control did not extend much further than suburban Paris (the *Ile-de-France*). This mini French state would have been hemmed in on the west by the trans-channel, Anglo-Norman mega-kingdom, which technically speaking, was a French vassal, but in political reality, a powerful threat. To the east, the Ile-de-France would also have been overshadowed by a sprawling German Holy Roman Empire, presided over by an emperor (Frederick Barbarossa) enjoying papal endorsement from Rome. Surrounding regional Paris were various fiefdoms such as Champagne and Flanders, ruled by their own dukes who also were technically vassals of the French king, but in reality played all sides to their own advantage, or sometimes for their very own survival.

Most importantly, all of these rulers were related to each other by blood or marriage, and international disputes were often reduced to the sordid level of family feuds. For example, the wife of Henry II, Eleanor of Aquitaine, had previously been the wife of Louis VII (see Chapter 4). Children from both marriages went on to become royalty and nobility in their own right, including one daughter, Marie, Countess of Champagne and patron of Chrétien de Troyes. She had married the great-grandson of William the Conqueror, Henry the Liberal, Count of Champagne, whose distant cousin (the Conqueror's other great-grandson), Henry II, now sat on the throne of England and was married to Marie's mother Eleanor. Marie's father (and

Eleanor's ex-husband), King Louis VII of France, then married Henry the Liberal's sister, Adele. From here it only becomes more complicated. This fluent, unstable political landscape would later allow large foreign armies to march into southern France during the early 13th century, spreading devastation and rapine, while the rest of the continent stood back and watched apathetically or even applauded. This was also the map of Europe that saw the dawn of the Arthurian romance under the pen of Chrétien de Troyes around the year 1170.

Before the author began this project he was quite familiar with the historical background of feudal Europe, and knew that it was from this checkerboard polyglot that the Arthurian legend originally emerged. What later came as a total surprise was the conspicuously secondary role played by the English in the entire process — that is, if one defines "English" during the mid–12th century as Anglo-Saxon. Not only were French romancers such as Chrétien primarily responsible for transforming Celtic myths into popular legend, it was French and Anglo-Norman politics, as well as social mores, that primarily shaped the creative impetus. This was true even for Chrétien's predecessor Geoffrey of Monmouth (see Chapter 9), who was writing to please the Anglo-Norman nobility and was probably of Breton extraction himself. During that time, the word "Britain"—*Bretagne* to be exact—emphatically signified lands on both sides of the English Channel. As for English history and geography in the modern sense, these were (not surprisingly) given nominal and obligatory recognition, after which European continental and French reference points became the main focus.

This filtering process began with the very first true Arthurian romance, Chrétien's *Erec and Enide*. "Erec" was a Breton name, as the poet himself informs us (line 652), and many non–English names used in Chrétien's tale appear to have been appropriated from the margins of a period document known as the *Mappa Mundi* in order to give the story a more international flavor.[2] Curiously, Arthur's final, fatal battleground of Camlann (in England) is never mentioned in any of Chrétien's romances, although it is found in Geoffrey of Monmouth and later became very important to the legend as a whole. Chrétien and his audiences may have simply been more interested in Arthur's knights (especially their amorous misadventures) than in Arthur himself; therefore, the place name of his downfall was not considered a crucial piece of information for storytelling purposes. It is also apparent that Chrétien was more interested in mixing tragedy with comedy (and, if necessary, attaching an artificial happy ending), as opposed to writing straightforward tragedy. Accordingly, Camlann had no essential or useful place in the poet's overall dramatic scheme.[3]

Chrétien did see fit, however, to conclude *Erec and Enide* with a spectacular coronation pageant for the title hero at Nantes in Brittany. He could not, of course, have Erec crowned in England where Arthur reigned, but there were many other locales besides Nantes where this easily could have been accomplished, even within the British Isles.[4] Erec was a king in his own right, but he was also a knight of the Roundtable and Arthur's vassal, much like King Hoel of Brittany in Geoffrey of Monmouth's account. The most overt connection between Chrétien's chosen setting and political events of the time — a strong one that can be used to reasonably to date the work — is that Henry II held court at Rennes and Nantes in 1169 while presiding over the installation of his son Geoffrey as Duke of Brittany.[5] Henry Plantagenet — a French and Latin-speaking Norman — had married Eleanor of Aquitaine in 1152, thus ambitiously positioning himself to become overlord of the massive and prosperous kingdom which now overshadowed his weak rival in Paris. This same rival also happened to be his new wife's ex-husband.

Perhaps the most dynamic aspect of Henry's vast kingdom was the political unification of the Welsh and Bretons. In theory this sounded quite good, but in practice, problems arose. One overt rivalry between the Welsh and the Bretons was the contested cultural ownership of the Arthurian tradition. As imaginative storytellers, the Bretons gave their Welsh kinsmen everything they could handle. Typifying this struggle between battling bards were multiple, disputed locations of Arthurian landmarks, beginning with the Isle of Avalon, mentioned by Chrétien in *Erec and Enide* (line 1907) as the home of Arthur's sister Morgan le Fay and her consort Guingamar.[6] In Great Britain, perhaps the most popular geographic candidate for the "Isle of Apples" (as it translates from the Breton and Welsh languages) is Glastonbury in Somerset, which is now dry land but formerly was surrounded by a marsh or lake. Located off the northwestern coast of Brittany, however, is the *Ile d'Aval*, which has its own traditional, mystical associations with the burial, rejuvenation, or resurrection of King Arthur.[7] This French-speaking island of apples is obviously much farther away from Camlann (wherever that was exactly) than Glastonbury, as well as on the opposite side of the channel; however, it still exists as a literal and attractive island destination with an enchanted reputation. Given the predominance of magic in the Arthurian world, not to mention the elasticity of the geographic divide between Wales and Brittany (as we shall see in a moment), its claim cannot be completely dismissed out of hand.

If the unrestricted geography of Chrétien's *Erec and Enide* is impressive, that of his next Arthurian romance, *Cligès*, is sweeping and in many ways, unprecedented. Cligès, along with his father Alexander, are Greeks from the

Byzantine Eastern Roman Empire, who travel west seeking to earn their spurs as Arthurian knights at the English court. This of course involves shuttling back and forth across Germany, France and Brittany, but the truly impressive geographic details come after the heroes land in England. There, the characters move between the towns of Southampton, Shoreham, Oxford, Wallingford, Windsor, London, Canterbury, and Dover, all within plausible distances, order, and time-frames of each other.[8] Both the exterior and interior of Windsor Castle, under renovation during the time that Chrétien's early romances were being composed, are described in detail.[9] When reading these passages it is quite easy to forget that they were produced by a French continental writer. This was an age, it should be remembered, in which geographic knowledge, even among the literate, typically did not extend far beyond the boundaries of one's own local fiefdom. The question is therefore naturally raised, where exactly did the poet get his English geographic data?

Beginning with Gaston Paris during the 19th century, there has been a growing and respectable school of thought among critics that Chrétien probably traveled to England at some early stage in his career.[10] Constance Bullock-Davies, who has conducted perhaps the most detailed analysis of the question, observed that "apart from his knowledge of France, which has to be taken for granted, the country he appears to have known best and which he so convincingly describes is England."[11] She stated the sound literary maxim, "When an author is writing of what he knows in depth he is able to transmit to a reader an unmistakable impression of authenticity."[12] This is true for Shakespeare or Twain, just as much as for Chrétien de Troyes. It has been observed by Joseph Duggan that, in contrast to his detailed geographic precision for England, Chrétien in *Cligès* gives few if any details about the Byzantine homeland of the hero, even though during his time Constantinople was one of the world's most famous and prosperous cities.[13] Moreover, the broad, trans-channel domain of King Arthur in *Cligès* and other romances strongly suggests the sweeping Angevin Anglo-Norman kingdom under Henry II and Eleanor of Aquitaine at the time these works were written.[14]

If one accepts Chrétien's disputed authorship of *Guillaume d'Angleterre* (see Chapter 18), then the argument for the poet's first- or second-hand familiarity with the geographic landscape of mainland Britain receives a further boost. In addition to its wide-ranging place settings, *Guillaume d'Angleterre* has an English sourcebook cited by the poet (who calls himself Chrétien) from the Abbey of Bury-St. Edmund's in Suffolk.[15] The house of Blois-Champagne, as emphasized by Ruth Harwood Cline, had close kinship connections with civil and ecclesiastical authorities in England, and therefore had regular and extensive dealings with them. Interestingly, Chrétien's patron Henry the Liberal had an uncle and two brothers who were both active leaders in the English church, one of whom, Hugh of Lagny, was for a time abbot at St. Benet of Holme in Norfolk, adjacent to Suffolk in the north. Furthermore, Bury-St. Edmund's and St. Benet of Holme had close historical and cultural ties, partly because of their regional proximity to one another.[16] Regardless of whether Chrétien personally traveled to Great Britain, it is definitely true that he would have had direct access to detailed information from this extensive family network of patrons. These ties would have been even more pronounced if Chrétien was himself a clerical member of that same family. Finally, it may well be that the poet was both a family member *and* traveled to England.

In Chrétien's next pioneering romance, *Lancelot*, physical geography becomes more nebulous and almost irrelevant to the story. Camelot — mentioned in *Lancelot* for the first time in world literature by Chrétien — is a perfect example of this. Like Avalon, the location of Camelot is disputed among those who assert that it was a real place. For Malory and many others, it was situated at Winchester, appropriately enough, near Glastonbury and the legendary Avalon. For Chrétien, in the opening of *Lancelot* (lines 30a and 33a), the fabled home of King Arthur's court was somewhere near the village of Caerleon in southeastern Wales, but this is not dwelled or elaborated upon.[17] Other Anglophiles who favor physical, concrete remains have identified Camelot with the dramatic archeological site at Cadbury Castle, located much further to the south in Somerset, England. The French, on the other hand, like to place Camelot at Nantes in Brittany, which might cause us to laugh until we realize that one of Chrétien's most famous and influential adaptors, the Bavarian knight Wolfram von Eschenbach, also strongly implied that Camelot was at Nantes in his 13th-century epic poem, *Parzifal*.[18] Clearly, the Nantes association is a very old and venerable tradition. The big question looming behind these competing speculations is whether Camelot, like King Arthur himself, ever existed. Confronted with a maze of reasonable choices, some commentators have sensibly concluded that Camelot is best viewed as a state of mind or source of inspiration, rather than as a physical place on the map.[19]

Although Chrétien does not expressly identify Lancelot as French — the character is merely referred to as "Lancelot of the Lake" (line 3660) — his Breton origin soon became part of the Arthurian tradition and has remained popular ever since. Today, the tourist trade in Brittany quite impressively milks it for all of its worth. About ten kilometers north of the charming village of Paimpont (located in the forest of that same name, also known as Brocéliande), is a murky prehistoric lake, fronted by the Château de Comper, and within that edifice, most appropriately, Le Centre de l'imaginaire Arthurien (see Chapter 19). These environs, by pretty much unanimous opinion, are the traditional home of Lancelot and his fairy-stepmother Viviane. To repeat, none of this is found in Chrétien, but the traditions are first established in his immediate wake. The neighborhood of Paimpont is the hub for an entire circuit of Arthurian tourist sites surrounding the remnants of the still imposing Forêt de Brocéliande. Some of these sites include Le Tombeau de Merlin, Le Fontaine de Berenton, and the rustic country church at Tréhorenteuc. The church is remarkable in that it features mid–20th-century mosaics depicting themes first utilized in an Arthurian context by Chrétien, such as the Holy Grail and the White Stag. This artwork seems (quite appropriately) to associate the Arthurian legend with the sacrifices of the French *Resistance* during World War II. As for Merlin's tomb, he was said to be imprisoned in a rock (still to be seen and touched) as punishment for his obsession with the enchantress Viviane.

Lancelot is logically assigned a French tomb as well at La Forest-Landerneau near the city of Brest on the far west coast of Brittany, within the romantic precincts of the Château de Joyeuse Garde. In Chrétien's poem, Lancelot discovers his own pre-prepared tomb and confirms his heroic destiny by easily lifting the heavy stone that covers it. The list of Arthurian landmarks in Brittany is lengthy and no doubt continues to grow as this is being written: the Forêt de Huelgoat (with Le Camp d'Artus and Le Grotte d'Artus) and the Monts d'Arrée, both located near the Breton west coast and having various legendary connections to Arthur and Merlin; the Sillon de Talbert on the north Breton coast, associated with Arthur and his half-sister Morgan le Fay; Saint-Efflam, where the local namesake patron saint upstaged Arthur by vanquishing a dragon; Mont-Saint-Michel, where in Geoffrey of Monmouth's account, Arthur killed a menacing giant in single combat ... and so forth.[20] Once again, many of these traditions do not appear in Chrétien's works, but it was he who first provided the imaginative spark by immortalizing *jongleur* oral tradition as epic romantic poetry.

To make Chrétien's French hijacking of the Arthurian legend from the British complete, he utterly ignores the "English" Channel in his superlative masterpiece, *Yvain*. During the story, the hero sojourns on horseback from Carduel (Carlisle) in England to Brocéliande Forest in Brittany within a space of two days, but with absolutely no mention of crossing water.[21] One's first inclination is to attribute this major omission to medieval ignorance; however, upon close inspection, the gap appears to be intentional. In *Cligès*, a work that everyone agrees Chrétien wrote before *Yvain*, a full awareness of the channel is demonstrated as characters cross water by ship between England and Brittany. In Chrétien's first work, *Erec and Enide*, the channel is not expressly mentioned, but a firm sense of time and distance is reflected by the author as it takes characters a week to travel from Tintagel Castle in Cornwall to Nantes (in Brittany, it is specified). Was the author becoming senile by the time he wrote *Yvain*? Is tectonic plate theory a possible explanation? To assert that the poet did not know any better is to risk reducing him to our own uniformed level. To say that he knew but did not care, or better yet, that he knew his audiences did not care, seems a more likely scenario.

This reader would surmise that Chrétien, like all educated Frenchmen of the time, knew darn well where the channel was but *chose* to ignore it for dramatic effect, thus intentionally flaunting all conventional notions of time and space. This was a poet who, in the very same work (lines 5713–5714), reminds us with hyperbole that the distant Seine and Danube rivers are impossible to connect. When it suited his purpose, Chrétien was perfectly capable of drawing upon accurate geographic minutiae. As for Yvain's horseback journey to Brocéliande and the magical fountain of Berenton, it represented, in effect, an adventure to places both supernatural and real. Normal laws of time and space would no more apply to Yvain than to Dorothy traveling to Oz from Kansas in a cyclone. It was this same stark gap between reality and fantasy that caused Wace and countless other tourists to shake their heads after visiting Brocéliande in search of wonders (see Chapter 3). As this type of magical adventure became one of Chrétien's trademarks, it also grew more pronounced as his romances evolved in complexity. Above all, to expect a French poet, or even an Anglo-Norman poet, to refer to the channel as "English" is absurd. A casual glance at any map labeled in French will reveal this same body of water consistently referred to as *La Manche*.[22]

By the time he wrote his last romance, *Perceval*, Chrétien had more or less abandoned all conventional notions of physical geography, as exemplified by the elusive castle of the Holy Grail. The title hero first ventures from remote Wales to King Arthur's court, which is plausible enough, but then the story's landscape becomes increasingly otherworldly, until the reader can do little except roll with each new turn of the poet's imagination. Perceval stumbles into the Grail Castle and the metaphysical realm of the Fisher King much the same way characters are transported to and from the wooded magic chateau in Jean Cocteau's classic film version of *Beauty and the Beast*.[23] As for the alleged location of the "historical" Grail Castle on the map, once again there is no shortage of choices, depending on one's personal preference. Perhaps the most popular site is Corbenic in Wales, derived from Malory.[24] Others identify it with Castell Dinas Brân in Wales, or Peel

Castle on the Isle of Man, or any other number of various locations in northwestern England.

Like English Avalon and Camelot, the Grail Castle has a French competitor, and a surprisingly compelling one at that. Isolated in the French Pyrenees, near the Spanish frontier, is the visually stunning Montségur, one of the last Cathar fortresses to be reduced during the bloody and morally-bankrupt Albigensian Crusades. While adherents to the Cathar heresy in southern France were not saints in any sense of the word, their credentials for religious martyrdom were plausible. Many of them, with or without putting up a fight, were massacred by orthodox Catholics eager for wealthy plunder and fearful of things for which they had little or no understanding. In the shadow of these atrocities, the Pyrenees region developed its own Holy Grail tradition, a tradition which in fact may have been present there from the very beginning (see Chapter 7).

The identification of the Grail Castle within a mountainous French wilderness provoked a bemused and fond tolerance from this writer until he realized that Richard Wagner's last opera *Parsifal* presents the same scenario. Wagner's libretto, as all his enthusiasts know, is based on Wolfram von Eschenbach's epic poem, which does not specify the Pyrenees location but heavily implies it with other French locations, calling the place *Munsalvæsche* or *Montsalvat*.[25] From these suggestions, Wagner (and others) have quite logically and sensibly deduced a Pyrenees site. It should be recalled that the German nationalists Wagner and Wolfram were not exactly pro–French in their political views, yet they still embraced these French geographic associations within the Arthurian legend. Moreover, in *Parzifal*, Wolfram openly criticized Chrétien for not telling the whole story. Wolfram repeatedly asserted that his version was based on a southern French source, one Kyot the Provençal, as opposed to a book that Chrétien says was given to him by Philip of Flanders.[26] This criticism, combined with myriad similarities between the two versions, especially in the middle sections of Wolfram's tale, suggests a common tradition. If Wolfram was simply making up things not found in or departing from Chrétien's version, then why would he seek outside justification? Chrétien's other continuators did not feel a need to do this, especially given that his *Perceval* was left unfinished with countless unanswered questions about how it should end.

As for the stance adopted by numerous scholars — namely, that the Kyot attribution is a literary fiction — this may well be, but there may be some truth to it as well. Wolfram states that Kyot accessed the story from an Arabic manuscript in Toledo, written by a non–Christian named Flegetanis. This was an age in which Arabic and ancient Greek learning were in fact flowing into France via translated Arabic manuscripts direct from Toledo (see Chapter 2).[27] Because a manuscript or other references to these sources may no longer exist does not seem like a very convincing reason to dismiss the possibility. Given ever-emerging connections between Andalusian and French medieval poetry, Spanish Islamic ties to the Arthurian legends, especially those transmitted through southern France, now seem less far-fetched. For example, the fact that Wolfram interpreted the Holy Grail not as a grail but rather as a kind of philosopher's stone (derived from Sufi mysticism), deserves more critical comment than it has received in the past. In any event, Wolfram's "fiction" may well have a basis in fact.

Modern obsession with the alleged Grail Castle at Montségur has led to many bizarre theories which have filled entire books of their own.[28] Lack of concrete, documented information always gives free range to the human imagination. Nevertheless, it is this imaginative world that forms the heart and soul of the King Arthur legends. Physical places and concrete objects do not count nearly as much as how we picture make-believe places and objects in our minds, and Chrétien would surely agree with this. Above all, it is useful to remember that whether one is studying the geography or any other aspect of the Arthurian universe, we should not concern ourselves so much with objective, historical truth as with subjective, imaginative truth.

Not so very long ago, this author thought that all Arthurian landmarks having historical basis (to whatever extent) were located strictly in England and Wales. Now, he would definitely add France to that list, and, quite frankly, Timbuktu, if only the Bretons would tell a good story about it. Ultimately, the Arthurian kingdom is best viewed as a kingdom of the human mind and heart, not unlike that endorsed by the character Balian in the film *Kingdom of Heaven*, portraying political events in the Middle East in the probable aftermath of Chrétien's death.[29] Chrétien devised his poetic opus not with indisputable, historical facts and figures, but rather from fables concocted by Breton *jongleurs* and Aquitainian *troubadours*. He was also inspired by Geoffrey of Monmouth's audacious attempt to create an English Virgilian epic, which we shall examine presently. He may have even glanced at a map while doing it. One thing, however, is for certain: any kind of rigid, fossilized thinking will surely cause one to trip in the constantly shifting landscape of Arthurian geography.

Chapter 9

Geoffrey of Monmouth Proves Reading Is Believing

> *During a period of five hundred years the tradition of his exploits was preserved, and rudely embellished, by the obscure bards of Wales and Armorica, who were odious to the Saxons and unknown to the rest of mankind. The pride and curiosity of the Norman conquerors prompted them to enquire into the ancient history of Britain: they listened with fond credulity to the tale of Arthur, and eagerly applauded the merit of a prince who had triumphed over the Saxons, their common enemies—* Edward Gibbon.[1]

Before the 1130s, all that had been written about Arthur (or at least, that which has survived down to the present), amounted to very little and practically nothing the average person tends to associate with the Arthurian legend. Then, around 1136, an amazing thing happened: the *Historia Regum Britanniae* (*History of the Kings of Britain*) was written by Geoffrey of Monmouth, the future Catholic Bishop of Asaph. Not only did Geoffrey make Arthur's story the focal point and climax of his epic, he effectively popularized the tale outside of Wales and Brittany to unprecedented levels. As a result, within a few short years Arthur's name would be on the lips of almost everyone in the western world, and one of the world's great literary traditions would be firmly established. Surprisingly, though, the King Arthur one reads about in the *Historia* bears only a vague resemblance to that which modern fans are used to seeing. If Arthurian geography can be challenging to those interested in pure historical facts (see Chapter 8), then wide discrepancies between Geoffrey's portrait of the hero and that presented eight centuries later by a skilled novelist like T.H. White are nearly irreconcilable. Nevertheless, within two generations of Geoffrey, French romancers on the continent—

Chrétien de Troyes being first and foremost among them — would creatively embellish the legend with innumerable details, subplots, and motifs now comfortably familiar to any young or adult reader of White's *The Once and Future King*.

Thus, in a very real sense, it was Geoffrey who got the ball rolling in terms of introducing King Arthur to the general European public in 1136, and yet (as we shall see in a moment), one searches the *Historia* in vain for most prototypical Arthurian details.[2] To put the work in proper perspective, we should remind ourselves that this was three centuries before the invention of Gutenberg movable type. That Geoffrey's impact was so great during an age that only knew illuminated manuscripts and word of mouth makes his achievement (as well as Chrétien's) all the more impressive. Any lingering doubts as to the tremendous advantages enjoyed by the 15th-century printing press when first introduced are quickly dispelled upon reflection. In 1485, Thomas Malory's *Le Morte d'Arthur* became one of the first major English books printed with the new technology. Malory's work was far more reliant on French continental sources than on Geoffrey's "English" *Historia*, which Malory "beat to press" by 23 years. It has rightfully dominated Arthurian studies ever since. When Geoffrey was finally printed (in Paris) in 1508,[3] he became better known as one of Shakespeare's primary sources for *King Lear* and *Cymbeline* than for the legendary British king that he glorified above all others.[4]

For many if not most readers, Geoffrey's panoramic, grandiose Latin prose in the *Historia*, along with a serious — indeed, totally humorless — tone, effectively disguises the fact that there is little if any historical basis for his version of the King Arthur story. Indeed, it is useful at this point to observe that the etymological roots of the words "history" and "story" in the Old French language are hopelessly blurred together.[5] For audiences back then (as today), there was often hardly any difference between fact and fiction. As for Geoffrey, his fabrications and falsehoods are much too numerous to list in detail within a study limited in scope such as this, but a few random highlights may suffice. For example, variant period manuscripts (of which there a large number, thanks to the work's popularity) cannot agree at which battle Arthur's nephew Sir Gawain dies a heroic death — some editions have him die twice, just to be safe. Arthur's antagonist on the continent, the Roman emperor Leo, is unknown to history, nor is there any corroboration for the Roman governor of Gaul, Lucius Tiberius. At the climactic, Armageddon-like battle fought near Langres in France, the king of Spain is given an Arabic name (Ali Fatima) even though the Prophet Mohammad had not yet been born and it would be another two centuries before Muslim Saracens invaded the Iberian peninsula from North Africa. In short, Geoffrey's history is really a story, or pseudo-history, as some commentators have politely called it. His geography, arithmetic, and dates are hopelessly confused.[6] He is obsessed with prophecy and magic; his genealogies are more suspect than the Bible's. But Geoffrey had one big thing going for him to offset all of these shortcomings: he was telling people exactly what they wanted to hear — particularly his Anglo-Norman overlords who most surely patronized him.

It does not take a trained historian to figure out that the Norman conquest of England in 1066 laid the essential groundwork for the production of a "best-seller" such as Geoffrey's *Historia*, along with the explosive growth of continental enthusiasm for Arthuriana over the next century. The Norman conquerors saw themselves as liberators as well as conquerors; specifically, they claimed to be liberating the Welsh — close kinsmen to the Norman's Breton allies — from centuries of Saxon oppression. This claim was, of course, a gross over-simplification, but the Welsh-Breton tradition of King Arthur could be easily adapted to buttress Norman expansionist propaganda in Great Britain.[7] One of Geoffrey's most recent English translators, Lewis Thorpe, wrote: "Geoffrey had several clear-cut political reasons for what he wrote, his desire to give 'a precedent for the dominions and ambitions of the Norman kings' and his wish to ingratiate himself with his various dedicatees."[8] As for Edward Gibbon, he was only stating the obvious when he wrote the quote under the heading of this chapter. *Acts of the Kings of England* by William of Malmesbury, written in 1125, was one of the earliest Anglo-Norman documents to sing the praises of Arthur's military victories, as well as repeat the popular tale of his undiscovered tomb.[9] William's *Acts*, however, was just a prelude to the wild success of Geoffrey's *Historia* the following decade, a success so thorough that it had unintended political consequences — ones that even far-sighted Normans did not anticipate (see Chapter 8). Within a few years (circa 1150), Geoffrey followed up his phenomenal success with the *Vita Merlini* (*Life of Merlin*), adding material on probably the second-most popular — some would say, *the* most popular — figure in the Arthurian legends after King Arthur himself (see Chapter 19). He also demonstrated in this sequel a total ease and adeptness at producing Latin verse, confirming his lasting reputation as a master of the written word.

In studying the legacy of Geoffrey, one is repeatedly struck by how his broad influence was simultaneously coupled with wild factual inaccuracies. Read what the critics say. Edmund Chambers, dean of 20th-century British literary scholars and himself a paragon of caution, marveled that "no one with any knowledge of ancient history could have a doubt as to his [Geoffrey's] wilful and impudent lying." Chambers labels Geoffrey's writings as "ridiculous figments," "fables," and "deceits," displaying "an unbridled lust for mendacity." He also strenuously objected to Geoffrey covering up his fictions by "clothing them in Latin speech to give the colour of honest history."[10] Another leading modern critic, Roger Sherman Loomis, who did more than anyone to establish the Arthurian legends firmly within the Celtic-Welsh tradition, called Geoffrey a "faker of history" but applauded his "cynical ingenuity," remarking that "the more one studies the *History of the Kings of Britain* and the methods of its composition, the more one is astonished at the author's impudence, and the more one is impressed with his cleverness, his art."[11] Nor is such criticism a modern trend. Geoffrey's more learned near-contemporaries, such as William of Newburg, wrote in frustration, "It is quite clear that everything this man wrote about Arthur ... was made up, partly by himself and partly by others, either from an inordinate love of lying, or for the sake of pleasing the Britons."[12] William attributed Geoffrey's astounding popularity to his uncanny knack for pandering to the "brutishly stupid" Bretons.[13] Infamously, he quipped that Geoffrey's *Historia* attracted more demons than any exorcist could ever hope to expel.[14]

During the Renaissance and Enlightenment, Geoffrey became fodder for serious historians, even patriotic English ones, who took pot shots at a very easy target. The downward trend in respectability for the Arthurian legends among scholars culminated with Gibbon, who dispassionately observed, "The severity of the present age is inclined to question the *existence* of Arthur."[15] In spite of all this intellectual hostility, however (or perhaps because of it), interest in the *Historia Regum Britanniae* today appears stronger than ever. Nowadays, it is William of Newburg who is forgotten to history, not Geoffrey of Monmouth. In hindsight, it is far more accurate (and healthier) to place him firmly within the context of French and Anglo-Norman epic storytellers, rather than to try to force him into the long tradition of serious British historians represented by figures like Gibbon. In this respect, he was a harbinger of Chrétien de Troyes, who in turn became the true father of Arthurian romance one generation later. As a preliminary step, Geoffrey's Latin prose *Historia* was transmitted into French verse by Wace in 1145 (titled the *Roman de Brut*, see Chapter 10). The *Historia* was also a close forerunner of the influential French *Roman d'Eneas*, probably written by Benoît de Sainte-Maure around 1160. Finally, every student of Geoffrey's *oeuvre* has noted that he overtly attempted to create an English national epic along the same lines as Virgil's *Aeneid*.[16] Was Geoffrey the clergyman really at heart a frustrated *jongleur*? It would seem so.

As for Chrétien, his countless, unique contributions to the Arthurian tradition become readily apparent with any casual reading of the *Historia*, which (to repeat) presents quite a different picture of King Arthur and his kingdom than the ones modern audiences are used to seeing. After dedicating the work to members of the Norman nobility,[17] and relating a long, fictional history of Great Britain from the fall of Troy to the fall of Rome, Geoffrey devotes the climactic final chapters of his *faux* chronicle to the reign of Arthur and its immediate aftermath. The basic outline is recognizable to all aficionados of the legend. The prophet Merlin facilitates the birth of Arthur through magic and intrigue. Upon his father's death, Arthur becomes king of Great Britain. He then proceeds to repel all Saxon invaders, leading to a long reign of peace and prosperity. His kingdom eventually falls, however, through the intrigues of his evil nephew Mordred and the infidelity of his wife Guinevere. Finally, after being "mortally wounded" while defeating and killing Mordred, Arthur mysteriously retires to the "Isle of Avalon" for healing treatment.[18] Both Arthur and Merlin abruptly vanish from Geoffrey's narrative after having served their dramatic purposes. Are these not all of the essential details typically found in Arthurian romance, one may well ask?

This writer would respond firmly in the negative. Yes, a well-known basic plot was articulated by Geoffrey, but it was not he who inspired reams of sequels and continuators in many different countries, languages, and over a period of several centuries. Chrétien, on the other hand, did, and the reasons for this become obvious enough upon close study. Geoffrey succeeded in getting everyone's attention, but it was Chrétien who got everyone else trying their hand at the same subject matter, the *matiére de Bretagne*. To begin with, almost all of Geoffrey's text is solely concerned with Arthur's military campaigns and triumphs. In this sense, it is not much different from the patriotic epics *La Chanson de Roland* or *El Cantar del Mio Cid*, both produced earlier during the same century. The main point, if not the only point, of the story is that Arthur exceeded the ancients as a warrior-king. A very small portion of Geoffrey's narrative — almost an aside — is devoted to Arthur's peacetime court, which attracts outstanding knights from other lands, and inspires good manners and courteous behavior (where there was only bad behavior before, it is strongly implied). Beautiful women inspired the men to courage, Geoffrey remarks in a single sentence. Conspicuously absent in the *Historia* are most of the great resonant themes and trappings of the Arthurian world: no Roundtable, no Holy Grail, no Camelot, no Lancelot, no Perceval, no Morgan le Fay, no spiritual quests, no courtly love — in short, no romance.[19] More sordidly, Guinevere's adultery in the *Historia* is with Arthur's nephew Mordred and not with Lancelot, who does not appear in world literature until Chrétien introduced him. Had it not been for Chrétien and his imitators, Geoffrey's King Arthur may well have been consigned to a narrow space within world literary history as a sort of ultimate tribal warlord, along similar lines as a Roland or Cid.

One thing subtly integrated into Geoffrey's *Historia*, though rarely commented upon (for whatever reason), is that the King Arthur legends, even at this embryonic stage, had strongly pronounced and inescapable French connections and overtones. In the narrative, after defeating the Saxons, Arthur conducts two major military campaigns on French soil, during the first of which he spends nine (!) years in France. His closest ally in both French and British wars is his nephew, King Hoel of Brittany. Thus Geoffrey immediately establishes close ties of kinship between the Welsh and Bretons. As he subdues enemies on the continent, Arthur hands out French dukedoms to Bedevere (Normandy) and Kay (Anjou), while receiving homage from French vassals such as Guitard of Poitou and the "Twelve Peers" from various regions of Gaul, led by Gerin of Chartres. His successful first French campaign culminates in Paris where Arthur defeats the Roman leader Frollo in single combat, much to the acclamation of the Parisians.[20] A detailed print depicting this duel, titled *Arthur à Paris* by Galliot du Pré and dated 1514, can still be viewed today at the metropolitan library in Rennes.[21] When Arthur invades France for a second time to fight the Romans, the French are more or less his loyal allies and view him as a liberator, just as the Normans wanted the Welsh to view them. First, however, Arthur must kill a giant who has been terrorizing the precincts of Mont-Saint-Michel. Geoffrey neglects to address another discrepancy. The western Roman Empire had permanently disintegrated before the beginning of the sixth century, and by Arthur's stipulated epoch, Italy was being contested between the Byzantines and the Ostrogoths.

Even more suggestive than Geoffrey's prominent French place settings is his own mysterious personal background as a writer. It is not unusual, especially in reference to Shakespearean source studies, to hear Geoffrey of Monmouth lionized as a prototypical English yeoman-chronicler, with academia occasionally reminding us that he was more likely "Welsh" than English. As noted by some of the most reputable scholars in this area, however (and always falling upon deaf ears), is the fact that during the 12th century Geoffrey was not yet considered an English name — it was Norman. Given the overwhelming unlikelihood of any Saxon or Englishman being given a baptismal name belonging to their conquerors one generation after the fact, only one reasonable conclusion can follow: namely, that Geoffrey of Monmouth came from a Breton family or, worse for Anglocentrics, a native Welsh family allied with the Bretons during William the Conqueror's invasion in 1066. While the heavy cavalry in William's invading army consisted mostly of the Norman nobility, the bulk of his foot soldiers were Breton fighting men who had been promised British spoils. Loomis, the leading advocate for a "Celtic" King Arthur during the 20th century, had no doubts about this, and subscribed to the theory of Geoffrey's Breton parentage.[22] Chambers, among many others, concurred.[23] Loomis also believed that Geoffrey's alleged sourcebook was Breton in origin.[24] These opinions come not from Frenchmen but from some of the best modern British and American specialists.

Such speculations about Geoffrey's ethnic heritage have been troubling, at least for those who take the trouble to scrutinize, as opposed to gloss over them. As a result, it has been seriously suggested in recent years that Geoffrey of Monmouth may have merely been a front man for an unknown "pseudo–Geoffrey" who actually wrote the original version of the *Historia*.[25] The idea with this particular theory is that once we remove the historical, Breton, and pro–Norman Geoffrey from the picture, then the true author (whoever he was) can go back to being a red-blooded patriotic Englishman—or at least a pro–English Welshman—in our imaginations if nowhere else. Under this scenario, the political convenience of the *Historia* to the Normans, along with its prominent Norman dedications, are thus reduced to the status of necessary window-dressing. The pseudo–Geoffrey theory is often calmly and rationally discussed in Arthurian circles without any acrimony or emotional baggage typically attaching to, say, the Shakespeare authorship question. A similar issue revolves around Chrétien de Troyes himself (see Chapter 24), since virtually nothing concrete is known of his personal or public life, despite the fact he was the most celebrated writer of the Middle Ages before Dante.

Perhaps the most intriguing question of all is how exactly did Geoffrey's tall tales—via the French translation of Wace—eventually spark Chrétien's poetic interest in *le matiére de Bretagne*? Urban Holmes speculated that it is theoretically possible that Chrétien met Geoffrey before the latter's death in 1155, assuming Chrétien (as a cleric) was part of Bishop Henry of Winchester's entourage to England that same year.[26] A more simple and likely connection to Geoffrey for Chrétien is that the *Historia* places the final battle between Arthur and the Romans near Langres in Champagne, not far from Chrétien's namesake town of Troyes.[27] Although this particular event was another one of Geoffrey's creative fictions, the huge popularity of the book itself would have probably put Langres on the international map. Although the debated precise location of this make-believe battle is a major topic within itself, most authorities agree that it allegedly occurred in the Champagne-Ardenne region.[28] To clarify, Geoffrey and Chrétien were not exactly singing "La Marseillaise" when they wrote their Arthurian works. On the other hand, to ignore this aspect of the *Historia* (as do some commentators) is to completely distort our understanding of a work that first made the King Arthur legend into an international sensation.[29]

Thanks to Geoffrey's energetic imagination, King Arthur had become a household name throughout the Latin-speaking world by the mid–12th century. At this point, Chrétien de Troyes enters the story. A bare outline for *le matiére de Bretagne* had been articulated and public interest piqued. People now wanted to know more about the Arthurian legend, and, moreover, to hear and read about these things in their respective, vernacular languages. More specifically — and this is where Chrétien's true genius manifested itself — audiences wanted to know more, not so much about Arthur, but about his knights. The individual knights of the Roundtable (and their ladies) would be the focus of all future Arthurian sequels and legends, beginning with Chrétien. Their adventures, or misadventures, were the stories that the European nobility, especially female nobility, wanted to hear. The personal conflicts between military duty and romantic love had become greater than ever in feudal society by this time in history. The dalliances and moral ambiguities of Lancelot and Cligès, as invented by Chrétien, were only one aspect of this dilemma. To these individual knights and the continually evolving code of chivalry in a Europe more economically prosperous than ever, we shall now turn our attention in Part II of this study.

PART II.
HISTORICAL THEMES: THE KNIGHT

Chapter 10

The Birth of Chivalry

The medieval discipline of knighthood, when faithfully observed, was not for the faint of heart. In theory, it entailed protecting the weak, enforcing the law, and upholding civilized manners; in reality, it usually meant fighting indigenous Muslim populations and guarding European economic interests in the Middle East. If one belonged to the elite military orders, such as the Templars or Hospitallers (Knights of St. John), then it also required, on paper at least, living a completely austere and monastic day-to-day life. That a number of these fanatical warriors (especially the Templars) often forgot their vows and indulged themselves in lives of rapine and luxury, might almost be excused in retrospect, given the otherwise harsh and unrelenting demands of their daily existence. European knighthood, particularly in the Holy Land, tended to be nasty, brutish and short, in the words of one famous philosopher.[1] To be married to a knight, or to be the mother of one, could be just as cruel a fate, with widowhood, mourning, and poverty as frequent rewards. In Chrétien's last romance, Perceval's mother was quite right to be upset when her son decided to leave the Welsh family farm and join the ranks of King Arthur's Roundtable.[2]

To examine the origins of the chivalric code is to be reminded that such concepts are given many different meanings by different people. Definitions can be tricky. To one, "chivalry" might mean victory in war and little besides; to another, winning is not so important as how one plays the game, no matter how deadly that game might be. To others still, prowess in combat is only one aspect of chivalry, a concept that must also entail good ethics, morals, and manners. A man might be referred to as "chivalrous" solely if his dealings with either sex are gentlemanly. Moreover, "courtly love" is a phrase frequently viewed as overlapping "chivalry" in meaning. This reader, like many others, leans towards a broader, more complex definition of the term. Those who prefer an all-inclusive outlook, for the most part, acquired it without ever having read the poetry of Chrétien de Troyes. Nevertheless, the concept began in a very real sense with the tradition he founded, although there are some who plausibly argue that a knightly code of honor existed in the Muslim world long before it took root in a Europe engulfed by the Dark Ages.[3] Those who later read his poetry certainly have their personal beliefs reinforced; it is Chrétien's deep exploration of the contradictions and conflicts in this value system that many of us now tend to dwell upon. We may initially acquire our definitions secondhand, and then perhaps discover their source in Chrétien's 12th-century epoch. Such has been the power of the poet's long-term influence, although he is not a household name outside of specialized academic circles.

One thing is indisputable; once the idea of chivalrous knighthood firmly took hold in Europe during the High Middle Ages, it spread like wildfire in every direction. After Spain had been overrun, seemingly overnight, by the great Saracen invasion of the 8th century, a long and relentless *Reconquista* began to gradually manifest itself at the turn of the first millennium. The lynchpin of this process consisted of aspiring petty Spanish monarchs learning to harness the boundless energy and selfless devotion of their irrepressible *cavalieros*. Predating the French romancers, this monumental enterprise was immortalized in literature by the *Cantar de mio Cid*. Across the continent in Germany, a society not previously known for sophistication or refinement in manners, *minnesinger* poets the caliber of Walter von der Vogelweide sang the praises of German virtues both in love and in war. At the same time, the Teutonic order of knights cut a swath of domination straight across northern Europe that barely stopped on the borders of Russia and France. Consequently, their kings enjoyed papal endorsement as new Holy Roman Emperors, eventually extending their influence as far south as Italy and Sicily.[4] Some of these Germanic warriors, such as the Bavarian knight Wolfram von Eschenbach (1170–1220), tried their own hands at writing epic poetry. The results included Wolfram's own, highly influential Arthurian masterpiece, *Parzival*, the relationship of which to Chrétien's earlier romance by the same title is still debated by scholars.[5] Whatever the sources and uses in fact were, it is clear that by the turn of the 13th century, the Arthurian ideal of chivalry was internationally accepted across Europe, even as its details were being disputed among its proponents.

Remarkably, however, long before German military might reached Italy and Sicily (and long after that, domination by the Spanish), the French, and particularly their expansionist-minded Norman brethren (see Chapter 13), had come to lord it over the entire Mediterranean world. With them came the Arthurian legends. Their concurrent, absolute conquest of England during the 11th century had enabled the rapid transmission of obscure British folklore across Europe to the furthest reaches of western civilization. Now King Arthur and his Roundtable knights belonged to all of Christendom, not just the Welsh. Back in France, the order of Templars had been incorporated in 1128 at Chrétien's namesake town of Troyes, where the nearby *Forêt du Templar* still bears their title. More than one commentator has noted the connection, perhaps coincidental but real nonetheless, between Troyes, the Templar knights, and the origins of modern Arthurian romance.[6] The most important aspect of this convergence is that Chrétien's unique poetic view of knighthood and chivalry is fascinating for its complexity and depth. Like the world in which he lived, there is nothing simple or cut-and-dry in his worldview. Despite the fantasy of its original conceit, it is a poetic world based on keen empirical observation of reality, and is therefore of permanent interest to future generations, whether they be fans of King Arthur or not.

The literary Frenchification of the Arthur legend began in earnest with the trans-channel popularity of works produced by Geoffrey of Monmouth during the early 12th century (see Chapter 9). Although Geoffrey was primarily concerned with pleasing his Norman patrons by establishing a heavily fictionalized Arthur as the European warrior-king *par excellence*, other admirable qualities are hinted at as well. In Geoffrey, it is briefly stated that Arthur was both brave *and* generous, that a code of courtliness was instituted, and that bravery of Arthur's knights was in turn inspired by the chastity and virtue of their women (and vice versa). All figments in Geoffrey's addled imagination? Perhaps. More likely, these features were compliments to his contemporary benefactors. Although Geoffrey did much to initiate a century of inventive Arthurian fiction, there is no way he could have foreseen in which directions other storytellers would soon take this same material. Within a few short years, Geoffrey's afterthoughts were greatly expanded into something new and completely different. His mere suggestion was about to become one of the permanent, major themes in world literature.

Because Geoffrey's preposterous mythologizing of English history had been written in Latin, a strong demand for his tales in the French language was immediately created. The void was filled with startling alacrity in 1155 by the Norman *trouvère*, Robert (?) Wace (pronounced *waz*). Wace identifies himself as a native of the French island of Jersey, a resident of Caen, and the canon of Bayeux, site of the monumental tapestry depicting Duke William's history-shaking conquest of England in 1066. Like Geoffrey before him and Chrétien after, Wace was an Angevin-era cleric writing to please French royalty and nobility. His *Roman de Brut*, an ultra-free translation of (and expansion upon) Geoffrey's work, was dedicated to none other than Queen Eleanor of Aquitaine, mother of Chrétien's future patron, Marie of Champagne.[7] Wace not only interpreted Geoffrey for the non–Latin-speaking French, he embellished, altered, and spun the text in a manner that would have deeply impressed even the tireless seamstresses of Bayeux. Whereas Geoffrey threw into his Arthurian history the notions of chivalry and courtly love almost as a footnote, Wace amplified these ideas into a more important, though not yet central, focus. As Edmund Chambers summarized, "Arthur's court is thus already in Wace, more definitely than in Geoffrey, reaching its mediaeval status as the mirror of knighthood and centre of romantic *aventures*. Geoffrey's hint as to the relation of *amour courtois* to military prowess is emphasized...."[8] It is a very good bet that these themes began receiving more attention by the French poets because their audiences, particularly the wives of knights, wanted to hear more about them.

Examples of Wace's French glossing onto the tales of Geoffrey (who was probably of Breton descent himself) are too numerous to catalogue here, but a few examples will perhaps suffice. Wace takes trouble to note that Arthur treated his servants very well, which presumably set him apart from other monarchs.[9] In Geoffrey, Arthur invites foreign knights to his court and has close connections with his nephew, King Hoel of Brittany. Wace expands upon this with Hoel crossing over to England to help his uncle in defeating the Saxons, Scots and Picts. During one curious interlude, Wace presents a Saxon villain and opponent of Arthur's named Baldulph, who disguises himself as a (presumably) duplicitous Breton *jongleur* in order to cross enemy lines.[10] Later, when Arthur makes his first military excursion into France, Wace multiplies his list of French vassals, which besides Sir Bedevere and Sir Kay (who are awarded French lands), include Holden of Boulogne and Borel of Le Mans.[11] Back in England, Wace specifies which regions in France were represented in giving Arthur homage: "Frenchman and Burgundian, Auvergnat and Gascon, Norman and Poitvin, Angevin and Fleming, together with him of Brabant, Hainault, and Lorraine...."[12] Later, Arthur returns to France, defeats the Roman (read: papal) army in the field, and then in Paris itself slays the Roman commander Frollo in single combat.[13] In the process of this conquest or liberation, Arthur wins over the Gauls, many of whom fight on his side. As Wace writes, "The very French began to regard him as their king...."[14]

Among many innovations, the greatest that Wace can claim credit for (or at least as being the first to record), is *La Table Ronde*, or the ubiquitous Roundtable of knights at the Arthurian court. In doing this, it is impossible to say with any certainty whether Wace was repeating an existing, popular tradition or making things up out of thin air. All we know for certain is that

after Wace, the Roundtable became a permanent fixture in the Arthurian landscape, and a very important one at that. Chrétien, with a few short years, would play it to the hilt, presenting it twice in his first romance, *Erec and Enide* (lines 83 and 1669).[15] Some scholars, such as Roger Sherman Loomis, have noted a similarity between the Arthurian Roundtable and the Last Supper table of Christ sometimes depicted in art.[16] Others have made the obvious point that it was an early symbol of democratization, a notion first expressly made in the Middle English prose version of the romance of Layamon.[17] Prior to this, Chrétien not only mentions the Roundtable, he makes it obligatory for comprehensive gatherings of Arthurian knights, thereby placing more emphasis on the image than previously found in medieval literature. This is probably yet another reflection of audience taste. The poet's mostly female patrons wanted to hear about Arthur's knights, and any assembly of warriors so jealous of their prerogatives therefore necessitated the existence of a Roundtable in order to level the playing field and keep the peace. If the primary focus had been entirely on Arthur, as it had been in Geoffrey, then it is questionable whether the Roundtable would have been invented in the first place.

Chrétien's attitude towards the knights of Camelot was unprecedented for its time, at least among western literature that has survived down to the present. His heroes are complex and flawed, sometimes likeable, other times definitely not; they are all fighters *and* lovers who must frequently deal with the conflicts naturally arising from these dual but often opposing roles. David Staines noted the shift in content and tone that took place in the time between Wace to Chrétien:

> Wace, an Anglo-Norman poet, pays less attention than Geoffrey, however, to Arthur's military successes and more to his social behavior. It remains for Chrétien, with his emphasis on Arthur's knights as the representatives or embodiment of the king's chivalric order, to complete the transformation of Arthur into a courtly monarch.[18]

Above all, Chrétien dramatized the conflicts of husband versus warrior (Erec and Yvain), and courtly lover versus royal vassal (Cligès and Lancelot). Finally, the poet presents in epic fashion the potential conflicts between ambitious knighthood and obedience to the church (Perceval). To a lesser extent, Sir Gawain is held up throughout Chrétien's romances as the perfect (for some readers, too perfect) exemplar of chivalry, especially in *Perceval*. Some critics have plausibly argued that Gawain would have eventually become the true hero of the Grail Quest, had Chrétien lived to complete it.[19] Standing in contrast to the shining exemplar of Gawain is Sir Kay, the embodiment of all that is unattractive in the warrior stereotype — boastfulness, meanness, sadism, hypocrisy, and, for good measure, ineptitude as a fighter. As for King Arthur, truth be told, Chrétien does not show much interest in him except as a surprisingly weak monarch and inattentive husband — one always in need of his Roundtable knights and often in need of a personal champion as well. In short, Chrétien always uses Arthur as backdrop material.

One of the more demonstrative hints of Arthur's weakness and impotence in Chrétien's presentation of the legend comes during his final installment of the romance cycle in *Perceval*. The very physical symbol of Arthur's worldly power — the sword Excalibur — is possessed not by the king, but rather by his nephew Gawain. Chrétien chooses to follow an old tradition in which Arthur gives his sword ("Escalibor") to Gawain upon the latter's achieving knighthood.[20] This is an indication of Gawain's status as Arthur's favorite knight and his foremost position among Roundtable colleagues, with both traditions traceable back to Geoffrey. Given the parallel plots in *Perceval* between the hero and Gawain, plus their highly personalized weapons — the sword belonging to Perceval is prophesized to fail its owner in one instance only — it is intriguing to speculate how the poet would have opted to tie together loose ends, or bothered to resolve these, had he lived to finish the work. We will not add to the host of critical theories on this subject. That which Chrétien did live to complete is too fascinating in and of itself to be shortchanged by detours on such hypotheses. The main point is that Chrétien's listeners seemed far less interested in Arthur than in his warriors. This holds true even for secondary foils such as Gawain and Kay.

In one of the most profound, simple, and touching vignettes to be found in the entire canon, Perceval is officially dubbed a knight, not by the king, but by a semi-retired knight-instructor, Gornemant. As if to emphasize the mysticism and solemnity of the occasion, Perceval's entry into the exclusive equestrian order involves not public pomp and grandeur, but instead, a quiet and private affair. The scene includes only Perceval and Gornemant with no apparent witnesses. The sanctity of the moment is inherent, and does not require a church or courtly setting — the latter typical for the period and in modern times presented as such for dramatic effect.[21] This is not the kind of knightly dubbing most people nowadays tend to imagine. At the other extreme end, and later in the same story, Gawain (rather than the king) awards knighthood in his capacity as knight extraordinaire to 500 youths *en masse*, and this only after an all-night church service (lines 9172–9188). Still further from these in style and feeling is the knighting of the hero's father Alexander in Chrétien's earlier romance, *Cligès*. Although King Arthur himself performs the dubbing, the gesture itself is not described and most of the lengthy focus in the passage is on the material gifts that Alexander receives from Arthur and Guinevere. Finally, the poet abruptly (and rather oddly) announces, "Now they were knights; enough's been said" (line 1199). In contrast to all these, Perceval earns his status by defeating and killing in one-on-one combat an enemy of the king (the Red Knight) and, with minimal preparation and no warning, is given a spur, a sword, and a kiss by his mentor (lines 1624–1628). One is struck by the rustic simplicity of the scene, which is neither a grand celebration nor a secretive ritual. It is possible that Chrétien's last patron, Philip of Flanders, had witnessed or perhaps personally administered many *ad hoc* knighthoods awarded in humble circumstances such as these, given his extensive wanderings as a Crusader in the Middle East. Somehow, the poet learned and apparently believed that genuine knighthood and chivalry took on a more special meaning under primitive and unpretentious conditions like this.

The passage in which Chrétien describes this pivotal moment early in *Perceval* makes another good comparison study in English translations. Ruth Harwood Cline, in rhymed eight-syllable couplets, conveys the seriousness of the moment in a tale which, up until that point, is filled with absurdity and buffoonery:

> The lord attached the sword in place.
> He gave the young knight an embrace
> and said he'd given with the sword
> the highest honor of Our Lord,
> an order made by God's decree,
> and it was knighthood, chivalry;
> that such an order must remain
> without deceit, without a stain
> [lines 1630–1638].[22]

Chrétien uses the word "chivalry" to climactic effect, although no mention is made of courtly love. Burton Raffel, writing in free-form verse, eliminates the term altogether, thus giving the same idea a somewhat more militaristic (and non-specific, depending on one's point of view) context:

> Then the nobleman took up the sword,
> Belted it on the boy,
> And kissed him, saying that thus
> He conferred the highest distinction
> God had ever created,
> The order of knighthood; knights,
> He declared, were sworn to honor
> [lines 1632–1638].[23]

"Knighthood" becomes a matter of "honor," a distinction that is divinely bestowed. This version highlights the poet's seeming total elimination (or at least distancing) of the connection between knighthood and *amour courtois*. Perceval is not married, but he does have a girlfriend (Blancheflor) and, before his dubbing, has no hesitation in kissing attractive women. His brutish behavior vanishes upon his becoming a knight. Perceval's counterpart (and implied role model) is Gawain, who, though himself the mirror of perfect knighthood, gladly exchanges kisses and embraces with the princess of Escalvon. This is before the townspeople riot in protest — not at the hugging and kissing — but upon their discovery that Gawain had in the past killed (in combat fair and square) their king and father of the princess. Thus courtly love retains some of its vestiges in *Perceval*, but to a lesser extent. Interestingly, no one except Arthur appears to be married, almost as if the poet was endorsing the monkish, celibate version of knighthood adopted so fanatically by the Templars and Hospitallers.

Chrétien's unfinished journey through his last Arthurian romance had begun years earlier when he created his very first work in the genre, *Erec and Enide*. It all started with perceived conflicts between the personal duties of medieval knighthood and the proper courtly duties of a knight towards his wife or lover. What was true chivalry? Whatever it was, however one defined it, its origins or birth in the modern sense probably began with the works of Chrétien de Troyes. While it is obvious that European knights and knighthood existed long before the time of Chrétien — in fact, these things appear to have existed outside of Europe even before that — something quite different happened during the 12th century, as C.S. Lewis once observed (see Chapter 4). The image of the warrior-knight — the one who successfully led the First Crusade and was still believed by many western apologists to be invincible, was being tempered (and softened, some would say) by more civilized values filtering into French-speaking domains and beyond. Being a successful fighter was no longer enough; now one had to be a good courtly lover as well, in order to legitimately represent the chivalric order.

Chapter 11

Erec, Enide, and the Pitfalls of Happiness

> ... *Erec and Enide played an essential role in the transmission of courtly ideals from France and the Norman nobility of Britain to other parts of Europe, one of the most significant developments in the history of Western civilization*—Joseph Duggan.[1]

Chretien's *Erec and Enide* is more than just a great romantic poem; it is a revolutionary synthesis, one that marks a great turning point in western literature. At the time of its composition (somewhere around the year 1170), the work represented something completely new under the sun, and nothing remotely like it had previously been heard or read by audiences.[2] Although the Arthurian genre as epic literature had been popularized during the previous generation, thanks to Geoffrey of Monmouth (see Chapter 9), and the French romance or *roman* had already utilized classical subject matter, no one before Chrétien had blended the two together, let alone in such a brilliant and seamless manner. More importantly, medieval notions of romantic chivalry and courtly love had yet to be fully incorporated into the Arthurian world before Chrétien applied his considerable talents to doing just that. While it is true that his French-Norman predecessor Wace (see Chapter 10) had earlier upped the ante to a significant extent with his free translation of Geoffrey, the arts of peace still played a largely secondary role in the story of Arthur, as opposed to the arts of war. It took Chrétien to bring the two more into balance, if not place more emphasis on the former. In this sense, *Erec and Enide* marked the true beginning of these new ideas being rapidly transmitted throughout western civilization. While European society remained largely illiterate and barbarous, everyone still loved a good story that was well told, and the French nobility were now in a strong position to sponsor and encourage this sort of activity. The result was a masterpiece still read for its pure entertainment value, causing even a discerning, informed critic like C.S. Lewis to declare that he enjoyed reading Chrétien's version of the same tale more than Tennyson's.[3]

At this point, it is useful to summarize some of the source material, at least that which has been identified to date, going into this notable creation. Part I of this study has already covered the broad intellectual currents coming together in Champagne during the time of Chrétien — the Arthurian legends from Wales, the new love poetry from Spain via the French troubadours, the revival of classical learning in the cathedral schools — and a few specific examples from *Erec* can illustrate the point for anyone still in doubt. In terms of Celtic lore, the poet begins his tale with conventional backdrop devices, including the hunt of a white stag and a sparrow-hawk contest, both of which are brilliantly interwoven even as it becomes slowly apparent that this story is going to be about much, much more than hunting and fighting.[4] As the poet informs his readers, Erec is a Breton name (line 652), and (as noted by scholars) is specifically derived from the Breton name of Guerec.[5] The basic outline of the story is Welsh in origin.[6] Urban Holmes speculated "that Chrétien had heard the basic plot of *Erec and Enide* recited by professional minstrels and that he felt this catchy tale could be improved by embellishing its plot (*matière*) with more meaning (*sens*)...."[7] Other Arthurian names and place names are sprinkled throughout like window dressing, yet in such a convincing manner as to suggest that the poet was thoroughly imbued with this lore, and possibly had traveled to England himself. Tintagel is mentioned twice as the castle seat of Erec's family, as well as the locale of his father's death (lines 1909, 6460). The knights of the Roundtable are catalogued, and this list includes the name of Tristan (lines 1242, 1687), making Chrétien perhaps the first poet to link the two legends (Arthur and Tristan) together. Isolde (line 424) or Iseult (line 2021) is mentioned twice. Other Arthurian names found in Geoffrey and Wace are also utilized, including those of Arthur, Guinevere, Kay, Gawain, Bedouer and Merlin.[8]

One of the more striking innovations possibly introduced by Chrétien in *Erec* is to transform the Avalon enchantress Morgan le Fay into King Arthur's sister (line 4194), a feature which then later became a permanent fixture in most versions of the legend.[9] Geoffrey had first mentioned Morgan as a sorceress (and healer), but then around the year 1170 two works suddenly turned her into the sibling or half-sibling of Arthur, one of which was Chrétien's *Erec*. The other poem to do this was the French-Norman chronicle *Draco Normannicus* (*Standard of the Normans*), usually attributed to Étienne de Rouen.[10] Chrétien may have picked up on this, or perhaps it was the other way around, or possibly both writers used a common lost source or oral tradition. More specifically, Chrétien has Morgan married to Guingamar, lord of Avalon, and both attend Erec and Enide's wedding early in the story.[11] Especially noteworthy is that in Chrétien, Geoffrey, and all early presentations of the Morgan character in Arthurian literature, nowhere is she given any of the sinister or evil traits that later became so pronounced in more modern interpretations of the myth. For the early French romancers of the High Middle Ages, she appears to have been viewed as a good enchantress rather than a bad one.

While the true feeling and style of courtly love poetry would not fully manifest itself in Chrétien's romances until *Cligès* and *Lancelot*, classical references to love and feminine beauty in *Erec* are abundant. Enide is described as being more beautiful than Lavinia, the idealized bride of Virgil's Aeneas (lines 5840–5843).[12] Moreover, there is a direct reference to the *Aeneid* with detailed, ivory-carved scenes from the epic on the saddlebow of Enide's palfrey (lines 5291–5299).[13] Ruth Harwood Cline noted that the poet favored referencing Ovid's tale of Pyramus and Thisbe, in which one lover mistakenly believes the other one to be dead, and this conceit appears in Chrétien's first four romances, including *Erec*.[14] For that matter, it is interesting to note that Chrétien, like his future English counterpart, Shakespeare, was sometimes attracted to the same classical material for inspiration, particularly from Ovid and Virgil. Some of these stories included that of Pyramus and Thisbe (*A Midsummer Night's Dream*), Philomena (*Titus Andronicus*), and Book II of the *Aeneid* (*The Tempest*). More fascinating still is the poet's prominent use in *Erec* of the "Patient Griselda" theme—the vindication of a long-suffering wife—except that Chrétien long predated other authors who are usually credited with inventing and developing it, such as Boccaccio, Petrarch, Chaucer, and again, Shakespeare (*The Winter's Tale*).[15] This leads one to suspect that all of these writers, Chrétien included, were drawing upon ideas far more ancient, and perhaps even Arab or Oriental in origins, than is commonly supposed.

As the first in a series of five, Chrétien's *Erec and Enide* establishes a formula in structure that the poet would more or less adhere to throughout his career. The work is a *tour de force*, and a prototype for everything that would follow: a prologue and opening scene at King Arthur's court, usually celebrating a religious feast; the hero (of noble blood or, in Erec's case, the son of a king), along with his heroine-counterpart, who both undergo various trials and tribulations; a temporary return to and reprieve at Arthur's court; the hero's friend Gawain presented as a model of chivalry; Kay held up as a foil, a mean-spirited and verbally abusive protagonist (though not much of a fighter); a climactic trial and test in the realm of the supernatural; and finally, a happy, triumphant ending in which conflicts are resolved.[16] All of Chrétien's romances have unlikely twists and turns. The plot of *Erec* is no exception in this regard; one aspect striking most readers as quite unusual — one that would be repeated in *Yvain*— is that the hero and heroine meet and are married in the opening scenes of the story. They do not, however, live happily ever after. Most of the action and conflict resolution comes long after the nuptials. This feature gives the romance an edgy, energizing dose of realism, a morally edifying subsurface, that most audiences were (and still are) not used to. Clearly, the poet had much more on his mind than simply telling a good, entertaining story, although he succeeds in doing this as well.

A major theme in both *Erec* and *Yvain* is pronounced by Gawain in the latter work when he declares, "Shame on those warriors, by Saint Mary, who grow less valiant when they marry!" (lines 2315–2316). This potential clash between chivalry and courtly love (within the context of conventional marriage) is jarringly introduced in both romances, although in *Yvain* the hero's fault is to break a solemn promise to his spouse, whereas in *Erec* he completely forgets his duties as a knight. In essence, the pitfall of the couple's wedded bliss is that Erec ceases to be the same person that Enide originally married. He becomes strictly a lover and no longer a fighter, let alone the knight *extraordinaire* he embodied before meeting his wife. Urban Holmes opined that *Erec and Enide* (and hence the Arthurian romance genre as a whole) grew out of an impulse to merge the old epics with the emerging concept of courtly love.[17] The result was what Holmes referred to as the "purifying quest" theme which became a defining feature in all of Chrétien's subsequent romances and the Arthurian saga as a whole.[18] As to the latent conflict between marriage duties and those of knighthood, the poet would more fully develop this concept in *Yvain* (see Chapter 16), to the point where, as Holmes noted, the entire adventure becomes one of spiritual progress and growth for the hero and heroine.[19] Even more surprising was the poet's complete equation of marriage with true courtly love. Ruth Harwood Cline appropriately reminds us that "*Erec* is the initial work in which Chrétien begins to develop his ideal of aristocratic love within marriage. The idea would have seemed novel to his contemporaries."[20]

Getting back to the story, problems arise for the married couple shortly after their honeymoon, when one morning (while still in bed) Enide announces the bad news to her husband that he, formerly Arthur's premier combat knight, is now publicly perceived as a washed-up has-been. Writing in octosyllabic verse as in the original text, Cline has Enide lament to her husband: "Your reputation has declined.... Now you are mocked by one and all..." (lines 2545, 2550). Using free form verse, Burton Raffel has her put it somewhat more forcefully: "your reputation, [y]our name, have tumbled to the ground.... Now you're a joke..." (lines 2545, 2546, 2551).[21] Other English translators are pretty much in unison. W.W. Comfort, D.D.R. Owen, and David Staines all write: "Your reputation has suffered," then add their own choice words: "Now they all go about making game of you..." (Comfort); "Now ... all go about mocking you," (Owen); and "Now all ... make fun of you" (Staines).[22] One is tempted at this juncture to wonder whether the poet and his mostly female audience at the French court had a specific, real-life knight in mind. If so, it would not have been the first nor the last time that art imitated life for the sake of amusing an artist's patrons.

In her long speech, Enide is careful not to simply browbeat her husband, and admits in sharing the blame for the situation. Cline has the heroine diplomatically prefacing her pillow talk with Erec as follows:

> ... the finest knight of all, avowed
> the boldest fighter and most proud,
> more than a count or monarch royal,
> and the most courteous and loyal,
> has now relinquished chivalry
> completely on account of me
>   [lines 2495–2500].

In the Raffel translation, Erec has done more than "relinquished chivalry"; he has "turned [h]is back" on it (lines 2500–2501).[23] Other English versions put it in similar terms. For Comfort, Erec "has completely abjured all his deeds of chivalry," while Owen sees him as having "utterly given up his whole practice," and Staines portrays him as having "utterly abandoned all deeds of chivalry."[24] All translators agree that Enide is understandably careful to acknowledge her own complicity in her husband's perceived transformation from superhero to pushover. If "Erec" was in fact a real person at the French court, then a lowly court poet had to be very careful and delicate in his portrayal of the situation. To amuse the ladies with caricatures would have been one thing, to offend their warrior husbands, quite another.[25]

Erec, genuine hero that he is, responds to Enide's startling revelation not with anger, excuses, or words, but instead immediately dons his armor, then orders his wife to put on her finest attire, not to speak a word, and to ride into the wilderness with him following shortly behind. Thus the couple ventures forth into a dangerous and chaotic medieval landscape. Erec essentially uses Enide as bait to attract trouble — not a very chivalrous thing to do—yet she willingly complies, implying that her own reputation needs to be restored as well as that of her husband. Amusingly, her only fault is that she tends to be a talker, and not very well suited to the code of silence that Erec attempts to impose. As they successfully pass though one adventure after another, with Erec rescuing his damsel in distress over and over again, one might say that an important lesson for Enide is to be careful what you wish for. In spite of these numerous tribulations, however, Erec gradually succeeds in winning back his lost reputation as a champion fighter, and no one seems more pleased about this than his submissive but high-spirited wife. Arguably, there is a subtle element of renewed sexual tension as the hero continually rescues his lady out of harm's way, often sustaining physical wounds in the process and in need of nursing afterwards.

The finale to this series of self-imposed trials is the famous *Joie de la Cort* ("Joy of the Court") sequence, in which Erec must defeat a supernatural warrior who is essentially his own giant, outsized twin. This he accomplishes with the help of divinely-inspired stamina and energy that eventually wears down his foe to the point of exhaustion.[26] Rather than deliver a *coup de grâce*, Erec spares his vanquished opponent and learns that he had previously been a knight who inappropriately vowed not leave that given spot for the sake of his lady love—essentially the same trap that Erec had almost fallen into himself—and was subsequently bewitched because of it. The scene, taken as a whole, plays out as both exorcism and combat. The odd and memorable title, "Joy of the Court" has itself been the subject of much critical commentary. Joseph Duggan believed that it was, in part at least, used by Chrétien "in accordance with the medieval predilection for deriving a name from its contrary: only when the ordeal is done away with will there be joy in the court."[27] There is also general agreement that the phrase was probably derived from a Celtic pagan source, but was then perhaps misunderstood by the poet and given an entire new meaning in *Erec*, much the same way Chrétien later adopted the pagan legend of the grail for a totally different kind of symbolic use in his last romance, *Perceval* (see Chapter 22).[28]

The character development of Erec, or rather the public perception of his character, moves like an inverted arch. He begins with renown, then falls into disrepute, but by the end of the tale ascends to even greater heights of fame and praise. If he represented a historical personage within the poet's court circle, then that individual would have been far more flattered than offended if he waited to hear the end of the tale. Erec's unimpeachable status as a holy warrior standing in high heavenly favor is confirmed in the aftermath of the fight, as local townsfolk proclaim a benediction while bestowing their thanks:

> The people greeted Erec, bowed,
> and kept repeating in the crowd:
> "God save him who restored anew
> the joy and bliss our court once knew!
> God save him, the most fortunate
> Of men that God strove to create!"
>   [lines 6320–6326].

The public acclamation is hyperbole, and yet so were the opening scenes of the romance in which Erec is portrayed as an Arthurian knight without peer, with the possible exception of Gawain. Throughout the story, it appears the poet kept trying to outdo himself by raising the bar for knightly and chivalrous accolades with every vignette, as if he were performing before a live audience (which in fact he probably did). Even Erec's victory celebration after "Joy of the Court," however, is a mere prelude to what follows in the concluding chapter of the work.

The coronation scene at the close of the romance in which Arthur has Erec crowned King of Brittany during Christmastide at Nantes is unique in the poet's output, and one not to be repeated, if for no other reason than that it could not be exceeded in terms of celebratory triumph. Critics have rightly noted that multiple aspects of the portrayed ritual strongly recall the historical progress and confirmation of King Henry II's son Geoffrey as Duke of Brittany at Nantes in December 1169. Chrétien may well have been part of the Anglo-French retinue that witnessed these notable events.[29] For these reasons, *Eric and Enide* has sometimes been referred to as "Plantagenet romance," although the truth is that Henry II and his wife Eleanor of Aquitaine were estranged during this same period, an estrangement that would soon break out into an open rebellion by their sons. The poet's depiction of the ceremony, however, focuses on the magnificence of material wealth displayed and bestowed, rather than underlying political tensions. In an obvious compliment to Henry II, Chrétien states that the gifts given from King Arthur to the newly-crowned couple exceed those given to their dependents by Alexander the Great and Julius Caesar, two ancient world conquerors known for their splendor and generosity (lines 6611–6620). It is an interesting way to bring to a close such a groundbreaking work of literature. Enide, who begins the story as the noble but impoverished daughter of a country vavasor, becomes Queen of Brittany and wealthy beyond imagination. As for Erec, the knight who endures every trial, risk, and hardship for honor's sake, he dramatically regains his good reputation, with kingship thrown into the bargain. This last item, however, comes at the expense of his father's passing at Tintagel, for whom the hero secretly grieves (lines

6465–6466). For all the trappings of victory and congratulations, something rings hollow in the tone of the entire proceeding, and the poet abruptly announces the conclusion of the tale as King Arthur distributes lavish presents among his friends. Perhaps Chrétien was himself hoping to receive some largess as well from his noble audience.

The moral certitudes attached to this idealized vision of knighthood and marriage would prove unsustainable, both within the medieval French society to which the poet belonged, as well as within his future work. Although Chrétien's *Erec and Enide* was obviously successful in that he was encouraged enough to produce four more works in the same genre (over a space possibly as short as ten years), his exploration of the human heart, both within and without the confines of marriage, would grow increasingly complex and subtle. Love, marriage, and happiness, it would seem, had many more pitfalls than merely the man neglecting his duties as a knight; in fact, Chrétien's masterpiece *Yvain* suggests that a knight ignoring his duty to a wife was a far greater concern. *Cligès* and *Lancelot* would go even further, hinting that true love and legal matrimony were not always one and the same. This must have been a difficult realization if the poet was, as many have maintained, a straight-laced clergyman. Lastly, *Perceval* would move into entirely new territory, vehemently preaching that both marriage and knighthood ultimately owed their obligations to a Supreme Being rather than any mere earthly authority. In retrospect, the most striking feature of *Erec and Enide* is its utopian-like presentation of a unified and harmonious British-French kingdom straddling both sides of the channel. Fast-forwarding three centuries after Chrétien's death, a disgraced and aged English knight, an eyewitness to the final disintegration of this longstanding political artifice, would then pick up the story where Chrétien and other French romancers had left off. The result was a redefinition of the Arthurian saga for the modern English-speaking world so thorough that many still believe Camelot was an exclusively English invention to begin with.

Chapter 12

The Achievement of Malory

Thus the knight prisoner, by the alchemy of his ardour and his cadenced prose, transformed lead and silver into gold — Roger Sherman Loomis.[1]

Almost exactly three centuries after Chrétien de Troyes invented the Arthurian romance as a genre with his *Erec and Enide*, a recently-released English knight prisoner (by his own self-description) died in London, presumably a broken and temporarily forgotten man. Before his death, however, Thomas Malory left the world a manuscript that would become one of the very first major books published in English with the new technology of movable type printing and forge together the unwieldy Arthurian tradition into one convenient literary template for future English-speaking generations to admire. Rather surprisingly, it would be almost another three centuries before this landmark opus would become the touchstone of English Victorian romantics adopting the King Arthur saga as their own. It has been ringing loudly in our ears ever since. Thus what began as a French cleric-turned-court poet trying to entertain a small group of noblewomen, ended six centuries later as arguably the number one cultural reference for all western secular humanities. While the name of Shakespeare remains on the lips of everyone who enjoys English poetry, it is the story line of King Arthur, his knights, and their ladies, that everyone remembers. Anyone who doubts the truth of this should simply type an internet search for King Arthur in reference to popular culture, then attempt to tally the blinding number of hits.

The purpose of this study is not to join the sometimes overwrought scholarly debate over the life, times and work of Thomas Malory. On the other hand, the often overlooked connection between this important figure and the equally (if not greater) achievement of Chrétien de Troyes is notable enough as to demand a detailed close-up, one which thus far has been disappointingly

The true protagonist in the Arthurian legends was not the king or his knights, but rather the 12th-century Angevin Empire of Henry II and Eleanor of Aquitaine. This geo-political backdrop was the impetus behind Chrétien's distinctive romances. Three centuries later, Sir Thomas Malory probably numbered among those who fought in vain for the preservation of the empire's remnants, after which he memorialized a fictional Camelot in prose.

scarce among professional academics. The personal life of Sir Thomas Malory (1405?–1471) of Newbold Revel, Warwickshire, is obscure; yet we seem to know far more about him than about Chrétien, not only because he lived three centuries later, but also because he seems to have been actively involved in some of the most important political events of his time. His most important achievement in the historical sense, however, was posthumous and artistic. In 1485 (14 years after his death), Malory's *Le Morte d'Arthur* was published at Westminster by William Caxton, England's first professional typesetter and also the man responsible for the first printed edition of Chaucer's works.[2] The very French ring in the title of this Middle English classic suggests that the author was intimately familiar with the original source materials from which these legends developed. It is doubtful whether anyone hypothetically fast-forwarding from the 15th to the 19th century and beyond could have foreseen the immeasurable popularity of this tradition. In the English language alone, writers as talented and diverse as Alfred Tennyson, T.S. Eliot, and T.H. White would all later draw inspiration from it.

Before examining the scanty but highly relevant details of Malory's life, it is useful to briefly summarize the times in which he lived, and how that era compared to the era of Chrétien. Succinctly put, the mid–15th century was a period in which all feudal institutions, particularly that of knighthood, were severely on the wane. In France, the culmination of the Hundred Years War in 1453 resulted in the permanent expulsion of Anglo-Norman rule from the continent. By that time, English kings had become far more English than French in their character and manners. During the 12th century of Chrétien, these same "English" kings were more along the lines of Henry II and his grandfather, William the Conqueror — Normans born in France speaking French as their first language. By the 15th century, these same monarchs had consolidated their hold on England — like their Norman predecessors in other lands, they went thoroughly native (see Chapter 15) — but in the process also gradually lost a grip on their continental homeland. With French victory over the English at Orléans in 1428, a victory inspired by the visions of an illiterate French peasant girl, events would move inevitably towards an independent and stronger French monarchy. This would mark the final division of a vast kingdom once unified under the reign of Henry II and Eleanor of Aquitaine, a trans-channel political entity idealized by Chrétien in his romances. This traumatic event in England would in turn be immediately followed by the War of the Roses — a horrific 30-year free-for-all of a civil war ultimately leading to the establishment of a Tudor dynasty which lasted until the time of Shakespeare.[3] Simultaneous with the English defeat in France, Europe itself would suffer a major setback with the loss of Constantinople to the Ottoman Turks, also during the year 1453. Although the recovery of Spanish Andalusia from Muslim rule in 1492 would somewhat compensate for this loss, Thomas Malory did not live to see or foresee it, dying in 1471, the same year that the Yorkists finally crushed the Lancastrians in England. In general, this was not a good time for the idealization of chivalry, which in truth had been receding from public favor with the advents of the Renaissance and Reformation, as well as the science of modern warfare. Curiously, the comparatively new (see Chapter 4) courtly view of relationships between the sexes seemed to survive and thrive even as its military counterpart of knights in shining armor became obsolete.

Thomas Malory, we can be fairly confident, was a close eyewitness to these discouraging (especially from an English point of view) political trends and experienced, at a minimum, deep disillusionment as a result. Having physically survived some of the worst dangers that the battlefield and intrigue could throw at him, the elderly knight at last found himself not in respectable retirement at an old soldier's home, but dishonorably incarcerated instead. Western pretensions about what knighthood was capable of achieving — trans-channel political unity, European control of the Middle East, even civil law, order, and justice in England — had surely vanished or, at the least, been dealt a permanent setback. This would have been profoundly true among those knights who had personally engaged in the fighting. Chrétien, in contrast, lived and wrote during a time witnessing the apex of chivalry's reputation in the West, a reputation initiated five centuries before when an Islamic attempt to conquer Europe was thwarted at the battle of Poitiers in the year 732. This western superiority complex began to deteriorate in the likely aftermath of the poet's death with European defeat by Saladin's forces at the battle of Hattin in 1187, and the subsequent failure of the Third Crusade (see Chapter 17). Thus the popular view of military knighthood in Europe spanned over 800 years and affected every literary trend associated with the West, from Chrétien to Malory to Cervantes. Loomis summed up how the Arthurian legends fit into this continuum: "If one were asked to sum up in a few words both the greatness and the limitations of the literature of the Round Table, perhaps the best answer would be that it produced Don Quixote."[4] In effect, what began at Poitiers ended at Lepanto, the 1571 naval engagement between Europeans and Turks in which a young Cervantes, future author of *Don Quixote*, was physically maimed and psychologically impacted for life. But we digress.

Aside from being a native of Warwickshire (like the traditional author of Shakespeare's works), the other surviving, documented information on the life of Sir Thomas Malory is provocative, particularly in relation to his singular achievement in English literature. After inheriting family estates in 1434 (at age 29), Malory, like many other English knights of his day, apparently marched off to the Hundred Years War in France, which was then winding down to its final, painful phase for the English. He appears to have been under the command of no less an imposing figure than Richard de Beauchamp, 13th Earl of Warwick, at the siege of Calais in 1436. By this time, however, with a pivotal Burgundian defection to France in 1435, the English were lucky to have any holdings left on the continent besides Calais. Beyond this, little can be learned of his activities, other than through his association with Warwick, one of the most cultured and widely traveled men of his times, praised during his own day as a paragon of chivalry by the Emperor of Constantinople.[5] Malory's connection with Beauchamp implies much. Though him, it is entirely possible that Malory had firsthand access to the very best that medieval French culture had to offer, including the incredibly rich legacy of the Arthurian French romancers.

The next we hear of Malory is when was sitting as a member of Parliament in 1445, the fateful year in which Henry VI married Margaret of Anjou, the "she-wolf of France." After the War of the Roses ignited, we catch another glimpse of Malory in 1462 as an ascendant Yorkist under the banner of the new 16th Earl of Warwick, Richard Neville (1428–1471), helping to mop up remaining Lancastrian resistance following the battle of Towton.[6] Like many others in this pitiless struggle, however (including his mentor Warwick), Malory seems to have switched sides, and in 1468 he was specifically excluded from a royal pardon granted to all Lancastrians by Edward IV. In 1471, after being freed from prison during the short-lived re-establishment of Henry VI as king, Malory died and was buried in the Franciscan church near Newgate prison. The extensive charges compiled against him by his accusers between 1450 and 1460 included rape, cattle theft, and non-payment of debt, plus attempted murder of the Duke of Buckingham. These accusations were likely trumped up by political motivation, but also probably contained some truth. Few who managed to stay alive during those times kept their innocence for long. Before being freed shortly prior to his death, Malory twice escaped his jailors, once by swimming a moat. He was considered too dangerous by the Yorkists to free or to pardon, but apparently not dangerous enough to kill outright.[7] It is obvious that they really hated him. As for history's final judgment of Malory as a person apart from his work — if such judgment must be made — he remains at best an enigma, and at worst, yet another example of a deeply flawed individual who, in spite of his shortcomings, made a tremendous contribution to world culture.[8]

As one might expect from a biography of this sort, the author of *Le Morte d'Arthur* presented the legends in a somewhat new light, one that was both nostalgic and tragic. It is true that Chrétien had also done this to some degree three centuries earlier, but with Malory the overall mood and atmosphere darkens considerably. Largely because of him, many tend to think of the Arthurian universe in dark, subdued, and somber hues. Moreover, this coloring carried over to and resonated strongly with British Victorian writers and the Pre-Raphaelites. To return to the 12th century depiction of Camelot in the romances of Chrétien, the reader is immediately struck by a far more optimistic viewpoint: endings are happy, comedy and irony abound, picturesque scenes are painted in bright and bold colors — this is quite different than the landscape drawn by Malory. This is not to say that the Camelot of Chrétien knows no sorrow, darkness, or anxiety; on the contrary, the poet injects strong doses of these elements at regular intervals, thus giving his romances an edge often lacking in the work of lesser artists. Frequently, there is a strong sense of unpleasant foreboding, particularly in his final romance, *Perceval*. For Malory in 15th-century England, however, things have become far more grim and the outlook totally serious. Malory's Camelot is unquestionably the self-defeated and demoralized England of his own time, with perhaps a hint of hope for the future (via the Holy Grail) tossed in to avoid complete despair.

It is not our purpose herein to catalogue innumerable examples of the manner in which Malory accomplishes this progressive effect; in fact, it was not new, strictly speaking, given the French continuators (after Chrétien) that he surely was drawing upon. Instead, a few short examples will suffice. Lancelot, the prototypical courtly lover first introduced into the Arthurian saga by Chrétien (see Chapter 1), becomes in the hands of Malory a far more serious and, many would say, sympathetic figure than when he initially appeared in 12th-century poetry.[9] Completely gone are Chrétien's humor, burlesque, and unspoken censoriousness. For Malory, Lancelot becomes a full-blown tragic hero in much the same vein as King Arthur himself. There is something about Lancelot's invincibility as a fighter combined with his hopeless passion for Guinevere that becomes a central focus in *Le Morte d'Arthur*. Was this theme hitting a little too close to home for the artist? Indeed the same could be said for Malory's Arthur. He is a victim of his own weakness for the Queen and misplaced over-trust in his friends and vassals. The identical observation can be made with respect to Malory's forceful inclusion of the Tristan and Isolde tragedy. The love triangle and its potentially devastating effects on an otherwise healthy body politic clearly engaged the English knight prisoner-turned-teller of cautionary tales. By dramatic comparison, Chrétien disdained the questionable morals of the Tristan legend and, when not making disparaging allusions, was always at pains to present healthy alternative models in behavior for his heroes and heroines. Arguably a more striking figure in Malory is Arthur's sister Morgan le Fay, who had progressed from benign enchantress in Chrétien to something akin to the Wicked Witch of the West by the 15th century. Malory retained her evil side, but in the final scene has her reconciled with her brother, thus turning Morgan into something of a tragic and sympathetic character, not unlike Lancelot. We should remember at this point that during Malory's era, political and military alliances in England often switched sides so suddenly and with such homicidal results that the modern reader frequently needs a scorecard just to keep track of whom was fighting whom to the death at any given moment in time.

To repeat, the dark life and times of Malory were not the only forces driving his reworking of the Arthurian story. The seeds of this transformation were already to be found in his French source materials.[10] After all, the 13th and 14th centuries had been no picnic for France either. After exhausting themselves by playing a leading role in the Crusades, the French found themselves at the mercy of the English. Not surprisingly, given the immeasurable popularity of Chrétien's romances in the immediate aftermath of their writing, Malory seems to draw primarily (if not exclusively) from the poet's prolific French continuators, rather than directly from Chrétien himself, for minute details.[11] Malory uses the same broad canvas painted by Chrétien but fills it in with brand new material, using an entirely different focus and emphasis. The result can sometimes appear disjointed in terms of disciplined literary structure. As Loomis reminded us: "Malory was an uneven writer."[12] Uneven perhaps, but he was also a superb editor, possibly one of the best ever, depending on how much posthumous help he actually received from his publisher Caxton.[13]

If Malory was not accessing Chrétien's romances directly, then one may well ask whether there was any connection at all. Yes, should be the resounding answer. At the very least, continuators before Malory were permanently indebted to Chrétien, and they were most certainly reading his work. It was Chrétien who first incorporated the Holy Grail theme, so near and dear to Malory's heart, straight into the Arthurian canon.[14] It was Chrétien who first introduced Lancelot and made courtly love a central theme in the saga — also a key element in Malory's version.[15] It was Chrétien, insofar as anyone can tell, who first associated the legends of Arthur and Tristan. It was also he who seems to have first made Morgan le Fay the king's sister. Without Chrétien, Malory's sources would have looked quite different, as would Malory's own writings.[16] More likely, Malory was quite aware of Chrétien, given the breathtaking synthesis he achieved, but opted to draw upon later French writers because of the totally different mood and feel found in the 12th-century poet's romances.[17]

In spite of these many uncertainties, it can be firmly asserted that the three-century period between Chrétien and Malory represented a crucial period in the overall development of the Arthurian legend. During this interval, it proceeded from the poetic and romantic innovations of Chrétien to the English gravitas and grandeur of Malory. Once again, we find ourselves turning to the insights of Loomis, who commented upon the Anglo aspects of Arthur with more authority and informed scholarship than anyone before or since. Loomis categorized Malory as a literary alchemist, turning lead and silver into gold. The lead and the silver, in our opinion, represented the continuators of Chrétien, rather than the poet himself. The gold stood for the knight prisoner's staggering achievement in the English language, from which we all still benefit. Chrétien's work was also gold, but from a completely different time and place that is now hard for us to comprehend, just as it would have been for Englishmen, and possibly Frenchmen as well, during the mid–15th century. And yet it was this strange and exotic world of the 11th and 12th centuries that gave birth to the legends in the very beginning. On thing that both eras did have in common, as shall be seen in the next chapter, was that both saw knights clashing in arms, and doing so on both sides of the channel.

Chapter 13

Restless Second Sons

Those interested in the astonishing military exploits of the past should look for these not in the pseudo-historical King Arthur of the sixth century, but rather in the documented, and very real life adventures of the 11th-century French Normans. Their stunning feats of territorial conquest, combined with political astuteness rarely rivaled throughout the ages, exceeded anything concocted by medieval romancers.[1] Clearly, in retrospect, Chrétien de Troyes and the French poets had more to draw upon than written, fictional tradition; the oral histories of their patrons would have been inspiring enough. Add to these histories the Welsh-Breton lore then achieving wider circulation, and the first flowering of Arthurian legends in France during the 12th century makes perfect sense. Indeed, the boundaries between these histories and legends were frequently blurred (see Chapter 9). As the Norman military engine forcefully swept across western civilization in seemingly every direction at once, the ultimate effect was to bring a good portion of western (and non-western) culture back to France. It also injected a heavy dose of French culture into the conquered outlying regions, especially England. As historian Christopher Tyerman reminded us, "Neither the Angevins nor their Norman predecessors as kings of England were in any meaningful sense English."[2] This, from an Oxford don. Such was the political background of England, France, and Europe that set the stage for the King Arthur of the imagination — the one most familiar to us today. The next phase of this development, as discussed in the previous chapter, would be a more forceful Anglicization of Arthur by Thomas Malory during the 15th century.

Why did the Normans suddenly burst out of northern France during the 11th century, pretty much overrunning everything in their path? The short answer is that a large number of their male heirs suddenly faced very reduced, meager circumstances, and this naturally proved a strong economic motivator for conquest. In an age of relative peace and prosperity, at least compared to the Dark Ages preceding it, eldest male heirs of the nobility still inherited everything under the law, but they also had more and more younger siblings than ever who received nothing.[3] Under such circumstances, the society having the most formidable martial traditions was bound to be a menace to the rest of civilization, and at the beginning of the High Middle Ages this particular society happened to be the French Normans. By the mid–11th century, Normandy was overflowing with able young men who had no property of their own but had plenty of weapons in hand combined with knowledge on how to use them. Worse, they had to live under the less-than-gentle dominion of their eldest brothers. Many of these restless second sons, however, knew how to fight, and many had just as much ambition and ability (if not more) than those less worthy who lorded over them. Many asked themselves why more prosperous but weaker neighboring societies should be richer and happier than they. It was like dangling treats before a child and then giving the goodies to a smaller child standing nearby. Predictably, Europe and the Mediterranean world soon became like the Wild West, except that this was eight centuries before the American West was "won" by pioneering settlers using similar justifications, sometimes characterized as "Manifest Destiny."

The first victim or beneficiary of restless Norman ambition was southern Italy, which up until that time had been an attractive but lawless cash cow for its ephemeral rulers, a land constantly fought over to a stalemate by competing factions of Italians, Lombards, Byzantines, and Saracens.[4] Within a generation of their first arrival, the Normans had taken over southern Italy much like the amoral Clint Eastwood character in Sergio Leone's spaghetti-western *A Fistful of Dollars* takes over a small, nameless town.[5] Sicily and Malta were soon added. Among this small but amazingly intrepid band of adventurers, perhaps the most famous was Robert Guiscard (1015–1085), who would eventually succeed in reinventing himself as the Duke of Apulia and Calabria. Originally, Guiscard had been the insignificant sixth son of a petty French nobleman, Tancred de Hauteville. By the time he was finished, Guiscard had become the undisputed lord of a huge and wealthy geographic area, with neighboring Italians, Lombards, Muslims, and Greek Byzantines trembling at the mention of his name.[6] Robert's equally talented younger brother Roger later migrated south to become King Roger I of Sicily. Even the eldest Hauteville son, William the Iron Arm, chose to join his younger brothers after becoming dissatisfied with the comparative meagerness of his own inheritance in Normandy. These conquests, along with near simultaneous incursions into Spain (see Chapter 15), represented the first direct

French contact with Arab culture which would decisively influence the French troubadours and *trouvère* poets such as Chrétien de Troyes during the 12th century.

The most crucial source materials for Chrétien, however, would come to France from across the English Channel. Once again, it was Norman military and political ambitions that facilitated the process. In 1066, William of Normandy, the illegitimate son of Duke Robert and known by many of his contemporaries as "William the Bastard," invaded England in full force. William laid claim to the English throne vacated by Edward the Confessor, who had died childless and, so claimed William, named him as rightful heir and successor. On the epic battlefield of Hastings, William's heavy Norman cavalry and allied Breton infantry defeated the most powerful of the English dukes, Harold of Wessex, whom the Anglo-Saxons had proclaimed as their own king.[7] William's brazen military conquest of England proved to be permanent, with ramifications that will continue to be felt as long as the English language is spoken. French-speaking overlords were imposed on England, and the native tongue of the Anglo-Saxons became gradually Latinized.[8] Consequently, the English language became unparalleled in the burgeoning scope of its vocabulary.

As for the Norman victors, they were directly (and quite willingly) exposed to the legends and traditions of the British Isles. The Breton storytellers or *jongleurs* had always known of these tales through their nearby Welsh cousins, but after the Norman conquest, a direct pipeline was established between the original Welsh-Breton sources of the Arthurian material and mainland France, then home to the most sophisticated literary society in the western world (see Chapter 3). Moreover, these skilled and innovative French poets enjoyed the full financial support and encouragement of the very same nobility that had recently appropriated Great Britain, temporarily uniting it with continental French Europe into an unwieldy, crazy-quilt mega-kingdom. Literary impact, though powerful, was purely incidental. The prime motivator was cheap real estate acquisition, as evidenced by the Conqueror's commissioning of the Doomsday Book in 1086 for the purpose of surveying (and assessing) his subjects' newly invested English properties. Like the institution of marriage (see Chapter 4), war and politics of the time were mainly concerned with the consolidation of wealth, but the unforeseen and more lasting consequences of both proved to be literary, particularly in the Arthurian arena.

Finally, for the French, came the East. The Greek Byzantine Empire and Middle East Holy Land felt the heavy weight of Norman arms, by now acting in irresistible tandem with other powerful French nobles wanting a piece of the action. By 1099 the Crusader Kingdom of Jerusalem had been forcibly established and Godfrey of Bouillon (1060–1100) — the second son of an obscure, wealthy French count — became its first ruler. Though not a Norman himself, some of Godfrey's crusader companions or rivals included the son of the English Conqueror (Robert) as well as the son (Bohemond) and great-nephew (Tancred) of Robert Guiscard. By the end of the 11th century, the first heirs of second sons from the previous generation (such as Guiscard and the Conqueror) were passing themselves off as legitimate royalty in their own right. Nevertheless, it was still Godfrey, the talented and ambitious second son, who was by general election voted the greatest of them all. This is not to say that the First Crusade was motivated strictly by the greed of French nobles unable to inherit their father's property; most of them were quite well off to begin with.[9] On the other hand, it would be more incorrect to say that insatiable greed was not a significant factor, especially given the recent Norman takeovers of England and Italy. As French Crusaders tore a bloody path through Byzantium and the Middle East, many (though not all) established their own fiefdoms in the Holy Land, never again returning to their French-speaking homelands. Although most of these kingdoms would collapse within a century (see Chapter 17), a more enduring legacy would be the crucial impetus they gave to the establishment of the Arthurian legends through French romancers such as Chrétien and his continuators.

Perhaps the most famous sibling rivalry between monarchs in English history occurred between two men who came of age just as Chrétien was inventing the Arthurian romance genre. King Richard I *Coeur de Lion* (1157–1199) and his younger brother King John I (1166–1216) were both sons of the same King Henry II and Eleanor of Aquitaine, who appear to have done so much to initially promote the Arthurian literary tradition (see Chapter 6). Both brothers were monarchs over the gigantic Angevin empire straddling the "English" Channel during the late 12th century, thus encouraging a unique cross-fertilization of poetic and storytelling innovations. While the Lion-Hearted elder brother spent most of his adult life crusading and fighting wars on the continent, his cunning and resourceful younger sibling stayed at home in England and Normandy to plot, scheme, wheel and deal. By 1190 John had successfully become English regent in Richard's absence during the Third Crusade, a sinister situation in and of itself that helped to inspire the Robin Hood legends. After Richard's death in 1199, John assumed the crown for himself. He proceeded to quarrel with the French king, the pope, and just about everyone else, but managed to hold his own remarkably well, except perhaps when his own barons forced him to sign the Magna Carta in 1215. Interestingly, one of John's many victims was his young nephew, Arthur of Brittany (1187–1203), who was perceived by the unpopular John (with good justification) as a potential rival for the throne.[10] This Arthur was most likely named after the legendary English hero so famed by that time throughout Europe, including French Brittany. His own tragic and somewhat fictionalized story was immortalized by Shakespeare in *King John* some four centuries later.

The theme of a disgruntled, less-than-fully-legitimate heir runs thick and heavy throughout the entire Arthurian corpus, as every reader of these legends readily appreciates. Arthur's stay-at-home nephew, and in later versions his illegitimate son, Mordred, proves to be the downfall of Camelot, combined with Queen Guinevere's adultery. This tradition began well before Chrétien's time with Geoffrey of Monmouth and has continued strong ever since.[11] Rather strikingly, Mordred is never mentioned in any of Chrétien's works. When the poet gives an exhaustive list of Arthur's Roundtable membership in *Erec and Enide* (1669–1706), the name of Mordred is prominently absent. Chrétien does see fit in this very same list to mention some obscure names, including that of Loholt (line 1700), a legitimate son of King Arthur generally unknown to more modern audiences.[12] In subsequent permutations of the tale, beginning with the Vulgate Lancelot-Grail Cycle, Mordred — originally Arthur's adulterous nephew — was transformed into Arthur's illegitimate, rebellious son. It also appears that the sordid adultery of Guinevere and Mordred was replaced in the Vulgate Cycle with a somewhat more palatable and sympathetic adultery between Guinevere and Lancelot, which Chrétien deserves credit for initiating (see Chapter 1). Hand-in-hand with this innovation, Guinevere becomes merely an adulteress (with Lancelot) and not a traitor (like Mordred) as well. After Chrétien's time, Mordred gradually evolves from a prototypical, dissatisfied heir into a treacherous villain of Iago-like complexity and diabolical cunning. It may be that Chrétien opted not to mention Mordred simply because he found this aspect of the legend distasteful, or perhaps because the pervasive theme of treasonous inter-family relations might have hit a little too close to home for his noble French patrons and audiences.

Standing opposite from the powers of evil in the poet's vast array of characters in the romances is Arthur's valiant nephew, Gawain.[13] Gawain, like his famous uncle, is given a prominent role in Geoffrey of Monmouth's early version of the story. Later, in Chrétien's hands, Gawain becomes the epitome and exemplar of knightly virtue, courtesy, and prowess. He fights Yvain to a draw, pacifies a violent Perceval, and successfully negotiates with a disguised Erec. He is Lancelot's closest companion and proxy in arms. Unlike Arthur's unpleasant and discourteous seneschal, Sir Kay, Gawain is both polite and indomitable. In the most conventional sense he is the "First Knight" of Camelot.[14] Nevertheless, Gawain is never the primary hero in any of Chrétien's romances; rather, he is always used as a foil. Because of his nearly too-perfect persona, Gawain is also rather one-dimensional as a character. Among scholars, Karl Uitti noted that although Gawain is repeatedly held up as the model of good knighthood, he consistently comes across less sympathetic and somehow inferior to Perceval, Yvain, Lancelot, Cligès, and Erec.[15] The same comparison holds true with his uncle Arthur, in spite of all of his personal foibles. Their flawed character traits make them more compelling. Gawain is the original template for the ideal knight, before being supplanted in that role by Galahad or Lohengrin in later continuations. Not until the anonymous 14th-century masterpiece *Sir Gawain and the Green Knight* is he given recognizable human frailties, thus finally becoming a sympathetic Arthurian hero in his own right. Therein lies that work's true greatness and timelessness.

Gawain is presented, at least by other poets and chroniclers who see fit to mention the name of Mordred, as the latter's brother or half-brother, at least until Mordred later transforms into Arthur's illegitimate, evil son during the Vulgate Cycle. Gawain's presumptive, preferred status over his brother or cousin Mordred is generally agreed upon by the romancers. This preference is based on actual knightly merit and possibly birthright as well. Even in pre–Chrétien versions (such as Geoffrey of Monmouth), Gawain is considered heroic by any standard, accompanying Arthur in all of his wars and eventually falling with his uncle while fighting against the rebellious Mordred at the battle of Camlann. In Chrétien's final work, *Perceval*, perhaps the greatest symbol of Gawain's favor with Arthur is his personal possession of the sword Excalibur.[16] This is the only time in his works that the poet mentions this famous weapon by name. Chrétien was drawing upon a tradition that had Arthur give Excalibur to his favorite nephew upon Gawain's becoming a knight. This same tradition was later used in the Vulgate Cycle as well, but later disappeared from the public imagination, much like the tradition of King Arthur's legitimate son, Loholt.[17]

The bottom line here is that, traditionally speaking at least, King Arthur has no truly legitimate, direct heir, either male or female. In the Camelot of Chrétien de Troyes, the various family relations and favorite knights of Arthur become his surrogate children, for better or worse. Using older traditions, Chrétien was able to help decisively shift the focus of audience attention away from the heroism of the king in favor of the Roundtable knights. The audience becomes engaged with the various escapades and misadventures of these knights — all of whom are profoundly flawed, imperfect human beings, with the exception of the early Gawain, who in Chrétien's romances is not a fully developed or multi-dimensional character. In spite of the personal foibles of the knights, or because of them, we are fascinated by their so-called fictional lives. This proved to be a long-term trend that the poet established, one that was seized upon by all writers who came after, and is still being embellished by modern continuators.

One question that naturally flows from this analysis is whether Chrétien was himself a first, second, or only son. We have no way of knowing with certainty and any opinion offered herein must be considered at best speculative. At the very least, a few general observations can be made, assuming that Chrétien, like most great writers, wrote about things he knew from firsthand experience. The first observation is that warm sibling relations are virtually non-existent in the poet's oeuvre; in fact, sibling relationships in general are scarcely portrayed and tend to be hostile. One example of fighting siblings is the bitter rivalry in *Perceval* between the "Maid with Little Sleeves," championed by Gawain, and her older sister. Another similar dysfunctional relationship is depicted in *Yvain*, with the hero again taking the side of the younger (and legally oppressed) sister.[18] The second observation to be made is that any close relationships dramatized (other than those between lovers) tend to be between cousins or friends, rather than immediate family.

From these examples, it might be deduced — with a big margin of allowable error — that Chrétien de Troyes was either an impoverished only son, or perhaps not a first son, pursuing limited career options. Given that the vast majority of scholarly opinion portrays him as some level of religious cleric, it would make sense that such an individual may have first sought security in the church, and then, later, fame and fortune as a court poet. If this textually-based guess is incorrect, it still remains certainly true that what first began as the misgivings of French youth over inheritance rights during the 11th century, ended with timeless world literature being produced by Chrétien and other writers during the 12th century. Unfortunately, literary activity was not the only sphere in which the influence of aggressive French expansionism was felt, and in other respects the consequences usually proved very destructive. Even these negative consequences, however, could play a significant role in shaping the fictional Arthurian legacy, as we shall explore in the next chapter.

Chapter 14

Legacy of the Crusader Kingdoms

In retrospect, the European Crusades of the High Middle Ages come across, at best, as ugly religious fanaticism, and at worst, vicious, deliberate genocide. The restless Norman spirit which plunged headlong into places like Great Britain, Spain, southern Italy and Sicily with spectacular and permanent repercussions, had a curiously short-lived impact in the Holy Land. Although the Crusades proper spread themselves out over three centuries, Christian rule in Jerusalem, such as it ever was, lasted only 88 years. More telling, its post-colonial influence in *Outremer*—again in stark contrast to other places—seems to have made even less of an impression on the locals.[1] The final insult to western values and mores in this region came when local Christians and Jews openly preferred the enlightened and tolerant rule of the Muslim Sultan Saladin (see Chapter 17) to his immediate Franco-Christian predecessors. As for the Crusaders' supposed Christian allies in Byzantine Constantinople, the latter probably suffered more in the long run from the invasions than their Islamic neighbor-protagonists, and were glad to be finally rid of their barbaric Latin neighbors. All of this suggests that if we are to look for any good things coming out of the Crusades, these should be sought elsewhere besides within the geographic boundaries of the Middle East.

One such consolation prize was the Arthurian legend, and in particular the romances of Chrétien de Troyes, although this was not widely recognized until hundreds of years later. At that time, and in the immediate aftermath, all that seemed apparent was widespread disappointment and disillusion. Essentially, the First Crusade "succeeded" only in the narrow sense of physically capturing Jerusalem; all that followed were failures of varying degrees, some catastrophic in scope. Writing of the European psychological trauma after the costly and unsuccessful Third Crusade, historian Christopher Tyerman observed, "God's purpose seemed more clouded than ever"; moreover, "the Third Crusade cast a long shadow over the future."[2] Philosophically, Tyerman noted that "the acquisition by wealthy nations of the cultural icons of conquered or exploited weaker lands is a staple of world history, as shown by glancing at ancient Rome, nineteenth-century England or the United States of America in the past century."[3] Regarding the miserable failure of the destructive Fourth Crusade, which looted Constantinople of its holy relics, he caustically added, "These relics provided the Fourth Crusade's most positive and lasting legacy in western Europe."[4] The covetous and superstitious attitudes of the Crusaders, barbaric as they were, provide insight into the mindset of the same audiences (at least those who were literate) that had propelled the Arthurian works of Chrétien and other romancers into sweeping popularity by that time.

Perhaps those hurt most by the Crusaders' misguided zeal were their own kinsmen left behind in Europe. Writing during the 18th-century Enlightenment, Edward Gibbon, who was no fan of the Crusades, strongly hinted that the eventual political ascendancy of England was greatly retarded by these events. While admitting that some social progress in Europe had resulted from the quick removal of omnipresent robber barons from the scene, he asserted that overall more harm than good, even on the home front, had resulted from Crusader escapades into the Middle East.[5] One gets the definite sense that Gibbon would have disagreed with Shakespeare's King Henry IV, who asserted that youthful military aggression had to be channeled into foreign directions in order to avoid civil disruption at home.[6] Nevertheless, Gibbon acknowledged that "the conflagration which destroyed the tall and barren trees of the forest gave air and scope to the vegetation of the smaller and nutritive plants of the soil."[7] Specifically, Gibbon recognized that the clergy, of whom Chrétien was probably a minor member, used this chaotic period in western history to study, preserve and revive the humanities. Thus the Arthurian romance became one of Gibbon's "smaller and nutritive" benefits stemming from an otherwise devastating historical event.

The aftershocks of the Crusades were felt worldwide, often indirectly in ways that textbooks tend to ignore or downplay. About the same time Chrétien was inventing the Arthurian romance, coming of age on the other side of the globe was a young Mongolian named Temüjin, better known to later generations as Genghis Khan (1162–1227). By engaging each other in an obsessive and ruinous conflict, both Christians and Muslims lost sight of a new and much greater mutual threat from the East, one for which they would have been much better prepared had they not been in the midst of a never-ending holy war or *jihad*. By the mid–13th century, the Mongol hordes had overrun vast parts of Europe and the Middle East, and would have kept on going had it not been for the death of its intrepid leader and growing internal divisions among his successors. Gibbon emphasized the seriousness of the situation:

> Since the invasion of the Arabs in the eighth century, Europe had never been exposed to a similar calamity; and, if the disciples of Mahomet would have oppressed her religion and liberty, it might be apprehended that the shepherds of Scythia would extinguish her cities, her arts, and all the institutions of civil society.[8]

If the Christian Crusaders and Muslim Jihadists alike were unable to decisively conquer each other, how terrified they must have been of this new, unanticipated and seemingly irresistible threat which obliterated their cities and shrines. Worse, defeat often meant more than subjection: it could spell total annihilation. In the case of Europe, that meant the Arthurian tradition as well. There is no indication that the Mongols would have respected western culture as it had previously respected, to a limited extent, Chinese learning in its earlier conquest of that nation. It should also be remembered that the Mongol threat from the East receded just as the Arthurian literary tradition expanded during the generations following Chrétien's era.

As early as the 12th century, the Arthurian tradition in Europe had become more than literary; it was by then making tentative appearances in the visual arts as well. The topic is one of speculative debate and routine disagreement, but a majority of experts agree that the oldest extant image of King Arthur is located, quite fittingly, in French Brittany. This work is to be found on the exterior of the Romanesque-style church of Saint Efflam situated in Perros-Guirec, near Lannion. The indefatigable Roger Sherman Loomis, in his magnificent guidebook, *Arthurian Legend in Medieval Art*, summed up the mystery of the sculpture known as the Perros Relief: "As one might expect from the history of the Arthurian legend, Brittany has given us what may be — or may not be — the earliest surviving representation of Arthur. There is uncertainty as to both subject and date."[9] As for estimated dating of this obscure piece of art, Loomis (almost with tongue in cheek) gives a 150-year range of 1025 to 1175, settling for circa 1100. This primitive bas relief depicts (possibly) the mythical legend of Saint Efflam, who once upstaged King Arthur by overcoming a local dragon. This was accomplished through devout prayer that the otherwise invincible sword of the king had been unable to vanquish with physical might alone.[10] The legend itself is juvenile by modern standards and somewhat hostile to the then-burgeoning popularity of Arthur, since it essentially asserts the moral superiority of church over the temporal power of the state. As for the intrinsic and aesthetic merits of the sculpture, its features are crude, worn and unattractive, but all of these qualities only seem to further its alleged distinction for being the first of its kind. In effect, there is no good reason to argue the contrary.

About the same time as the Perros Relief (or not long after), a far more elaborate and skillfully-executed sculpture was produced for the exterior of the Modena Cathedral in the Po Valley of northern Italy. This bas relief, found in the archivolt of the façade section known as the Porta della Pescheria ("Gate of the Fishmarket"), depicts a scene from the Welsh *Life of Saint Gildas* legend, written by Caradoc of Llancarfan in approximately 1130. In this tale, Arthur's queen is abducted by a rival king and held captive in a tower while Arthur and his knights come to the rescue. As in the legend of Saint Efflam, however, it takes the mediation of a holy man (this time Saint Gildas), to secure the queen's release.[11] As at Perros-Guirec, secular legend finds its way into sacred art as part of a moral lesson on the superiority of church over state, although in this case, rather interestingly, the intervention of the saint is not depicted. All we see are the secular players in the drama. This same abduction theme was later used by Chrétien in his pivotal romance, *Lancelot* (see Chapter 1). The image from Modena is of particular interest because the names of the characters are labeled, thus there can be no doubt as to its subject matter, although the exact dating is still debatable. Loomis placed it between 1100 and 1110, while more specialized experts such as René Jullian dated it somewhat later, around 1130 to 1140.[12] The latter range would seem to make more sense if the *Life of Saint Gildas* was in fact written around 1130. All of this analysis, however, is highly uncertain. If one disputes or doubts the exact dating or topicality of the Perros Relief (as many do), then the Modena archivolt becomes the earliest known treatment of the King Arthur legends in visual art. It is certainly more attractive in any case.

That the legend of Saint Gildas should be associated with King Arthur is not surprising, given that both were supposed Welsh contemporaries of each other and that both were allegedly buried at Glastonbury, a traditional British placement for Avalon (see Chapter 8).[13] The labeled names on the bas relief are also interesting, particularly that of Guinevere, identified as Winlogee. This is a name which, as Loomis pointed out, is derived from the Welsh version of Arthur's queen, Winlowen.[14] Also included are the names of Artus de Bretania (Arthur), his knights, including Galvaginus (Gawain), Che (Kay), and Isdernus (Ider).[15] Conspicuously absent are well-known names among the Arthurian nobility such as Lancelot and Perceval, both of whom were later French creations by Chrétien.[16] Clearly (it would seem),

Italian craftsmen for the Modena Cathedral were getting their story material from Welsh or Breton sources. The point is worth remembering because at this early stage during the 12th century, the Arthurian storyline was still developing and would have been quite unrecognizable to most modern perceptions. This was also likely many years before Chrétien applied his inimitable poetic and imaginative genius to the same tradition.

"Why in Italy and why in Modena?" the reader may well be asking at this point. The short answer, in a word, is "Crusaders." Loomis points to documented evidence of Breton Crusaders passing through Italy en route to the Holy Land and wintering in Bari (on the southwest Italian coast) during the winter of 1096 to 1097, before embarking by ship to their final destination.[17] A not unreasonable hypothesis — a rather obvious one in fact — is that the Breton contingent of the expedition, with their boisterous storytelling tradition in tow, passed through the Po Valley in 1096 (probably before and after this time as well), leaving their popular legends with the local craftsmen as proposed artistic material. When the Modena Cathedral went up shortly after this, it incorporated, like many other new churches of the day, popular artwork with crusading themes.[18] The Breton tradition of Arthur, especially a scene from the life of Saint Gildas, was particularly suited for this purpose. The full story (though only partially portrayed in the bas relief) confirmed the supreme authority of the Christian church while also advertising the unbeatable, warlike prowess of King Arthur and his chosen knights. We hesitate to say "knights of the Roundtable" because, at this early date, there is no evidence whatsoever of an Arthurian Roundtable. This ubiquitous symbol would first appear a few years later in the French poetic elaborations of Wace (see Chapter 10).

If the bas relief for the Modena archivolt is impressive with its audacious blend of religious and political propaganda for the period, then the work used as cover art for this book must be viewed as completely over-the-top in terms of juxtaposed symbolism. At the very tip of the geographic heel of southwestern Italy in the port city of Otranto is another town *duomo* or cathedral, within which lies one of the most unique and fascinating floor mosaics in all of Christian religious art. Spread out over a large area is a Tree of Life representation — a prevalent motif in medieval art — and to the right of one branch, among many other colored, mosaic figures, is "Rex Arturus." The image belongs to a small group in the ensemble that is clearly labeled.[19] The author recently viewed a reproduction of this image in the 2008 exhibition at Les Champs Libres in Rennes, and it is perhaps even more impressive in person than in photographs.[20] Startlingly, Arthur is seated upon what appears to be a mountain goat, a very utilitarian animal in Apulia and throughout southern Italy, to be sure. Loomis helpfully conjectures that in Welsh pagan lore, the goat was sometimes used as a symbolic creature of supernatural royalty. He also points out that the goat was typically a symbol of lechery as well, which could be viewed as Arthur's mortal weakness.[21] This would be in view of his insistence (against Merlin's advice, according to tradition) on marrying Guinevere, a stubborn act which ultimately led to his downfall. To the left of Arthur and his strange mount, Adam and Eve are seen being expelled from Paradise, while around him earthly chaos and mayhem prevails — not in Arthur's direct path, though. Crowned with a scepter in his left hand, the king gestures with his right towards a wild beast as if to say "Begone!" The beast, whose same species is wreaking havoc on humanity elsewhere in the mosaic, is reeling backwards, possibly having just received a head-butt from Arthur's magical goat.

According to a preserved and precise record, this fantastical work of art was commissioned by the archbishop Jonathan and executed by the priest Pantaleone in the year 1165.[22] This is approximately five years before Chrétien de Troyes is generally believed to have invented the Arthurian romance with his first surviving major work, *Erec and Enide*. The Otranto church floor mosaic is as visually rich in symbolism as Chrétien's romances are poetically complex, plus just as open to varying interpretations. For example, there has been some debate over exactly what kind of varmint is being driven back by the king. Loomis suggested a panther, based on a legendary combat between Arthur and Capalus, the giant cat of Lausanne. This was possibly taken from the same source for short Arthurian episodes such as those found in the *Bataille Loquifer*, written by Graindor de Brie circa 1175. Holmes and Klenke, however, took exception to Loomis' interpretation, and suggested that the wild beast portrayed in the Otranto mosaic is really a fox. They assert that a fox would tie in better with the overall biblical and religious symbolism of the work.[23] This writer's own subjective view is that the images look more like big cats, given their white spots and long tails, but wolves or jackals are admittedly possible. Foxes, though, have never seemed very threatening to him. Whether one prefers to view the Otranto beasts as feline or canine, there can be no mistaking that this is the earliest surviving color image of King Arthur, and one that is literally set in stone. The Otranto mosaic is also exactly contemporary with Chrétien and was completed on the very eve of his reshaping these disparate Arthurian literary traditions into their first, sustained masterpieces.

It is more than mere coincidence that such a work of art should be found in this particular place and time. To repeat, Otranto was (and continues to be) a port city. During the 12th century, it was, like Bari to the north, a convenient point of sea departure to the Holy Land and the Middle East. In 1165, the city was under the rule of powerful Norman monarchs who, during the previous century, had carved out kingdoms for themselves in Sicily and southern Italy. These may not have been Crusader Kingdoms in the strict sense of the term, since they were not located in the Middle East. On the other hand, these areas had now in fact come under monolithic Norman rule, though this was admittedly challenged on occasion and eventually overcome by the German Holy Roman emperors. By achieving this conquest, the Normans had expelled or subdued many anarchic elements from the region, including non–Christian ones such as the Saracens, as well as other endlessly competing factions (see Chapter 13). Immediately after the Otranto floor was completed, the Norman King William II of Sicily ("William the Good") came to the throne and presided over the final economic and cultural prosperity of that dynasty. It coincided with the 12th-century renaissance taking place on the continent, which simultaneously saw the genesis of the Arthurian romance in France. Wherever Norman influence went, so did the advancement of society, or at least so it seemed. At a minimum, this was certainly true in both southern Italy and northern Europe. In satellite areas such as Champagne and Troyes, the indirect Norman influence was as strongly felt as it could have been, short of being domineering.

The surviving Arthurian church artwork at Otranto and Modena represents two small, tangible legacies of the Crusader kingdoms, the latter from Breton Crusaders passing through the Italian Peninsula, and the former from the peaceful benefits of later Norman conquest, settlement, and rule. Places like Bari and Otranto may not have been Crusader destinations in the strict sense, since these never were the conscious or ultimate goals of the enterprise; in a broader sense, however, these were the towns where true Crusader influence came to a halt. If the western adventurers made little positive or long-term impression on their Muslim and Byzantine adversaries, their cultural influence in mainland Europe through which they traveled was permanent. The Arthurian corpus and its artistic ornaments were only a few conspicuous examples of this among many. Although the Crusades failed in their stated object, and Crusader Kingdoms rapidly crumbled, their psychological impact was enormous both at home and abroad. We still feel it today with the King Arthur tradition as one byproduct.

Perhaps the last word in this regard should be left to Loomis, who, near the end of his long and distinguished career, offered a somewhat jarring observation. Appropriately reminding us that many of the Crusaders very likely had King Arthur on the brain as they marched off to kill and be killed, Loomis (like Gibbon) reflected on the domestic impact these stories had as well, beginning with Geoffrey of Monmouth. He asserted, "By one of history's bitter ironies, then, Geoffrey's pushing the conquests of Arthur into western Europe was a factor which made possible the advances of the Turk into eastern Europe."[24] In other words, the unification of Great Britain and continental Europe in Arthur's kingdom ultimately contributed to the Hundred Years War between England and France. Both were encouraged to fight one another, thus allowing the Ottomans to advance into eastern Europe with minimal opposition. We would only add that while this may certainly be true, the same unifying dynamic allowed the French and the Bretons to enormously enrich western literary heritage through peaceful means. This process included the intrepid Normans resettling and intermarrying with different cultures. If one includes the conquest of England as a forerunner of the First Crusade, then the biggest legacy of the crusading spirit may have been nothing less than the creation of the modern English language.

Chapter 15

Normans Gone Native

> ... *they renounced their gods for the God of the Christians; and the dukes of Normandy acknowledged themselves the vassals of the successors of Charlemagne and Capet. The savage fierceness which they had brought from the snowy mountains of Norway was refined, without being corrupted, in a warmer climate; the companions of Rollo insensibly mingled with the natives; they imbibed the manners, language, and gallantry of the French nation; and in martial age, the Normans might claim the palm of valour and glorious achievements*—Edward Gibbon.[1]

Of the many legacies left to civilization by the military excursions of the Normans during the 11th and 12th centuries (which included the Crusades), the most valuable by far has been the English language itself. This notable development in the course of human affairs began with, and ultimately resulted from, a heavy and forcible injection of Latin-derived, Old French into the Old English, Anglo-Saxon dialect of the recently conquered British Isles. Contemporary with this process was the initial development of the Arthurian legend in France and England. On the surface this may seem like a surprising coincidence, but even a tiny bit of reflection will correct any initial, false impressions. Great changes and innovations rarely (if ever) occur in isolation, though some commentators do their best to make us think that. Instead, true originality, the type that has lasting influence, tends to come in bunches, and bunches that are interrelated at that. New stories—which is exactly what the Arthurian legends of the 12th century were, despite their ancient roots—came contemporaneously with linguistic innovations. Although the tales were at first told in older traditional languages such as Old French and Latin, their subsequent development would have an inevitable adoption by the English vernacular and Malory in the 15th century. During the age of Chrétien, everything was being propelled by a new sense of curiosity and invention.

It is fair to assert, though rarely commented upon, that all of these momentous events were facilitated by — indeed, made possible and hastened along by — the Normans bursting out of northern France. This they did either by hiring themselves out as knights and soldiers, or in concerted effort to expand their own worldly dominions. While the French Normans were certainly not the first or last tribe in history to successfully do these things, they possessed yet another societal trait that placed them within a far more exclusive class — namely, they were adaptable. The amazingly complete and enthusiastic assimilation of the Normans into the foreign cultures which they conquered is one of the great and relatively untold stories of history. In effect, this massive integration enabled the sweeping cross-cultural fertilization that in turn sparked the literary creation of the Arthurian romance by writers such as Chrétien de Troyes. Without the Normans to act as a forcible conduit for new ideas and values being transported across Europe, the great intellectual melting pot that was 12th-century France would have been delayed or perhaps forever postponed, much to the detriment of western culture as a whole. As much as it may pain a scholar of romance languages to admit it, it all started with the Vikings, to whom we should all be grateful.

The strange-but-true story of the Normans began in Scandinavia during the Dark Ages. As the Carolingian Holy Roman Empire founded by Charlemagne collapsed during the ninth century, Viking marauders stepped into the breach and made large parts of coastal Europe their new and permanent homes, particularly in northern France where Frankish and Gallic settlements were overrun by these irresistible migrations. Then something very unusual happened. Instead of simply killing, enslaving or expelling the vanquished locals, the Vikings intermarried with them and quickly blended in, almost as if to go into hiding. Most sources agree that in Normandy the entire process of assimilation was completed within the span only a few generations. This was the first indication that the Normans, whose name probably derives from a combination of "Norseman" with "Roman," were quite different from other barbarian invaders that had preceded them.[2] In retrospect, and within the context of the Arthurian legends, this incursion was doubly unusual in that the invaders not only contributed to the story's development (as patrons), those who stayed home in Scandinavia eventually contributed to it as well. For example, the 1954 film, *Prince Valiant*, despite its unintentional campiness and Robert Wagner's famously bad wig, goes more to the core and true international spirit of the Arthurian world than most other movies on the same subject matter attempting to claim historical authenticity.[3] It also serves as a useful reminder of direct ties between the Arthurian legends and Scandinavia, as, for example, in the source material utilized by Marie de France (see Chapter 4).

As the Normans were consolidating a hold on their namesake territory in France, another unlikely bedfellow was emerging in Andalusia at the other extreme end of Europe — one completely different in climate, religion, politics, race, and culture. The Muslims and Jews of southern Spain had by that time built up one of the most impressive societies the world had ever seen, centered around the fabled city of Cordova. It was here, among major advances made in all of the arts and sciences, that Arabic love poetry flourished and rose to new heights as well. Perhaps the most famous of these literary achievements was the poem today known as the *Tawq al-Hamāma*, or *The Neck-Ring of the Dove* by Ibn Hazm (994–1064).[4] There is a growing (and logical) acceptance among scholars that Arabic lyrical verse exerted, at the very least, a powerful indirect influence on the Aquitainian troubadours who would in turn later cast their complete spell over the style of northern *trouvère* poets such as Chrétien (see Chapter 6). Though written and recited in an alien tongue, the spirit and subject matter of Andalusian Arabic poetry was something completely new to Europeans. To deny its influence one must assert that entirely new themes and moods were being espoused by the troubadours that just happened to be identical to the ones their next door Muslim neighbors in Spain had been producing for some time previous.

These versatile Viking immigrants to Normandy inevitably collided with the refined artistic pleasures of Iberia during the 11th century, the result of military aggression by allied French Christian armies into Muslim Spain.[5] One of the first documented instances of this direct contact came in 1064 (two years before the battle of Hastings) when forces under Duke William VIII of Aquitaine crossed the Pyrenees and laid siege to the wealthy and cultivated Muslim-Jewish city of Barbastro.[6] Supporting the Aquitainians were auxiliary mercenaries from Normandy who by then were gaining a reputation as the finest soldiers in Europe, thanks to recent, breathtaking successes in southern Italy against the Byzantines, Lombards, and Saracens. After taking the city, the Normans followed their near ancestors' pattern of behavior and, instead of killing and destroying, appropriated lifestyles and tried to blend in as best they could. Historian Maria Rosa Menocal described the Normans' victory lap at Barbastro: "Nearly all report that the strangers among the troops, the contingent from the northernmost reaches of the Frankish lands, the Normans, walked into this first Andalusian city they had ever seen and immediately went native."[7] Menocal then repeats the oft-told anecdote of a displaced Muslim sending a Jewish neighbor friend back to negotiate for the release of his captured daughter, only to find her the wife of a Christian (presumably Norman) conqueror. The Christian head of the household was by then dressed, speaking, and eating like the indigenous population, listening in rapture to Islamic love songs being performed by local singing girls (or *qiyan*) who specialized in this highly-developed art form.[8]

As for the Aquitainians, they, along with their duke, returned to southern France, taking with them bits and pieces of the mesmerizing culture now claimed as their own, including the Andalusian singing girls.[9] The duke's son and successor, William IX of Aquitaine (1071–1126), was born seven years after the siege of Barbastro and would have been raised amidst the "spoils" of his father's Spanish conquests. William IX, as has been often noted (see Chapter 6), is widely acknowledged as the first of the troubadour poets. He himself would later take more than one wife from south of the Pyrenees.[10] Like his father before him, William IX was a military adventurer in Spain, as well as the Middle East.[11] There can be little or no doubt that he was familiar with, if not immersed in, the poetic arts of his Islamic neighbor-antagonists. It is noteworthy, however, that the famous troubadour duke, while immortally successful as a poet, was also a military failure without the Norman help that his father had earlier enjoyed. It can furthermore be argued that the Normans were even greater transmitters of literary traditions than the Aquitainians. Despite the crucial role played by William IX's granddaughter Eleanor (and her lavish court at Poitiers) in laying the groundwork for the beginnings of Arthurian romance, it was the Norman-Angevin kingdom anchored in mainland England and Brittany that produced and patronized the pioneering works of Geoffrey, Wace, and Marie de France. Eventually, this Norman stream of influence would coalesce at Champagne in the work of Chrétien de Troyes. Aquitaine was certainly an essential link in the chain of transmission, but not the one nearest (or most politically powerful) in direct relation to Chrétien, it would seem.

If one accepts the basic premise that Arabic culture (poetic culture in particular) played a central role in the development of the Arthurian legends, then the importance of the Normans in the process becomes magnified to an even greater degree. Moreover, to deny this Arabic influence, especially that coming out of 11th and 12th-century Andalusia (see Chapter 2), is to take an extremely blinkered and limiting view of literary history. Menocal repeatedly emphasized that "the spongelike and extremely mobile Normans played a crucial, if somewhat inadvertent role at the end of the eleventh century in familiarizing Latin Christendom with Islamic Europe."[12] This was certainly true in Spain, and it was also true in Sicily and southern Italy, where advanced Muslim cultures not only heavily influenced Christian art and literature, but were energetically embraced and thoroughly incorporated into it (see Chapter 13). During the late 12th century, as Chrétien was creating his groundbreaking romances, Sicily enjoyed a cultural and artistic heyday under the last of its resplendent Norman kings, William II.[13] Without this unlikely familiarization between otherwise hostile societies, without this enthusiastic integration of popular styles and themes, it is difficult if not impossible to imagine the King Arthur legends taking shape in the manner that they eventually did.

The greatest and most complete assimilation of the Normans into a foreign culture, however (and the one most typically taken for granted), involved their absolute and unequivocal conquest of mainland England in 1066 (see Chapter 13). In 1086, one year before the death of William the Conqueror in 1087, the self-made king commissioned the famous Doomsday Book for purposes of census and taxation in the newly Norman-controlled England. This was partly the result of William's successful elimination of the old Anglo-Saxon nobility and total replacement of Old English with Norman French as the new language of court. This shift had important consequences for the development of Arthurian romance over the next century. First, it brought the Welsh and Norman cultures into direct physical contact with each other. Secondly, the old legends could now be disseminated in a widely-spoken and widely-written language (Old French) that represented political power and prestige. Chrétien would later exploit this last advantage to full effect.

It served Norman political purposes as well. On the surface, the King Arthur legends may have seemed like the battle cry of an oppressed people (the English and the Welsh against their French Norman overlords), but once successfully co-opted by the Normans, it became their own vehicle. In this, the Normans proved adept at appropriating the machinery of propaganda, like everything else they came into contact with. Though often illiterate themselves, they seem to have possessed a keen appreciation for the power of the written word and what it could help to accomplish if properly cultivated and patronized. Like Arthur, the Normans had fought against the Saxons (read: Germans) in the past and would continue to do so intermittently. The name of Arthur had also become such a potent symbol of national unification by the time of the Norman Conquest that it could now easily be used as a brand name for the Angevin kings ruling territories on both sides of the English Channel. After all, the fictional King Arthur had supposedly done the same in the distant days of yore.

The establishment of the Angevin dynasty in England and Normandy (among other places) had itself been a rather unusual and unlikely affair. The stage was set in 1128 when a non–Norman, Geoffrey Plantagenet, Count of Anjou, married a granddaughter of William the Conqueror, the future Empress Matilda.[14] After a disputed succession to the English throne and bloody civil war failed to obtain the English crown for Matilda's family, fate intervened and awarded her son, Henry II, the prize with the natural death of King Stephen in 1154. Stunningly, Henry Plantagenet had ensured that his future domains as King of England would be even more expansive, having wed the much older and recently-divorced Eleanor of Aquitaine in 1152. England, Normandy, Brittany, Anjou, and Aquitaine had, within the span of one generation, become a single kingdom, and a new kind of propaganda vehicle was needed to justify it. King Arthur suited the purpose quite nicely.

The Norman conquest of England would also gradually transform and expand the English language into expressive, flexible proportions still exceptional by world standards. This — the "story of English" — would be its biggest legacy of all.[15] While fanciful Arthurian romance would be invented and developed by Chrétien and his continuators during the 200 years following the Norman takeover of England, the language normally associated with Arthur would develop separately but simultaneously. Not until four centuries after the conquest, would the English writer Thomas Malory (see Chapter 12) adopt the legends for his own use, and not until the 19th century would English poets such as Tennyson truly versify them. As Urban Holmes observed, the Anglo-Norman milieu and the 12th-century renaissance began as an imitation of the classics and then combined itself with a new, subjective spirit, much akin to 19th-century Romanticism.[16] Thus Arthurian lore and the modern English language would have a rendezvous in the distant future; they both began, however, in close proximity to one another during the 11th and 12th centuries. One essential element in this process — the key, if you will — was the French Norman assimilation into English and Welsh native lands and the gradual adoption of their customs and language. Many conquerors would not have bothered with this, but the Normans did.

There is no evidence that Chrétien de Troyes was of Norman background; then again, there is not much evidence of him as a person at all (see Chapter 24). Although most critics correctly agree that he must have spent a good deal of time in Champagne, the region of his namesake town, this does not rule out the possibility of Norman, Breton, or any other kind of ancestry beyond Troyes.[17] As a member of an elite circle at Troyes, he also would have had (if nothing else) direct contact with a number of individuals having documented Norman connections, including his patron Henry the Liberal, who was a great grandson of William the Conqueror. This Norman affiliation would have been even more pronounced if Chrétien at one time or another traveled to England, as many critics think he in fact did. Given that Champagne, though technically a satellite of the French monarchy, was also not far from, and often aligned with, the dukes of Normandy, it would be little wonder if one of its most famous sons could have claimed some of that ancestral heritage for himself. To repeat, quickly intermarrying and intermingling with other societies, French and otherwise, is what the adventurous and ambitious Normans tended to do. Their influence and dominance touched everyone in the western world at the time, including Chrétien de Troyes.

In the Middle East and the short-lived Christian kingdom of *Outremer* (see Chapter 17), French Norman domination at the time seemed more permanent, as well as more important, but in the long run proved to be nothing more than illusory pretension. Curiously, although no fewer than eight crusades were launched over the course of less than two centuries, Norman interaction with indigenous populations, though certainly present, seems to have been uncharacteristically hesitant (if not reluctant) and produced fewer tangible benefits for society. Advanced Arab cultures appear to have impacted Europe far more from the direction of Spain — not surprisingly since this close physical contact was unavoidable, whereas in the Middle East it was geographically distant and had to be aggressively initiated by one side or the other. While Syrian influence on Europe during and after the age of crusading was undeniable, it often tended to be roundabout through the Iberian Peninsula, rather than directly from East to West.[18]

As for the Normans, by the early 13th century, their name and prowess among nations had completely vanished. Edward Gibbon aptly summarized their nearly imperceptible decline and fall:

> ... the French monarchs annexed to their crown the duchy of Normandy; the scepter of her ancient dukes had been transmitted, by a granddaughter of William the Conqueror, to the house of Plantagenet; and the adventurous Normans, who had raised so many trophies in France, England, and Ireland, in Apulia, Sicily, and the East, were lost, either in victory or servitude, among the vanquished nations.[19]

One could well argue that this Norman retreat from the world stage had been mostly voluntary on their part, with the notable exception of *Outremer*, where their lasting influence had been the least felt. The objective failure of the Crusades and loss of the Holy Land may have provided the Arthurian romancers with material and inspiration, but these romancers, like Chrétien, were mostly in France. The distinctive Norman ability to empathize with and blend into their conquered territories, a crucial quality that made them so successful, also led to their eventual disappearance or rather (one might easily argue) their complete assimilation.

The Normans were perhaps the first European society during the Middle Ages to turn foreign integration into a civil (and military) virtue, similar to dominant and influential societies in the ancient world such as the Greeks and Romans. In our own modern age, when stone-cold racism is often disguised or gussied up with specious, cockeyed rationalizations, the Norman enthusiasm for blending in with conquered foreign populations strikes us as refreshing, if not revolutionary. At a glance, the geographic domains of their migrations and conquests — France, England, southern Italy, Spain, the Middle East — read like a map of the disputed source materials for the first Arthurian legends. The scholarly debate over the origin of the Holy Grail alone is perfectly illustrative of this, and there are many other examples as well (see Chapters 6 and 22). Without the Normans traversing these same domains in search of conquest and adventure, it is unlikely that one of the most beloved and treasured literary traditions in western civilization would have ever come into being. If one had to name a single event that truly set the stage for the poetic achievements of Chrétien de Troyes, it would be the marriage of Henry Plantagenet to Eleanor of Aquitaine in 1152. This act of foreign hypergamy, far from being obligatory, was nonetheless typical of the militarily triumphant Norman nobility, just as Henry's forebears had done before him. It was not unlike many of the marriages that take place in Chrétien's romances, where bride and groom more often than not come from opposite sides of the English Channel. One such example was the unusual and troubled marriage portrayed in Chrétien's *Yvain*, to which we shall now turn our attention.

Chapter 16

The Fragile and Hard-Won Sanity of Yvain

Unlike the French-speaking Normans of the Middle Ages, who integrated and intermarried into their various conquered lands (then completely disappeared from history), the hero-knights of Chrétien's Arthurian romances tend to remain rooted in the forests and castles of Wales and Brittany, at least in the reader's imagination. Even Cligès and his father Alexander before him, both of whom hailed from (and eventually returned to) Greece, seem more to inhabit Arthur's world as prototypical foreign princes in service of the English king rather than their own native land. Chrétien's Arthurian knights, on the other hand, do often share with the historical Normans a definite sense of mental imbalance. This typically stems from a loss of face or chivalric honor, rejection by or separation from lovers, the inherent conflicts between personal and social loyalties in feudalism, or some combination of these. Just as the behavior of the Normans often seemed deranged as they glorified in physical danger and long-shot risks, Chrétien's heroes are frequently viewed by other characters in the story either with fear or pity. Yvain, in many respects, is the ultimate exemplar of this.

Yvain, subtitled *The Knight with the Lion*, is considered by many critics (including this one), to be Chrétien's greatest work among his five romances, all of which were highly influential in their own way. Burton Raffel rightfully asserted that "*Yvain* can be considered his masterpiece."[1] Ruth Harwood Cline classified it as "one of the best constructed, most captivating tales in medieval literature."[2] A generation earlier, C.S. Lewis waxed euphoric: "How nobly the poem of *Yvain* approaches to the romantic ideal of a labyrinthine tale in which the thread is never lost, and multiplicity does no more than illustrate an underlying singleness."[3] Urban Holmes recorded matter-offactly, "*Yvain* is today the most popular of Chrétien's poems."[4] Paradoxically, and despite this near-universal admiration and acclaim, Yvain (or "Owen" as he is sometimes called in modern Welsh and English), pales in popularity as an Arthurian knight compared to other members of the Roundtable such as Lancelot. This state of affairs is especially strange given that Lancelot was invented by Chrétien, although he is never given credit for this outside the rarified world of medieval scholarship. One encounters Yvain infrequently at best in fictional books, movies, or plays about the Arthurian knights. For example, in the well-known (though slightly deranged) film, *Monty Python and the Holy Grail* (1975), Lancelot, Galahad, and Bedevere are all portrayed, while Yvain is not.[5]

Another unlikely aspect of Yvain's comparatively obscure status within the Arthurian pantheon is that he, far more than any other knight of the Roundtable (and perhaps more than King Arthur himself), has a firm basis in 6th century historical fact. Even before Geoffrey of Monmouth identified him as son of the Welsh king, Urien (one of Arthur's vassals), other older and independent sources had referenced Yvain-Owen as a real, living, breathing person. One of these was the Welsh bard Taliesin, who may have been a member of that particular royal household.[6] Thus Chrétien turns Yvain, barely a footnote in Geoffrey and Wace, into his masterpiece. In Chrétien's romance, Arthur, Guinevere, Morgan, Kay, Gawain — all familiar Arthurian characters — are brought forth, but, with the exception of Gawain, we merely used as backdrops to the hero of the story, Yvain. Since he is the one individual in the Arthurian canon having some historical justification (and was Welsh, to boot), he seems like a natural choice as the focal point of Chrétien's *tour-de-force*; yet, he remains one of the least known to the general reading public. By Chrétien's time, Yvain had become a prominent figure in popular fiction, as well as historical fact. It is curious that, after Chrétien's day, this prominence gradually declined among Arthurian enthusiasts. One reason may have been in part because Chrétien's artistic achievement was so complete and impossible to match that his poetic continuators and adaptors lost interest and turned to other material. Accordingly, by the time of Malory in the 15th century, Chrétien's quintessential hero had been demoted to (at best) secondary status within the literary tradition.

There has never been much dispute about when *Yvain* was written. The range of dates is quite narrow based on internal references. The action of the plot is concurrent with events in *Lancelot*, as these are mentioned in three separate places (lines 3511–3520, 3713–3724, and 4517–4523). It is quite reasonably deduced by almost all analysts that *Yvain* was written around the same time as, or even simultaneously with, *Lancelot*, between the years of

1177 and 1181.[7] A four-year time frame for both romances combined is not too long because these total over 13,600 lines of rhymed octosyllabic couplets and include some of the poet's finest work. It may well be that Chrétien turned his exclusive attention to *Yvain* after he had farmed out the completion of *Lancelot* to another writer (see Chapter 1). The final illness and death of his patron Henry the Liberal between 1179 and 1181 also may have prompted Chrétien's shift in priorities. Another point of reference in the text of *Yvain* is the unusually close chronology (two weeks) between the dates for Christian Pentecost (lines 5–6) and the feast day of Saint John the Baptist (lines 629–630), a correlation which did in fact occur during the year 1180.[8]

The only significant challenge to the conventional dating of the romance stems from a present-tense reference by the poet to Sultan Nureddin Mahmud (or "Noradin," line 557), who died in 1173. This would seem to argue against a dating of 1177–1181, until one looks more closely at the text and the context in which the remark is made by a boastful (and inebriated) Sir Kay. Jean Frappier pointed out long ago that by the 1170s, Christian references to Nureddin had become proverbial due to the many defeats the sultan had prominently inflicted on Middle Eastern Crusaders.[9] Kay mentions the name of Nureddin side by side with that of Forré, a completely mythical Saracen king of Naples and Christian antagonist in epic poems. Thus, Nureddin, a dead man, is equated with Forré, a mere literary conceit, if the line was written after 1173. This would make some sense. Moreover, within the action of *Yvain* and other Chrétien romances, Kay does not know what he is talking about more often than not, drunk or sober. It would also be absurd to expect strict historical accuracy with a character who, according to Geoffrey of Monmouth, lived during the 6th century (before Islam existed), but who is associated with a famous 12th century Islamic military leader. In the final analysis, the reference appears to be more a literary conceit than a topical allusion.

Like most great masterpieces of literature, *Yvain* displays a brilliant synthesis of multiple sources, the combination of which may seem unlikely to most readers. As a result, surprise and delight come with every turn of the page, and these only increase upon re-reading. Although numerous ancient Welsh tales lend various aspects to Chrétien's version of the story, main elements of the plot, as identified by the dean of scholars in this area, Roger Sherman Loomis, share a common source with *The Mabinogion* collection, especially the tale "The Lady of the Fountain."[10] Many modern authorities, such as Joseph Duggan, agree that the oldest surviving Welsh manuscript is derived from Chrétien's French original, but that both drew upon an even older tradition.[11] While the trappings of Chrétien's *Yvain* are traditional Welsh, however, the spirit and mood are purely French, and often southern

French at that. As C.S. Lewis observed, for example, the lengthy allegory of the Body and the Heart presented when Yvain departs from Laudine (lines 2467–2488) is taken directly from the tradition of the Provençal troubadours.[12] Of the physical settings in the story, the ones that dominate by far are the environs of the mysterious, magical Forest of Brocéliande and, within that, the Fountain of Berenton. All of these places, with or without magic, are still popular landmarks in French Brittany today (see Chapter 8).

As in other romances, the poet expressly acknowledges his primary Breton source material from the very beginning. In writing of King Arthur, Chrétien maintains, "and I agree with Breton lore: his name will live forevermore..." (lines 35–36).[13] As one compares the various English translations of this passage made over the years, their similarities are striking with the exception of the one made by D.D.R. Owen, who, working out of Scotland and alone among all translators, changes "Breton" to "the people of Britain."[14] Although it may be debated whether "Britain" in this context connotes French Brittany as well, there can be no denying that, for the average reader, "Britain" unequivocally means Great Britain — on the English-speaking side of the channel and not in France. A tiny objection, to be sure; nevertheless, this is a prime example of how the very slightest word-change in translation can obscure old, original meanings and lead to radically new ones. It also may demonstrate (literally, in textbook fashion), Anglocentric cultural bias, although in fairness it may well have been that the Scotsman Owen was merely catering to the majority of his Anglocentric, culturally-biased reading public. Given that the Owen translation of Chrétien's romances as a whole is elegant, compelling, and deservedly popular, it represents yet more proof that even the best and most informed efforts can occasionally slip into inadvertent prejudice.

And then of course there is the lion, who becomes one of the most famous animals in medieval literature after the rehabilitated hero rescues the beast from the clutches of an evil dragon near the middle of Chrétien's tale. Indeed, Yvain must momentarily deliberate which of the two threats needs to be eliminated first. What follows is a poignant and humorous scene much appreciated by all animal lovers since, as the lion genuflects in human-like gratitude, imitating the gestures of feudal fealty and submission (lines 3205–3208). From then on, Yvain's unnamed and omnipresent lion-companion is anything but a pet.[15] Devoted servant, ethical role-model, comrade-in-arms, symbolic Christ figure — the lion has been termed all of these things by modern critics.[16] For example, Duggan observed that "the lion's unalloyed fidelity acts as an antidote to the selfish lack of concern for others whose consequences drove Yvain to madness. The beast's moral characteristics begin to rub off on his master."[17] During the 19th century, pioneering German scholar Wendelin Foerster maintained (correctly, it would seem), that Chrétien drew upon the ingenious conceit of a lion-protector from ancient, classical sources such as *Androcles and the Lion*.[18] Intriguingly, it appears that the historical Yvain — who was very successful in war — was in fact associated with the lion as an image on his shield.[19] By the time the French poet is through, however, the lion reminds one more of the powerful savior from the *Narnia* children's tales of C.S. Lewis — who himself was most certainly influenced by Chrétien's timeless work.

The symbolism of Yvain's lion, however engaging in and of itself, is a storytelling device that enters only to assist the hero in his main challenge, which is to somehow keep his sanity in a world of constantly shifting and conflicting obligations. Particularly thorny for Yvain are the conflicts in his duty to a beloved wife, Laudine, and his all-consuming desire to excel as a knight in combat. Unlike Erec, Chrétien's earlier, one-dimensional hero, Yvain breaks his word to Laudine and fails to return home after a year of tournament jousting with his close companion, Gawain. Add to this Laudine's strong character — one far less passive and submissive than that of Erec's long-suffering wife, Enide. The end result, not surprisingly, is total marital estrangement, one which shockingly sends Yvain straight into deranged insanity after he is informed of the consequences by a stern message sent from Laudine. The same woman who forgave the hero enough to marry him after killing her first husband (in self-defense) now will have nothing more to do with him, and Yvain knows she means what she says. The poet is now taking us into groundbreaking, psychological territory, the tragic byproduct of a far more serious (and realistic) breach of human trust. Entranced medieval audiences had no doubt never encountered anything quite like this before.

Such a pivotal moment in the history of world literature deserves a bit of comparative study among the various English translations. Professor Cline, in rhymed eight-syllable couplets like the original Old French, gives us the following:

> A whirlwind broke loose in his brain,
> so violent that he went insane,
> and clawed himself, tore off his clothes,
> and fled across the fields and rows.[20]

In the same number of lines and words (27), but in free-form verse, veteran translator Burton Raffel provides readers with a more externalized (and hence, more visual) image of the hero's mental disintegration:

> And such a storm broke
> Into his skull that he lost his senses,
> And he tore at his skin and his clothes,
> And crossed meadows and fields....[21]

By opting for phrases such as "a *storm* broke *into* his *skull*" (versus "a *whirlwind* broke loose *in* his *brain*") [emphases added], Raffel paints a vivid, objectified picture for readers and listeners, even though the action is taking place in the subjective and distracted mind of Yvain. Other English translators have used similar terms in prose, but with ever so slightly different results. For example, Comfort (during the early 20th century) originally wrote, "a *storm* broke loose *in* his *brain*," which contains elements later used by both Cline and Raffel.[22] Similar to these is the rendition by David Staines, who, like Cline, seems to favor a more interior reading with "a *whirlwind* broke loose *in* Yvain's *head*."[23] More aligned with Raffel is Owen, whose reading is definitely more objective and unusual in its word choice: "His *head is assailed* by so *wild a delirium*...."[24] At the end of the day, readers can chose their individual favorites, and perhaps we all understand the text best if there are multiple interpretations, updated by new ones every few years to reflect changes in literary fashion and taste.

Returning to the storyline, Yvain is slowly restored to sanity by the charity of a hermit and the Lady of Noríson, his own various heroic exploits, and the friendship of the lion, but is still nearly driven back into insanity by the memory of his alienated wife. This searing reminiscence is triggered by a return trip to the Fountain of Berenton, where he had first gone at the beginning of the tale to seek adventure, eventually leading to his winning Laudine's hand in marriage. This passage, too, presents issues in translation. In order to compress the text into rhyming, octosyllabic English verse, Cline opts not to mention arguably superfluous or redundant details such as a chapel near the fountain, or that the number of Yvain's sighs before collapsing was figuratively "a thousand."[25] All other English translators include these additional, express details, but at a cost of using more words to debatable added effect.[26] What matters most in this particular episode is that Yvain manages to hold on to sanity, thanks to philosophical reflection, the suicidal compassion of the lion, and news that his benefactor Lunette needs immediate rescuing. The lesson here is that the more one elects to restrict form in language, the more it necessarily follows that content is potentially restricted as well.

Yvain eschews several moral lessons as well, some quite profound and not the type that society is typically used to hearing. In addition to the obvious (that one should keep promises to one's spouse), and unlike Chrétien's hero Erec, who neglects chivalric obligations in favor of love, Yvain does the opposite: he neglects the duties of love in favor of chivalry.[27] Thus, resolution of the inherent personal conflicts in medieval society between the pursuit of romantic love and military glory is presented by the poet as a kind of balancing act. In short, there are no simple answers; however, from this tug of war within the conscience of knights (and their ladies) naturally flows many a contradiction. Rhetorically, the poet excels at meditating upon these. Perhaps the most famous example in *Yvain* comes from the episode in which Yvain is obliged by duty to fight to the death in trial-by-combat against his Roundtable colleague, Gawain. Both knights are incognito in armor and do not recognize each other; therefore, both unknowingly are determined to kill their best friend. Chrétien uses this as an opportunity to expound on the seemingly inextricable ties between human love and hate, beginning with the famous lines, "I wonder how a Love so great can coexist with mortal Hate?" (lines 5751–5752). The theme of civil conflict, sometimes between erstwhile friends and loved ones within a single household, was just as poignant during the Middle Ages as it is today, perhaps even more so. For Chrétien, lesson number one is that life and love are not simple, nor are the answers to their problems, and that these realities are to be ignored only at the peril of one's own sanity.

Because Yvain and Gawain do not truly know who they are fighting against (only what they are fighting for), it may well be argued that the two men do not really "hate" each other in this situation. On the other hand, given that the two knights hack away at each other with swords until exhaustion leads to a stalemate, the point seems a bit academic. Once Yvain and Gawain finally do recognize each other, both volunteer to capitulate and surrender, before Arthur declares the contest a draw. In the story, Love triumphs over Hate. A sophisticated modern reader may smile at such a device, and yet, it has serious overtones on multiple levels. For one, the Love-Hate debate also represents Yvain's estranged relationship with Laudine, who married him under very unusual circumstances, to say the least.[28] As in Shakespeare's *Richard III*, the bride must first forgive the groom for killing her previous husband, although Yvain's actions are admittedly more justifiable and forgivable than those of the Bard's ultimate villain-monarch. Yvain then forfeits this extraordinary forgiveness by leaving Laudine for a year and breaking his promise to return in a timely manner. This is the result of his own shallow forgetfulness. In the end, though, even this is forgiven by Laudine, through the helpful intervention of Lunette, and, above all, by Yvain becoming a totally different man, one with a new identity and (more importantly) superior moral values.

The appealing thing about the new value system of the reborn Yvain is that it has nothing to do with sex. Unfaithfulness and abstention are never issues for him. Were it not for his incredible prowess in combat, one would almost think of him as a monk — as many medieval orders of knighthood considered themselves to be. Yvain's moral transformation in the middle of the story has less to do with his wife Laudine than his relationships with other members of society, and with his God. After his spiritual and moral rebirth, Yvain scrupulously hears Mass before each fight, including before his contests with a menacing giant (line 3822) and two half-demons in the climactic struggle near the end of the tale (line 5211). As Professor Cline emphasized:

> ... on a deeper level, one of the lessons which Yvain learns is that, splendid fighter though he is, he is nothing in himself. Without the help of a charitable society he would have died insane in the forest, and without the help of God, whose aid is requested before every battle except the early ones, he would never have survived his combats with gigantic or supernatural foes.[29]

Many commentators have also noted that Yvain's lion-companion appears to be an overt symbol of this newly-realized, "no one can do it alone" philosophy. Yvain's victories and reputation become tied to his unique association with the lion, and this is fine with him. Thus, the primary focus of the hero's moral reform is social, not sexual. In the end, the things that really matter are the ones that he accomplishes for the needy of society — not for himself— and certainly not how he talks about doing any of these things. In fact, like many of the classic warrior heroes, Yvain is a man of few words.[30]

Particularly impressive in this regard is the final confrontation between Yvain and his two half-demon adversaries in the Castle of Evil Adventure. As in all of Chrétien's romances, the readers, along with the hero, are transported into a setting beyond the realm of normal human experience.[31] Despite this supernatural atmosphere, however, the stakes being fought over are as down-to-earth and perennially relevant as ever, namely, the alleviation of inhumane conditions for laborers within the castle. Yvain and the lion fight for (and win) the freedom of female "sweatshop" weavers enslaved by the demons. This is pretty radical stuff for the 12th century, although it cannot be used as an example of Chrétien showing sympathy for the common man, since all of the enslaved maidens are expressly of noble birth. Some critics have seen an allusion to textile workers in Champagne, but a more likely reference is to Christian slaves in the Muslim world at that time.[32] Supporting the latter interpretation is the appearance of the two demons, who resemble Moorish warriors in many respects, including their "hideous and black" physical appearance (line 5258), "round shields" typical in Islamic armies (line

5268), and who, like Islamic warriors, fight with their "heads and faces free" (line 5264), that is, without armored helmets or visors. Above all, the poet has his hero win renown in the cause of helping others who are unable to help themselves. For Chrétien, and for the idealized feudal system, this was the only kind of activity that constituted true merit and virtue for the medieval knight.

Before leaving this interesting subject, it would be remiss not to mention in passing the poet's unforgettable description of poverty in the castle sweatshop. After being unsuccessfully dissuaded from entering the castle by fearful, local plebes, Yvain and his lion behold a pitiful sight within:

> The maids were so poor, many wore
> No belts and were untidy, for
> They'd worn holes in their clothes at breast
> And elbow and were poorly dressed.
> Their shifts were soiled, their necks were gaunt,
> Their faces pale and starved with want
>   [lines 4965–4970].

The effectiveness of this highly descriptive passage defies any bad or obscure translation. Readers get it. While Chrétien rarely shows much deep sympathy beyond the aristocracy, images of his impoverished nobility tend to stay with us. Another good example of this is Enide's poverty when Erec first meets her. This is one thing that Yvain and Erec do have in common: they rescue the needy, by marriage or by any other means necessary. Was the poet himself poor? Assuming he was a clergyman, during those times clerical status did not necessarily imply being poor. If, on the other hand, he was completely dependent upon patrons for his daily bread, then these portraits may have well represented a subtle plea to them.

The problem with these lofty ideals is that during Chrétien's time there was a major disconnect between these and reality. Christian knighthood was becoming more and more associated with banditry and rapaciousness, especially along the perimeter of the European Christian world. Particularly in the Middle East, crusading knighthood seemed to be in the midst of a moral crisis. Maybe that is why the poets were harping about values. Less than a decade after *Yvain* was written, the Christian kingdom of Jerusalem abruptly crumbled into the dust as many of its diverse subjects concluded that God was no longer on the side of Christian knighthood. Though Chrétien may not have lived to see this collapse, he, like other astute observers at the time, probably sensed it was coming. It was prescience of this shattering event which likely had a great influence on the content of his last, unfinished romance, *Perceval*.

Chapter 17

A Dreadful Foreboding

We will never know for sure how or why the genius of Chrétien de Troyes came to interweave the Arthurian legends with the symbol of the Holy Grail (see Chapter 22), but we can perhaps develop a better appreciation of external forces that inspired him. The decade of the 1180s, sometime during which Chrétien composed his *Perceval* or *Conte du Graal*, witnessed one of the most significant historical turning points during the High Middle Ages. This involved the permanent collapse of the *Outremer* Crusader Kingdom in Jerusalem, an event whose ramifications are still, in some ways, felt by the modern world. Although the downfall of Christian Jerusalem had been anticipated for decades among Europe's more perceptive observers, when it finally did transpire, Christendom went into widespread shock and introspection. The effect was probably not unlike that recently felt by 21st-century American society after the 9–11 terrorist attacks. Some had seen it coming for a long time; many others, however, were taken completely by surprise. That Chrétien's work was deeply affected by this milieu has never been seriously questioned; the only real issue is whether he was among the few who vaguely foresaw calamity, or reacted immediately after it occurred. In either event, *Perceval* was left unfinished at the time of his death and includes 9,235 lines of some of the most influential poetry ever written. It also marked a major departure in style and content for Chrétien's vast Arthurian output.

British historian Edward Gibbon summarized well the political and military state of European affairs in the Holy Land by the 1180s when he wrote: "All without now bore the most threatening aspect; and all was feeble and hollow in the internal state of Jerusalem."[1] After less than eight decades since its violent and unnatural establishment, *Outremer* had become a case study in dysfunctional leadership and bloated weakness. Its newly crowned monarch, Guy of Lusignan, along with most of his top military decision-makers, were burdened by incompetence, corruption, vanity, and superstitious overconfidence. Guy's ascendancy to the throne the previous year had been an unlikely and disturbing event, achieved through marriage and intrigue, rather than merit or popular assent. The "threatening aspect" cited by Gibbon referred to the recent unification of the Arab world under its dynamic new sultan, Saladin, who was a paragon of virtue compared to most of his Christian adversaries. Thus the stage was set for a large-scale disaster in a region that Christians felt belonged to them by divine right.

The fall of Edessa to the Turks in 1145, and subsequent failure of the Second Crusade to recover it, were preludes to the overthrow of Jerusalem some 42 years later. The Second Crusade (led by French king, Louis VII, among others)[2] had facilitated the massacre of innocent Jews in France and Germany, as well as the plunder of eastern Christian states through which it passed. It was no match, however, for disciplined Turkish arms in Anatolia. One generation after the conquest of the Holy Land by the First Crusade, indigenous Islamic peoples were beginning to get measure of their oppressors. By the early 1180s, Latin Crusaders found themselves overmatched against the ascending power of Saladin, combined with their own massive internal divisions and grasping avarice. Worse, many did not seem to appreciate either their own shortcomings or the burgeoning power of their enemies, exhibiting a blithe arrogance in the supposed invincibility of their military orders and religious justification.[3] Not everyone in Christendom, however, was deluded. Among the realists was Pope Alexander III in Rome, who on January 19, 1181, issued a rare Apostolic Letter summarizing the gravity of the situation, and urging Christians everywhere to repent, reform, and hopefully prevent an impending disaster. This epistle would have been read in churches throughout western Europe, and it is very likely that Chrétien was among those who heard it.[4]

During the 1950s, maverick Arthurian scholar Helen Adolf advanced a thesis that the legend of the Holy Grail — in many respects the central theme of the King Arthur stories — was a direct outgrowth of the Crusades, in particular, the political-military crisis of the 1180s. This theory is now well-respected among professional specialists, yet remains essentially unknown or unacknowledged in the popular realm.[5] In the first chapter of Adolf's study, *Visio Pacis: Holy City and Grail*, titled "The Warning — Chrétien's *Perceval*," she asserted:

> The Grail legend is the fruit of the Crusades. More precisely, the legend owes its development to the transformation of the crude Crusading creed, with its reliance on "fetishes" (relics), into a religion of personal experience supported

by symbols. This transformation began around 1180, when the Latin Kingdom of Jerusalem fell.⁶

In other words, after the Christians lost control of Jerusalem as a physical place, along with its religious landmarks and relics, they sought out symbolic substitutes, the Grail legend being an example. This period coincided exactly with the composition of Chrétien's last and most famous poem, which saw him embark on a major shift in tone and content. Oxford historian Stephen Knight agreed that "the story of the grail, like so much else in medieval Arthurian literature, can be traced to Chrétien de Troyes ... he established the notion of the grail as a symbol of Christian perfection in a human world."⁷ Thus the traumatic setbacks about to engulf the political and military orbit of western Europe would later become a boon for western literature, which is still developing and being enjoyed today. The first spark, however, came from the pen of a Frenchman who, in all likelihood, had a vision of this symbol that was considerably different from those typically adopted by later poets; nor could he have foreseen the nearly thousand-year trend he inaugurated with his poetic conceit.

After several decades of decline and repeatedly ignored warning signals, the Latin Kingdom of Jerusalem came crashing down so quickly that it ceased to exist before many even realized it was in trouble. Both Christian and Muslim historians agree that Saladin's strategic moves leading up to his conquest were heavily provoked by recent Crusader lawlessness in the region. Foremost among the offenders was the infamous Reynald of Châtillon, who commanded a fortress along the borders of the kingdom and used this base to plunder peaceful Arab caravans that came within striking distance. King Guy either turned a blind eye to Reynald's criminal activities or covertly supported him. In the words of Gibbon, "Saladin condescended to complain; rejoiced in the denial of justice; and, at the head of fourscore thousand horse and foot, invaded the Holy Land."⁸ The beginning of the end came when Saladin captured the Latin city of Tiberias in Galilee. Saladin in fact had little interest in Tiberias except as a means of luring the Christian army into pitched battle. The Latins took the bait, consolidating all forces in the region for a march on Tiberias, believing they were on their way to routinely punish the careless insult of a heathen interloper.

The battle of Hattin (pronounced *Hah-TEEN*), located near Lake Tiberias, was fought on July 4, 1187, exactly 589 years to the day before the signing of the American Declaration of Independence.⁹ Historian Christopher Tyerman accurately observed that Hattin was "the greatest defeat of western arms by a non–Christian army since the tenth century."¹⁰ Most of the standing Christian military force in the Holy Land, to the tune of some

10,000 troops, including its elite orders of Templar and Hospitaller knights, were wiped out in a single day. Like most previous Crusader armies, this was not an English or Italian or German force — it was primarily French, in rank and file as well as leadership. King Guy and a small group of noblemen were spared for ransom, although Saladin made it a point to execute Reynald as a miscreant exemplar. Even Reynald, however, was offered a chance to save his life by converting to Islam.[11] He declined — his first and last recorded act of principle — and was promptly struck down. At the end of the day, a huge army had been annihilated and a Christian king taken hostage, but the greatest losses were psychological and symbolic. Also captured by the victors was the holy relic of the True Cross, purportedly discovered in Jerusalem during the original conquest of 1099, and routinely carried into battle by Crusaders as a presumed guarantor of success.[12] After Hattin, the aura of Frankish-Norman invincibility was gone forever. Although smaller European armies had been previously defeated, this time they had given it their best shot on a level playing field, and were still completely swept away.

The prelude and aftermath of this watershed moment in history was vividly portrayed in the award-winning 2005 Ridley Scott film, *Kingdom of Heaven*, featuring an all-star, international cast. Though historically inaccurate in multiple respects, the movie does convey the momentousness and pathos of the disaster, as well as its irreversible and permanent consequences for the Western mindset. Poetically, the film is right on target.[13] As for factual history, several things about Hattin stand out in retrospect. One is that few if any leaders in the Christian camp opposed going into the fight, yet this is precisely what their enemies wanted them to do.[14] Another is that is that the jihad had been sparked by wanton Crusader disruption of Arab commerce, rather than any stated religious doctrine or dogma. The most charitable thing that can be said about the westerners is that they were laboring under massively false assumptions regarding their opponents. Whether it was written before or after Hattin, Chrètien's *Perceval* dwells repeatedly on the theme of false perceptions.

Within three months after the battle, Saladin's victorious army occupied Jerusalem. After many of its remaining Latin defenders made it clear they preferred death to slavery, Saladin permitted them to safely evacuate without ransom.[15] Greek Christians, who had always lived within the precincts of the city, were allowed to stay. Latin Christians were guaranteed future access as pilgrims in return for a toll payment. The most enlightened act of Saladin, however, was not to summarily kill all Christians, as Crusaders had previously killed all Muslims and Jews in 1099, indiscriminately massacring every man, woman, and child.[16] Going against all expectations (and no doubt, many of his closest advisors), Saladin opted for clemency and achieved the moral high ground. Thus he won for himself not only Jerusalem, but eternal fame and universal admiration. Gibbon, who wrote with a strong Western Anglo-Christian bias, was deeply impressed: "In these acts of mercy, the virtue of Saladin deserves our admiration and love; he was above the necessity of dissimulation...."[17] This civilized behavior stood in marked contrast to the rapacious and murderous acts of the Crusaders. Some of them had the novel epiphany that certain Muslims may be more righteous in the eyes of God than many pretended followers of Christ.

When news of Hattin and the fall of Jerusalem reached Europe, it was received as an earth-shattering event. Christopher Tyerman summed up the impact: "The disaster produced profound shock. Pope Urban III reputedly died on hearing of it." Then the new pope, Gregory VIII, wrote that the situation was "a great cause for mourning." Tyerman added that Gregory,

> ... [w]hile laying most of the blame for the calamity on the sins of the Franks...extended the burden of responsibility to include "the whole Christian people." It was a Christian's duty to repent past sins and restore past mistakes in the service of God and the recover "of that land in which for our salvation truth arose from the earth."[18]

It was time for sackcloth and ashes in Europe. This was especially true in France, where the Norman military tradition had been dealt a blow from which it would never recover. At the time, however, the permanence of the setback was not fully realized, so it was thought that sincere repentance and firm resolve might remedy the situation. Thus the bloody and futile Third Crusade under King Philip II of France and his Norman-Anglo colleague, Richard Plantagenet (*Coeur de Lion*) was immediately organized and launched to the great misfortune of all mankind. This venture would eventually succeed in depopulating large parts of Europe and the Middle East (as well as killing Chrétien's last patron, Philip of Flanders), but would be unsuccessful in terms of regaining the Holy Land for Christendom.

Both before and after Hattin, for those who uneasily foresaw the event and later for those deeply sorrowed by it, the Western worldview underwent a shift. There is little reason to doubt that Chrétien, as reflected by *Perceval*, was among those who at least anticipated disaster. To accept or mentally process the catastrophe, many European Christians were inclined to adopt at least two new opinions. First, the defeated French had to be faulted. It was as if the Crusaders had been struck down by heaven itself. Second, their great adversary, Saladin, was raised to the status of worthy opponent. It was certainly acknowledged that the villainy of the Crusaders compared unfavorably with the chivalrous virtues of Saladin. Thus the disheartening result at Hattin was re-explained and justified in terms of Christian theology. European literature began to lionize Saladin as much as it did its own subsequent and rather dubious role model, the bloodthirsty King Richard, *Coeur de Lion*. After all, it took a true knight to beat a knight, whether pagan or Christian. Saladin's generosity, temperance, and magnanimity were praised by European poets contemporary with him, such as the famed Walter von der Vogelweide in Germany. Over a century later, Dante Alighieri in his *Inferno* would portray the good pagan Saladin perpetually jousting with the bad Christian Richard in the underworld.[19] Thus Saladin became perhaps *the* symbol of a new western cultural phenomenon — the proverbial virtuous heathen.

Chrétien's Perceval is certainly no Saladin or Richard, but it is interesting to see the hero depicted as a knight who is indomitable in combat and yet still a novice who lapses from religion. Before fortuitously meeting a penitential Good Friday procession in the wilderness, and immediately after that, his pious hermit-uncle, Perceval completely falls away from the Christian faith. Citing his mysterious source materials, Chrétien writes, "And the book tells us that Perceval had so completely lost his memory he'd even forgotten God."[20] This spiritual amnesia continues for five years. Perceval is on the path to salvation before Chrétien's unfinished narrative breaks off, but unlike his previous Arthurian tales, this path is the main point of the story. Perceval's transgressions are relatively innocent compared to those of, say, Sir Lancelot or Sir Kay. Most of Chrétien's other characters are primarily concerned with the conflict between their duties as soldier-knights and courtly lovers. They struggle with moral choices (usually involving relations with the opposite sex) while considering themselves defenders of the traditional faith. Perceval, by contrast, is a novice on a spiritual journey as he fights battles both physically without and psychologically within his own conscience. His unique characterization marks a departure in the history of European romantic literature, one that is found within the work of a single author, making it even more noteworthy. Before the time of Chrétien, it was assumed that any successful knight must also be a good Christian. As Crusader footholds in the Middle East eroded, however, both Christian and Muslim stereotypes became more nuanced and complex.

This new kind of warrior-knight in literature — one who feels guilt and seeks to reform his life — is a reflection of the times in which it was written. In the popular view, *Outremer* had disintegrated because of its own moral shortcomings. The French nobility not only plundered defenseless Arab caravans, they stole from each other as well. For example, in 1187 (shortly before

Hattin was fought), Christian barons confiscated treasure donated to Jerusalem in 1170 by the Norman-Anglo King Henry II (father of Richard I) as expiation for his covert involvement in the murder of Thomas à Becket.[21] The stated justification for this suspicious appropriation was to pay soldiers — the same troops whose corpses were soon to be scattered across the arid precincts of Hattin. Blood money offered earlier in exchange for Becket's religious martyrdom in England, however, continued to be tainted when used for homeland defense. In the end, it probably would have done more good if left in the state treasury. In contrast to these sordid transactions, Chrétien's Perceval is a guilt-ridden knight whose spiritual quest cannot be corrupted by material wealth, although he often finds himself surrounded by riches.

One year after the Crusaders were defeated by Saladin, Chrétien's namesake home of Troyes suffered another blow. On July 23, 1188, most of the center city burned to the ground.[22] While the origins of this conflagration appear to have been accidental, French Christendom in Champagne was probably beginning to wonder whether there was any end to the seeming divine displeasure directed against it. Although Troyes would be rebuilt thanks to its strategic trade-route location, the physical world that Chrétien knew had vanished forever. Along with it probably disappeared clues that may have answered many puzzling questions about the great poet and his work. The most provocative facet of this tragedy is that Troyes, in addition to being forever associated with the dawn of Arthurian romance, was, more than any other European city, associated with the Templar knights who had lost Jerusalem the previous year. The Templars officially founded their famous order at Troyes in 1128, and their name has been connected with that place ever since.[23] The double whammy of Hattin and the Troyes fire likely caused serious questions to be asked in this part of France. For example, had God allowed Troyes to be burned because of its sinful and secular attitudes? Was it because of earlier tolerance towards its Jewish population, or later intolerance of them?[24] Was the city being chastised because of the Templar presence, along with their perceived moral shortcomings and military failures? And so forth. More importantly, to what extent did these perceptions impact Chrétien's original creation of the Arthurian romance?

Unfortunately, we will probably never know exactly how external forces influenced Chrétien, because the exact year of his death is a mystery. 1183–1191 is the range usually surmised, but so much happened in between those dates that precise cause-and-effect relationships cannot be established. If Chrétien was still alive in 1188, then he probably wrote *Perceval* in reaction to these calamities, a reaction shared by most people living at that particular time and place. If, on the other hand, Chrétien was dead by 1183, then he must be viewed as a visionary, one who — like a small number of other visionaries at the time — foresaw (at least three years in advance) the misfortunes to come. More precisely, he may have foreseen that a certain way of life in Champagne would soon vanish, not unlike his influential Arab predecessor the previous century, the Andalusian poet Ibn Hazim.[25] In this latter scenario, the linking of the Holy Grail with the Arthurian legends would have been a creative act of anticipation, a dreadful foreboding of imminent, catastrophic events. The Grail became an abstract symbol of Christian spiritual fulfillment after real, physical places such as Jerusalem had been lost. This is not to assert that Chrétien, before his death, dreamed that *Outremer* would fall (or that Troyes would burn down), although we do not rule out the remote possibility; more likely, he may have foreseen that an old worldview and attractive way of life were soon to be lost, especially after the death of his earlier patron, Henry the Liberal, in 1181.

The psychological impact or anticipation of these disasters on the mentality of creative artists in Western Europe should not be underestimated. By the end of Chrétien's career, a preoccupation with the adultery of Lancelot had been replaced by Perceval's pursuit of moral and spiritual improvement. This portrayal of a higher pursuit had in turn been foreshadowed by Chrétien's tale of *Yvain*, prior to *Perceval*. Popular modern notions of the Grail, however imprecise, are typically shaped by English lore produced several centuries after Chrétien's time. Most readers (including this one) have assumed that the Grail pursuit related strictly to the ancient and traditional Christian veneration of holy relics. It may come as a surprise that the beginning of the legend was more likely an imaginative response to impending or recent disasters. Also surprising is the reality that knight errantry was itself originally an institution more French than English, and (some would argue) an Islamic ideal long before either. The same can much be said for the code of chivalry and poetry of courtly love.

As for Arthurian romance, it took its distinctive form while Christians were being confronted with the unwelcome truth that holy places and things do not perhaps, in a more exalted realm, belong by right to any single religious creed. In the third and final part of this study, we will see how the ostensive justification for the Crusades (i.e., religious piety), by the end the 12th century, was being expressed more fervently than ever. At the very heart and center of the crusading enterprise, as well as the Arthurian legends, lay a very determined ecclesiastical impulse. The church, through its burgeoning and omnipresent influence, was in the process of imposing its will on everyone and everything. This imposition extended to the non–Christian world, and above all, to the sphere of written ideas, both sacred and secular, then beginning to flourish. Thus Chrétien, whose life and training appears to have straddled these diverse environments, appropriately made the first great leap toward achieving a revolutionary combination of unlikely elements.

Part III.
Religious Themes:
The Clergyman

Chapter 18

Good Guys, Bad Guys, and No In-Betweens

The iconic image of the Arthurian Roundtable automatically conveys to modern western audiences a sense of democracy, freedom, and equality. In point of fact, the medieval realm which spawned this symbol was quite the opposite. In reality, it was a feudal society of serfdom and autocracy, except for a tiny minority of nobility (and their immediate circle of patronage) who enjoyed some degree of privilege and latitude. Rather than being an inclusive world, the historical counterpart to the Arthurian Camelot was quite exclusive, and even then, one could only belong if the same religion and social code of conduct were shared with those who wielded absolute power. A more fitting symbol of this epoch was probably Magna Carta, a legal document which codified the personal rights of the nobility in relation to the English monarchy — that is what the political struggle of those times was really about. Above all, it was an era of crusading, military aggression, and conquest — usually all justified through religion, in which there was little or no room for discussion or compromise. One either followed a designated leader without question or paid for it to the extreme. Into this harsh dynamic entered the newly empowered churchman and his understudy, the church cleric, a class of society to which the inventor of the Arthurian romance probably belonged.

Perhaps no clergyman of the 12th century more embodied or symbolized the potential clash between church and state than Saint Thomas à Becket (1118–1170). This illustrious, English-born Archbishop of Canterbury was beatified by Rome after his martyrdom at the hands of Henry II's Norman barons (for defying the king) at almost the exact same point in time that Chrétien de Troyes was inventing the Arthurian romance in the France of

King Louis VII.[1] Becket was a good illustration of a very talented person who easily strode across the fluid boundaries of cleric and statesman. Upon close examination, the connections between Becket's life and the family network of nobility that would later patronize Chrétien are impressively extensive. To give just a few examples, Becket was consecrated as archbishop by Henry of Blois, the uncle of Chrétien's first great patron, Henry the Liberal.[2] Later, Count Henry's brother, Guillaume aux Blanches Mains ("William the White Hands"), negotiated Becket's case against Henry II with Rome in his capacity as Archbishop of Sens and papal legate in England.[3] Chrétien's last outstanding benefactor, Philip of Flanders, was a key go-between in the temporary reconciliation between Henry II and Becket (shortly before the murder of the saint), and afterwards made a pilgrimage to his tomb at Canterbury in 1184.[4] Strikingly, when Becket fled incognito from England to France in 1164, he used "Chrétien" as a pseudonym to disguise his identity.[5] If the poet's own moniker was an alias (see Chapter 24) — not an impossibility, given, among other things, the name's unusualness at the time — it may well have been that the English saint provided the original precedent for its use. In any event, it seems highly unlikely that Chrétien the poet did not have the life and model of his older contemporary in the back of his mind when he began to write the famous works for which he would be remembered. Becket was an exemplar of the times in terms of how a clergyman could and should be a good influence on the king, as well as his military vassals, even if the faithful exercise of that duty meant paying the ultimate price.

Clergymen did not of course always have to be martyrs and saints. They could also be poets and writers, and many more of them excelled at these peaceful activities. Although the personal identity of Chrétien is quite hazy, many of his fellow clerics who came before and after present a sharper image of the churchman (or churchwoman) gladly assuming the role of entertainer for noble patrons. In addition to the (possibly) earlier example of Marie de France, perhaps the most overt foray into secular literature by a member of the religious orders was made during the late 12th century by Andreas Capellanus ("Andre the Chaplain"). His memorable mock-treatise, *De Amore* or *The Art of Courtly Love* (see Chapter 4), was produced for the same Champagnois court that had earlier supported Chrétien's artistic efforts. As summarized with dry understatement by the English translator of Capellanus, John Parry, "The picture we get of Andreas from his book is that of a man who is connected with the Church, but for whom spiritual affairs are not the first consideration."[6] As for Chrétien, the overwhelming majority of modern commentators view him as a member of this newly emerging class of society, one difficult to fathom or grasp by 21st-century readers who imagine medieval churchmen as strictly monkish in lifestyle and spiritual in their concerns, heavily removed from the day-to-day, rough-and-tumble world of politics, war, and (most surprising of all) romantic love poetry. Some critics have gone so far as to postulate that Chrétien was specifically the Augustinian Abbot of Saint-Loup in Troyes mentioned by that same name in contemporary sources.[7]

As in our present times, the dividing line between cleric-writers such as Chrétien and cleric-activists such as Becket could often become quite blurred. Sometimes, in extraordinary cases, they could be one and the same individual, as shall be presently examined. More often than not, both types could be seen working towards identical goals, especially in support of the Crusades. Their intervention (or, some would say, meddling) into the affairs of state and civil society was justified by the brutal, chaotic condition of Europe before that time during the Dark Ages. Referring back to one of the foremost chroniclers of that earlier period, Saint Gildas (himself a transmitter of the original Arthurian tradition in its unvarnished, unromantic form), religious historian Karen Armstrong puts it bluntly, reminding us:

> The famous knights who, cleaned up and Christianized, would later inhabit the legends of King Arthur and his Round Table get a very different treatment in the writings of the Christian historian, Gildas. They are "sanguinary, boastful, murderous, addicted to vice, adulterous and enemies of God," and "...although they may keep a large number of wives, they are fornicators and adulterers."[8]

Before French poets injected these promiscuous warriors with a heavy dose of the courtly love ethos, there was little to recommend them as lovers; in fact, there was little to recommend them for much of anything except prowess in war. Into this breach stepped the highly educated and moralistic clergy who, before that time, had spent most of their energies living reclusive, monastic lives of piety. A few of the more daring and idealistic had tended to the ever-present needs of the sick and poor. Politics, war, and love poetry, on the other hand, were strictly off limits. All this changed with the onset of the High Middle Ages, and came to full fruition during the 12th century, especially in France, as churchmen now became prime instigators at every level of society, including literature. One outgrowth of this remarkable trend was French romancers such as Chrétien who branched out as poets and entertainers, thus inventing the Arthurian legends (as we tend to think of them) in the process. Just as the church had goaded European kings and knights into undertaking the Crusades, they soon followed by attempting, with varying degrees of success, to refine their morals and manners.

The epitome of this new breed of ecclesiastic was represented in the extreme by Saint Bernard of Clairvaux (1090–1153), who wielded his pen and voice with such effectiveness that he impacted the politics of his epoch probably more than any other individual. Unlike Thomas à Becket, who came from the lowest social ranks of the conquered English Saxons, Bernard's parentage belonged to the highest echelons of French nobility. Also, unlike Becket, Bernard was not a martyr; he was a mover and shaker — a prime instigator of the Second Crusade, advocate of monastic reform, and shaper of Catholic theological doctrine, among many, many other accomplishments. Royalty and popes hung on his every word. With respect to knighthood, Bernard was one of the most important advocates leading to the formation of the Templar Knights at the Council of Troyes in 1128. French nobility known to have been under the spell of Bernard at that notable event included Hugh of Troyes, Thierry of Alsace, Count of Flanders, and Theobald, Count of Blois. These events proved to be a prelude to the disastrous Second Crusade of 1146–1149, an ill-conceived endeavor personally promoted and blessed by Bernard, and later enthusiastically supported in his treatise, *De Laude novae militiae*.[9] Thus the immediate forebears of Chrétien's family network of patronage were heavily invested in the enterprise pushed by Bernard. While Chrétien himself probably belonged to the lower orders of French clergymen, he would have come of age at a time and in a place that fell under the enormous shadow of Bernard, one which also heavily cast itself over his future benefactors and mentors.

Chrétien's romances are not about Saint Bernard or Saint Thomas à Becket or even about the Crusades; they are about the King Arthur legends — more specifically, King Arthur's knights and their misadventures, especially in love. Nevertheless, behind the poet's entertaining stories is a very serious political and religious backdrop, one which his mostly female audience may have wanted to temporarily escape from, but one that was, in reality, inescapable and constantly exerting its influence on audiences and poet alike. As is often the case, the things that go unsaid in literature of any period tend to be those same things which are most influential in its creation. When Perceval meets up with his hermit uncle in the wilderness during the latter part of Chrétien's final work, the scene reflects in a microcosm an important ideal of the times — the indomitable but wayward knight being corrected, instructed and tempered by an older, wiser and more authoritative churchman. In an era of fanaticism and religious warfare, a time in which people and events were judged strictly in terms of black and white, the poetry of Chrétien stands apart. Great minds always tend to break out of the mold, no matter how conservative their training. Chrétien's own adherence to the rigid theology of St. Bernard is obvious (see Chapter 20), yet his Arthurian characters, especially his knights, are fascinatingly complex and deeply flawed. As for his female characters, they are vivacious, liberated, and completely unpredictable. All of these characters, to varying degrees, despite their personal virtues, need more stability in their lives, as well as outside help to achieve it. In a world of magic, enchantment, and superstition, they frequently turn to various Christian rituals in preparation for severe trials or in thanksgiving of success after a trial. Interestingly, though, Chrétien's clergymen characters in the romances are few and far between. Chrétien was not a Becket nor a Bernard; it was not the place of a court *trouvère* to remind his benefactors of their religious duties, only to entertain and, on occasion, possibly to inspire.

These qualities, particularly the light and subtle touch of the poet with respect to religion and politics, seems to have been completely lost in the immediate aftermath of his death. By the early 13th century, a total and militant Christianization of the Grail Quest legend had been completed by western writers. This heavy-handedness came in the wake of European defeat in the Middle East at the battle of Hattin (see Chapter 17), as well as widespread disillusionment following the costly failure of the Third Crusade. Although Geoffrey of Monmouth and Wace had seen fit to make their King Arthur an unequivocally Christian king, and although Chrétien had ornamented his romances with various Christian trappings, this aspect of the legend was not pushed to the forefront until a few years later. This last phase occurred after multiple military and political setbacks in the Holy Land had led to Europe's re-evaluation of its alleged moral superiority to the rest of the world.[10] Things that in Chrétien's romances had been inscrutably attractive or left to the reader's imagination now became overt, rigid, and dogmatic. In distant retrospect, it is noticeable that many facets of the Arthurian legends today held up to comic ridicule or satire do not apply to the poet who did so much to popularize the legends in the first place. Irreverent cinema such as *Monty Python and the Holy Grail* (1975) and its Broadway spin-off, *Spamalot* (2005), were partly inspired as a 20th-century backlash against (and parody of) the super-pious version of the Arthurian legends created by Chrétien's continuators, not by Chrétien himself. The same is true of Mark Twain's 19th-century novel, *A Connecticut Yankee in King Arthur's Court* (1889), a bruising, satirical send-up of the gravely serious Arthurian landscape then being promoted by Alfred Tennyson and the Pre-Raphaelites. Unintentionally funny films such as *Knights of the Round Table* (1953) now come across that way for the same reason.[11] Part of the reason Chrétien's style and content cannot be mocked in a similar manner is that he himself often gave similar treatment to the same myths. This over-the-top parody most notably occurred in his pioneering masterpiece, *Lancelot* (see Chapter 1). The poet may have been a cleric, but he certainly knew how to laugh.

Today, one does not usually visualize a medieval churchman writing comedy, let alone romantic poetry. More likely, today's reader would think of a cleric writing stories — to the extent that he might write stories at all — like the moralistic, non–Arthurian, 12th-century French romance *Guillaume d'Angleterre* ("William of England"). This enigmatic work, interestingly enough, though not half as entertaining or enjoyable as Chrétien's Arthurian romances, has generated its own small body of critical literature, mostly devoted to speculating on its indeterminate authorship. A significant number of scholars view *Guillaume* as being an earlier, and artistically less successful effort by Chrétien de Troyes. Urban Holmes presented a good, short summary of the pros and cons for this theory, and within these pages we will very briefly add a few observations of our own. Holmes cited Wendelin Foerster's belief that it was composed after *Cligès* but before *Lancelot*, thus placing it in the middle of the poet's output at a crucial stylistic juncture in his career.[12] Others, such as the venerable Gaston Paris, completely rejected it as an authentic work of Chrétien.[13] Very loosely adapted from the legend of Saint Placidas and Saint Eustace, the story is preachy, uninspired, and deadly serious, not to mention completely lacking in all of the magical, mystical trappings automatically found in the Arthurian universe.[14] A casual read of *Guillaume* does not yield a fraction of the delight, humor, or sparkling complexity of a work such as *Erec and Enide*, which supposedly predated it by several years.

The strongest argument against the poet's connection with *Guillaume* is that the story is just not very good compared to the other long works attached to his name, all of which are outstanding in this respect. Some critics have further argued against Chrétien's authorship because *Guillaume* is not included in the catalogue of his works listed by the poet in *Cligès*; however, if *Guillaume* was produced after *Cligès*, then it should be viewed as a later, experimental detour by the artist. Moreover, even if *Guillaume* was produced earlier, perhaps the poet did not wish to claim credit for, or to publicly boast about this particular effort. It would be silly in either event to insist that Chrétien listed *all* of his works in *Cligès*. Of the ones that he did choose to list, all reflect some degree of influence from Ovid or the Tristan legend, both of which were very popular at the time. *Guillaume* has neither, although at one point an allusion is made to the Tantalus legend found (among other places) in Ovid.[15] In retrospect, it is difficult to disassociate Chrétien's style with that of his greatest Roman influence.

If one can get past the comparative, inferior quality of *Guillaume*, however, arguments in favor of Chrétien's involvement are powerful and persuasive. For starters, the author twice names himself as "Chrétien" (or Crestien, to be more precise, a spelling typically used by the Bard of Troyes), and the principal manuscript source for *Guillaume* also contains *Erec and Enide* and *Cligès*.[16] These factors alone would, at the very least, suggest that the true author was likely either Chrétien de Troyes, someone from his circle, or someone trying to capitalize on his famous (and rather unusual) name. As for the fact that *Guillaume* does not measure up artistically to a *Lancelot* (or even a *Cligès*, for that matter), some critics want every Shakespeare play to be *King Lear*, and try to deny that the Bard had a full hand in writing many lesser works in the canon. Even the greatest writers, on the other hand, can produce flops, and oftentimes these are more interesting than the best works from less talented hands.[17] As for dating issues, it is best to remind ourselves at this point that the earliest surviving manuscripts for Chrétien's romances come from the 13th century, long after the poet's death. Thus all written evidence for authorship must be viewed with extreme caution rather than in total isolation. This is not, nor should it be, a comfortable area for making sweeping judgments of any kind.

In contrast to these manuscript uncertainties, the text of *Guillaume* provides ample support for those critics who wish to promote the work as a sort of failed, non–Arthurian excursion by a famous Arthurian poet. Regarding source material, the text expressly credits a book by one Roger Le Cointe from the Abbey of Bury St. Edmunds in southeastern England (Suffolk).[18] As discussed elsewhere in this study (see Chapter 8), there is a good possibility that Chrétien traveled to England or, at the very least, had access to English data through an extensive network of family patronage, even if he did not travel there personally. For example, Hugh of Lagny, the half brother of Henry the Liberal, was the abbot of St. Edmunds.[19] Assuming that *Cligès* was written no later than 1176 and that it predated *Guillaume*, the latter could have also been produced around that time.[20] While *Guillaume* is very similar in style to *Erec and Enide*, this is less true with respect to *Cligès*. On the other hand, it may well be that the rebellion of Queen Eleanor's sons against their father Henry II during the early 1170s made the poet reluctant or hesitant to reiterate these potentially sensitive themes that were so prominently displayed in his previous work, *Cligès*.[21]

While source materials for *Guillaume* could have easily been available to the poet, the thematic similarities to his Arthurian romances are quite numerous if one takes the trouble to look past its lackluster entertainment value. Prevalent among these shared motifs is a surprising contempt by the poet for anything connected with the lower classes, and especially anything to do with commerce. At one point, it is bluntly pronounced that "the peasant is a very foolish animal."[22] Although Guillaume goes in disguise as a merchant to the French city of Troyes,[23] and is quite successful in his business dealings, covetousness, greed, and their ill social effects are roundly condemned along the way. The Troyes locale is interesting for a number of reasons, not the least of which is the automatic connection with its most famous namesake poet. The author, whoever he was, seems to have been very familiar with the city as a renowned commercial hub. When a merchant townsman remarks to Guillaume, "The legacy of poverty is harmful, and you have been deeply harmed by it,"[24] this recalls an early scene in *Erec and Enide* in which the hero stumbles upon his future bride and father-in-law living in highly reduced circumstances. The only bargaining depicted occurs when Guillaume's lost wife Gratienne bargains to delay her forced, bigamous marriage to Gleolais, calling to mind similar tactics used by Fenice with the Greek emperor in *Cligès*.

Other multiple details in *Guillaume* suggest similar concerns found in Chrétien's Arthurian romances. Guillaume declares to his wife, "God grant me and you joy!" evoking images of the climactic trial scene from *Erec and Enide*. Reference is made to the stag hunt,[25] also found in the opening scene of *Erec*. Guillaume and Gratienne's lost twin children do not know who their father is,[26] similar to Perceval and Lancelot, while the hero becoming lost in his own thoughts[27] is another foreshadowing of *Perceval*. The unwitting conflict between Gratienne and her sons is not unlike the incognito combats between Gawain and the heroes of *Yvain* and *Cligès*.[28] Crusader allusions are scattered throughout like afterthoughts, such as a reference to the city of Aleppo[29]—compare, for example, the mention of Beirut in *Perceval*. Gratienne swears by Saint Paul, who is misquoted by Chrétien in *Perceval* and *Cligès* (see Chapter 21).[30] Chessboards are among the displayed merchandise[31]—a chessboard also figures prominently in one of the latter episodes of *Perceval*. The list goes on, and none of this proves Chrétien's authorship of *Guillaume*, but taken together it is enough not to dismiss the suggestion out of hand simply because the work is not very exciting as a romance.

As dull as *Guillaume d'Angleterre* may be in terms of storytelling, it throws into good perspective Chrétien's prodigious gifts otherwise displayed in his Arthurian works. Although he was probably a cleric, he was not a very good moralizer, except to remind his audiences (and future generations) that, in matters of love and war, things are rarely simple. The human heart cannot be contained by the powers of reason, no matter how hard one might try. On the battlefield, friend and foe are often indistinguishable. In short, right and wrong are sometimes very hard to discern. These are pretty good life lessons, and not bad ones coming from a poet-churchman who apparently did not have it within himself to write a good, straightforward morality play. In this sense, Chrétien's romances always seem fresh and contemporary. For this artist, the grey zone between good and evil was often that which was most inspiring as material, and, for that matter, most real. Curiously, however, the most morally equivocal character in the Arthurian legends is barely mentioned (once) and never makes a personal appearance in Chrétien's works. Just as subsequent storytellers in the same tradition felt a need to fully Christianize Arthur himself, they channeled much of their pagan and non–Christian lore into the ambiguous personality of Merlin.

Chapter 19

The Problem with Merlin

Chrétien's natural bent was toward realism — Roger Sherman Loomis.[1]

The polarized and illiterate society of 12th-century western Europe, so insistent on the absolute moral supremacy of the Catholic Church, was also a community in which the vast majority of its members believed wholeheartedly in magic, witchcraft and superstitions of the most juvenile sort. Pagan traditions long predating the advent of Christianity largely held firm, especially among the uneducated who comprised the overwhelming majority of the population. Rather than engage in the futile task of eradicating these beliefs, the church often found it more convenient (and practical) to incorporate non–Christian symbols, legends, and heroes into its own orthodoxy. Subversive things were thus more easily monitored and controlled if kept close at hand. The Arthurian legends as a whole fall broadly into this interesting category, although there is debatable evidence that King Arthur, assuming that he ever existed, was a Christian. The individual figure within the saga who best represents these old pagan traditions, however, is not Arthur, nor any of his knights, nor even their protagonists, but rather the wizard Merlin.

Today Merlin in many respects is a more popular character than the king to whose story his own was grafted upon sometime shortly before the era of Chrétien de Troyes. Remarkably, Chrétien shows little if any interest in Merlin, or (more likely), was very interested in the sorcerer's burgeoning popularity with audiences and sought deliberately to either deflect this or to take the Arthurian material into entirely new directions. Whatever the poet's true attitudes and motives were, however, there was no apparent stopping the public's fascination with Merlin as a kind of behind-the-scenes master choreographer of world political events. This popularity continues into the present day. Fair or not, it is thoroughly accurate to say that in the 21st century, almost everyone knows the name of Merlin while very, very few know the name of Chrétien de Troyes. This is rather unfortunate.

Like King Arthur himself, the historical existence of Merlin remains an open question. The earliest of the sources refer to one or more Welsh poet-soothsayers by the name of Myrddin, but these individuals are not given any explicit connection to the Arthurian saga.[2] Not until the mid–12th century, only a generation prior to Chrétien's time, did the two traditions merge under a highly imaginative pen being guided by Geoffrey of Monmouth (see Chapter 9).[3] Geoffrey presented in writing many of the details now associated with the character for the very first time, and given his penchant for bold fabrication in other respects, it is at the very least possible that he was drawing mainly upon his own personal muse rather than any written sources or pre-existing oral traditions. It is much more likely that the Merlin of the Arthurian universe was a rare example of a literary creation coming straight and exclusively from a storyteller's fanciful invention. Perhaps surprised by Merlin's popularity from his deviously-titled *History of the Kings of Great Britain*, Geoffrey followed up this influential work with an epic Latin poem, the *Vita Merlini* ("Life of Merlin").[4] In one sense, Geoffrey found his true calling with this unapologetic versification of pagan lore. By this time, Merlin was being equated in Judeo-Christian circles with the biblical prophet Isaiah.[5] This morphing of a pagan Welsh soothsayer into the reincarnation of a monotheistic icon was yet another reflection of how established religion and old magic were an easy mix during that era, particularly with respect to popular pagan traditions being adopted and incorporated into a Christian context. Today, many scholars and specialists question Merlin's very historical existence, and some hypothesize that his name may have derived originally from a Welsh landmark rather than an actual person. It is certainly true that Geoffrey's fictionalization of him represents an aggressive amalgamation of several historical and/or non-historical individuals, one or more of whom may have had a somewhat similar, but non–Latinized name.

These various uncertainties in "historical" accuracy vanish if we opt to view Merlin strictly as the ever-evolving product of a continuing literary process, and in many ways, this approach is more informative in terms of understanding how the character came about and what lies behind his never-ceasing popularity. It is useful to remind ourselves at this point that, during the eras of Geoffrey and Chrétien, literary fact and fiction had an extremely porous divide. The main difference between the two writers is that Chrétien never pretends to be anything but a poet and storyteller, whereas Geoffrey tries to hold himself out as both poet and historian. Geoffrey tells a stirring yarn and attempts to add the force of historicity, while Chrétien's tales move at a much slower pace as he creates verbal music and simultaneously explores the uncertainties of the human heart. In fairness to Geoffrey, it should be added that in the end he did prove himself to be an able poet (again, in Latin), and without his work there likely would have been no Arthurian romance as it was later developed by Chrétien and other French writers.[6] Nevertheless, it often seems forgotten by modern scholars that all of these poets were working with Breton as well as Welsh material and often it was the former that stuck most in the public imagination. For example, Geoffrey, in his *Vita Merlini*, in a rare (for him) acknowledgment of outside source material, credits a Breton tradition with the story of a seriously wounded King Arthur being taken the Isle of Avalon for healing after the climactic battle of Camlann.[7]

How does Chrétien fit into all of this? In short, he does not. The poet, we can be fairly certain, was writing for a mostly female audience who probably had little or no interest in the Merlin aspect of the Arthurian legend. Merlin is a guy thing. Whenever Merlin appears in the saga, it is all about Merlin and his machinations of history; it is not about Arthur or his knights, and certainly not about their lady loves. This last item was the domain of Chrétien, not surprisingly since it was also the domain of his patronesses. In modern cinematic terms, no woman ever watched *Camelot* to see Merlin, who makes no appearance except in Arthur's imagination. This movie (and musical) are much more in the spirit of Chrétien de Troyes. Men and adolescents, though, could care less. They would be more interested in Disney's *The Sword and the Stone*, which heavily revolves around the character of Merlin. To repeat, Chrétien's storytelling emphases (and alternative vision of the Arthurian world) likely resulted from his audience patronage. An earlier, though lesser example of this same phenomenon is the French translation of Geoffrey by Wace, which inserted heavy doses of courtly love values into the story, which also happened to be dedicated to Eleanor of Aquitaine. This was surely no coincidence. Eleanor was the living symbol of women's liberation during the 12th century, as well as a generous patron of the arts and a key figure in the literary development of the Arthurian corpus (see Chapter 4).

In terms of physical space, no place on earth better represents the convergence of these three threads — the legend of Merlin, the poetry of Chrétien, and the writings of Wace — than the Forêt de Paimpont, also known as Brocéliande, located in Brittany about 40 kilometers west of Rennes. Today, Brocéliande and its environs are home to the delightful Centre de l'imaginaire Arthurien, as well as numerous legendary Arthurian landmarks, not least of which is "Merlin's Tomb," a large rock in which the magician was, according to tradition, imprisoned by the enchantress Viviane as punishment for his lecherous obsession with her.[8] In Chrétien's masterful romance, *Yvain*, Brocéliande is the focal point of events leading to the hero's courtship of (and later reconciliation with) his wife — specifically, at the Fountain of Barenton, another local landmark still visited by tourists coming from near and far. For Wace, however, Brocéliande becomes a symbol of foolish superstition, based on his own personal experience as he relates in his prose work, *Le Roman de Rou*: "I went there seeking wonders; I saw the forest, and I saw the countryside; I looked for wonders, but I found none. A fool I returned, a fool I went; a fool I went, a fool I returned; I sought foolish things, and I think myself a fool."[9] A fairly convincing example of direct literary influence in *Yvain* occurs when Chrétien seems to paraphrase the same passage from Wace: "And so I went, and so I came, and called myself a fool by name, and foolishly I've told you all. I didn't want to tell at all!" (lines 537–540). In addition to this, the poet had also utilized nearly identical wording in his early poem on the ancient tale of Philomena.[10] Clearly, it seems, Chrétien had read or listened to the self-deprecating work of Wace with great interest, as have many generations of readers ever since.[11]

Like Wace, this writer traveled to Paimpont and came back a bigger fool than ever. Lovingly referred to by the author's wife as "Bill's big brain book excursion," they found themselves alone and on foot in the same forest reputed once to be the haunt of Merlin and those characters associated with him. After remarking (somewhat loudly) that the entire legend had been made up in the imaginations of the Bretons, he suddenly realized that thousands of threatening bees (to which he is allergic) were swarming in the tall trees overhead. Immediately losing all courage, he retreated out of the woods and potential harm's way.[12] The incident was, in some respects, reminiscent of the episode from the hit television mini-series *Merlin* (1998), in which the title character (played by Sam Neill), recruits the help of a bee swarm to ward off an attack of mythical, hostile griffins. Perhaps they were warning the author not to take lightly or downplay the veracity of the Arthurian tradition, particularly relating to its most popular figure. It is also probably a good thing that none of the locals heard my dismissive comment. If Americans have their multitudes of dedicated Civil War reenactors, the Bretons have the rich King Arthur saga to express in costume a similar and well-deserved pride in their longstanding cultural heritage.[13]

Although Chrétien's romances contain numerous episodes of magic and the supernatural, these are judiciously employed and take a distant back seat to concerns of love and psychological drama. The wilderness is never viewed by the poet as a friendly or desirable place. Joseph Duggan observed:

> ... one has to remember that in the Middle Ages the deep woods were not an inviting place of repose from the hubbub of town life. Rather, they were considered primarily as threatening, the locus of encounter with savage beasts and with creatures that we nowadays consider fantastic and legendary but which for medieval society were very real.[14]

This prevalent attitude is firmly established at the beginning of the cycle in *Erec and Enide*, as hero and heroine foray into an uncivilized and uncouth landscape. The same mood continues throughout his subsequent works. Magical, pastoral elements make obligatory appearances, but obstacles are overcome not through spells or incantations, but rather with piety, heroism, and charity. Merlin still has no place in this scheme. Whenever a reader might expect the magician to save the day, church doctrine is instead interposed, or better yet, a helpful and clever young maiden. In *Perceval* (see Chapter 21), a hermit or holy man (Perceval's uncle) makes a rare appearance in the overall narrative to guide the hero along the path of righteousness.

As rare as clergymen are in Chrétien's tales, Merlin is non-existent. Considered by many to be the chief protagonist of the Arthurian legends, the name of Merlin is mentioned by Chrétien de Troyes a grand total of one time, near the close of *Erec and Enide*, in a dismissive, passing manner. Specifically, Merlin is credited as the inventor of sterling currency — a dubious distinction, to be sure — and this takes place within the context of a somewhat hollow, materialistic anti-climax to the story (see Chapter 11).[15] The poet also had Merlin arguably in mind when he wrote *Yvain*, in which the hero fights and wins his climactic battle versus two other-worldly demons, one of whom is suggestively portrayed as being "born of a woman and a fiend" (line 5034). This was also Merlin's parentage, according to one tradition. Clearly, the poet was not fond of the magician, nor anything he stood for.

Referring to the Middles Ages in general and Chrétien in particular, C.S. Lewis perceptively noted that "they have destroyed more magic than they ever invented."[16] As an alternative to magic and spells (and by extension, paganism), Chrétien and writers like him preferred realism and human emotions. Their fascination with the newly emerging scientific thought of the era, including physiology (see Chapter 2), led them to explore the "magic" of the human heart, one might say. This quality is precisely what Roger Sherman Loomis identified in the opening subtitle quote from this chapter. The poet seems to have had little interest in fairy tales, nor do we suspect, did his audience; moreover, this particular audience, upon whom the poet depended for a livelihood, knew from personal experience that world affairs are directed from domestic situations affecting the rich and powerful, far more often than from potions or spells. Magical enchantment served well as a literary ornament, and fighting *mano-a-mano* may have been what the knights were primarily interested in, but for the women, love was what mattered the most, and rightfully so. A court poet would have been expected to cater to all of these interests, and to have prioritized them properly as well.

In fairness to Chrétien, he was not the only great writer to have a strongly negative reaction against the Merlin tradition. In his satirical (and widely misunderstood) novel, *A Connecticut Yankee in King Arthur's Court* (1889), Mark Twain attacks with gusto the prevailing sanctity of the Arthurian tradition, and seems to hold Merlin as a character in special contempt. Without going into too much detail (and thus straying too far from our subject), Twain assigns the role of antagonist, rather than protagonist, to Merlin, viewing him as a kind of huckster con-artist or, worse, a second-rate scientist turned Rasmussen-like opportunist and meddler into affairs that are none of his business, properly speaking. The disconnect between the real American New England world of the industrial revolution in which Twain lived, and the fantasy realm found on the popular printed page of his time, must have indeed seemed far too great. It is no wonder that someone of his extraordinary talent, situated in his particular time and place, reacted the way he did—that is to say, in a derisive manner.

Given the prevalent cultural climate of the English-speaking world during the late 19th century, it is likely that Twain, aka Samuel Clemens, was relentlessly bombarded by fellow literati waxing euphoric over King Arthur and his knights of the Roundtable. This was the era of Tennyson, the Pre-Raphaelites, and American *nouveaux riche*, who, in their heart of hearts, secretly wanted to be the equivalents of British aristocracy.[17] The latter group is still with us today in force. We suspect that Clemens became fed up with it all and wrote *Connecticut Yankee* as both an irritated response to overly-rampant Arthuriana and as a cautionary tale to those who held up the Arthurian world as some kind of utopian ideal. Whereas Chrétien was silent or insinuatingly hostile towards Merlin, Twain attacked him openly and without reserve. Other examples of this alternative view might be cited, but for purposes here, Chrétien and Twain both well demonstrate how imaginative responses to these old stories have been very far from one of lockstep, universal adulation.

The problem with Merlin is that he tends to be a divisive figure, despite his runaway popularity. Christian moralists are put off by his pagan and demonic heritage, while fans of pure romance understandably find him to be decidedly unromantic. Chrétien, it would seem, disliked him on both accounts. In either event, the poet had no place for the magician in his own vision of the Arthurian world. He did have room, however (probably at the direction of his patrons), for the likes of Lancelot, Gawain, Guinevere, and a host of intelligent, independent-minded noblewomen who were usually very good at getting what they wanted, especially through intrigue. Praise of magic may have been considered off limits, but not praise of love, even love outside the bounds of conventional marriage. The controlling long arm of the Catholic Church in 12th-century France may have been able to temporarily hold back or blunt the effects of old pagan superstitions, but it could not ignore the ever-pressing demands of human sentiment. Remarkably, Chrétien managed to invent the Arthurian romance as a literary genre just as the church (of which he was very likely a member) achieved its first high-water mark as a strict enforcer of public morality and religious doctrine throughout the western world.

Chapter 20

Triumph of the Gothic

Cistercian piety seems to have influenced the legend of the Holy Grail, which describes a spiritual journey to a symbolic city that is not of this world but which represents the vision of God— Karen Armstrong.[1]

In their beginnings, the Arthurian legends were heavily laced and intertwined with tales of pagan magic and superstition, with the character of Merlin being perhaps the best known manifestation of this trait. This aspect of the saga has survived prominently down to the present day. Less appreciated by the contemporary world, though just as critical to the creation of the genre, were the driving forces of 12th-century religious and intellectual trends, particularly in France. Although one does not normally associate the word "gothic" with the romances of Chrétien de Troyes, the poet lived at the very center of a society now universally acknowledged as the birthplace of gothic architecture, art, and everything that this famous aesthetic stood for. This is certainly not say that Chrétien's poetry should be rigorously equated with the gothic style; on the other hand, to completely deny a significant connection between the two would be much worse a distortion. Given that the city of Troyes was itself a great cultural crossroads of the period, it should not surprise us that such an innovative poet was affected by the environment immediately surrounding him. The impact would be especially profound if Chrétien was by training a cleric — a surmise considered likely by a growing number of scholars — and educated in the cathedral schools then proliferating all across Europe. While one may normally associate the term with the innovative cathedral style of building then coming into vogue, it should not be forgotten that these magnificent edifices were being first constructed before the very eyes of the same genius who is the subject of this study.

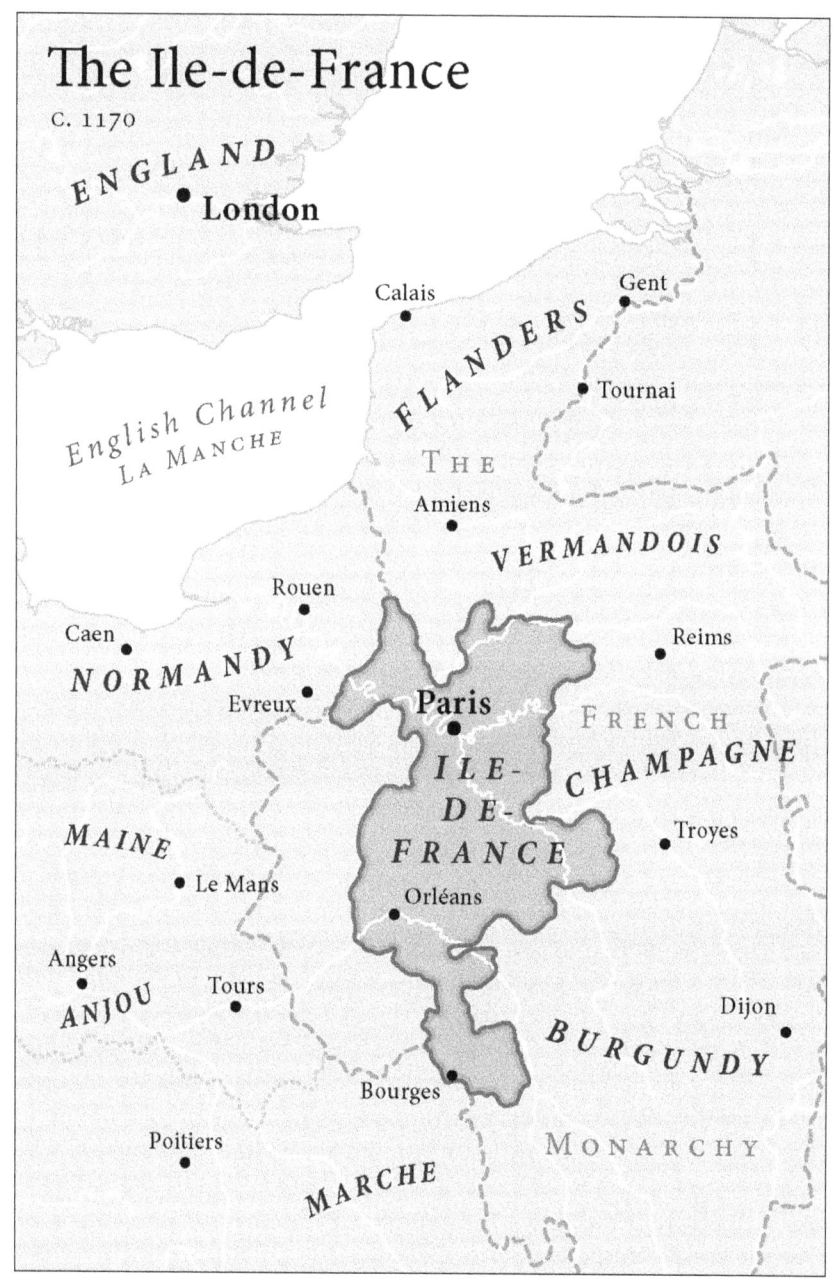

Paris, its suburbs, and the surrounding region, including adjacent and nominally loyal dukedoms such as Champagne, were all front row spectators to (and occasional participants in) neighboring events to the west in Normandy. It was the advanced cathedral school education and cosmopolitan worldview of French poets that provided the final, essential ingredient for Chrétien's groundbreaking synthesis.

To trace the beginnings of gothic architecture in France, and how this dramatic trend converged with the Arthurian legends, one could hardly do better than to visit the imposing Benedictine monastery of Mont Saint Michel, located atop a rocky island along the French shores of the English Channel at the precise geographic point where Normandy and Brittany come together.[2] According to tradition, the abbey began construction in its lower phases during the early 8th century, culminating in a series of imposing 12th and 13th-century structures, financed in part by King Henry II, the ambitious Anglo-Norman monarch for much of Chrétien's adult life. Named after Saint Michael, commander of God's armies for Christians, Muslims, and Jews alike, tradition also holds that the site was personally dictated to abbey founder Saint Aubert by the archangel himself. With respect to King Arthur, Mont Saint Michel is the locale in Geoffrey of Monmouth's account where the hero defeats an evil giant (Harpin of the Mountain) in single combat. The incident is later alluded to in Chrétien's *Lancelot* (lines 6074–6075).[3] Connections between the King Arthur legends and Saint Michael abound, not surprisingly, since European crusaders of the period often turned to both for inspiration. Thus shrines to Saint Michael can be found in remote places such as Otranto in southern Italy (a locale also providing the Arthurian cover art for this book), as well as more famous English sites, including Glastonbury and Cornwall. The Mont Saint Michel shrine in France is especially interesting, given that its layered and upward spire of development provides a dramatic visual lesson on how all of these period trends could potentially intertwine with each other.

True gothic architecture, though, represented far, far more than a mere trendy, ephemeral style of the times. It was a major byproduct of reformatory spiritual and intellectual trends defining the High Middle Ages in Europe. As discussed in the beginning of this section (see Chapter 18), the one individual who perfectly embodied these tides and currents for better and for worse was the Cistercian abbot, Saint Bernard of Clairvaux. Religious historian Karen Armstrong identified Bernard as "arguably the most powerful man in Europe" during the mid–12th century, with Pope Eugene II and King Louis VII of France "both in Bernard's pocket."[4] If Chrétien was, as most suspect, a French cleric trained in the cathedral schools, there is no way he could have avoided Bernard's far-reaching influence; indeed, the tone of his romances often reflect that he, like most everyone else at the time, was under Bernard's spell. Bernard could accurately be called the most politically correct person of his era; as a result, he left his indelible mark on Chrétien and all French romancers who developed the Arthurian legends as we know them. He was also, by growing consensus today among commentators, a somewhat narrow-minded, intolerant fanatic. Whereas Chrétien, as a groundbreaking poet, explored the insolvable mysteries of love and the human heart, Bernard belonged to a long tradition of writers who insisted on interpreting the most sensual book in the bible, *The Song of Songs*, as strict allegory.[5] Armstrong unfavorably summarizes Bernard's writings as a prime example of "unbridled subjectivity that fails to examine its prejudices critically," thus leading "to the worst excesses of religion."[6]

These "excesses" took many forms, one of which involved Bernard's attitude towards Muslims and Jews. Regarding Islam, Bernard could only advocate holy war and took no interest in alternative religious doctrines. Then, after actively preaching in favor of the highly destructive Second Crusade, which resulted not in victory for Christians over Muslims, but rather in a major Holocaust for European Jewry, Bernard did what he could to stem the massacres through personal intervention. Even he recognized that his misguided zeal had led to unintentional, evil consequences. Chrétien, though in his poetry a far more dispassionate and sympathetic observer of human sensuality than Bernard, appears to have also been an anti–Semite (see Chapter 23). Whether the poet would have ever attempted to save Jews from persecution, as did Bernard or Chrétien's patron, Henry the Liberal, is an open question. More certain is the basic premise that Chrétien (as a poet) wrote his romances under the heavy sway of Bernard's legacy, either consciously or unconsciously. Arthurian scholar Karl Uitti summed up this important but often overlooked aspect of the tradition:

> The contributions of Anselm, Abelard, and Saint Bernard of Clairvaux to the new sense of human individuality that was forged in the twelfth century can hardly be overestimated; they were among those who helped bring about and record the transformation of sensibility without which later twelfth-century vernacular romance (and the works of Chrétien) would have been inconceivable.[7]

Bernard may not have been the most brilliant thinker of his age, but his passion was contagious; moreover, he was intelligent, and intelligence combined with great passion usually will have a great effect on those within earshot. Chrétien, as the most talented poetic storyteller of his age, was no exception. On the other hand, the mind of a great poet is rarely confined by any narrow indoctrination, and will often break out of the very same mold that it seeks to glorify, promote or uphold.

To fully appreciate Bernard's limitations as a thinker — whatever greatness of heart he may have possessed — one should also look at other great intellects of the same period. One such figure was the famed Peter of Montboissier, better known as Peter the Venerable (1092–1156), Benedictine Abbot of Cluny. Peter seems to have been one of the few contemporaries that Bernard was willing to listen to in a disagreement, and rightly so, given Peter's distinguished track record. In contrast to Bernard, who showed little curiosity or outright hostility towards other faiths, Peter was one of the prime movers and shakers behind the first European Latin translation of the Qur'an. On top of this, he was also a voracious student of all new scientific and philosophic developments of the period, yet apparently accomplished this without compromising his personal faith or revered status as leader of the most important monastic institution in Europe. Bernard was not so deferential towards another Peter, the French philosopher Peter Abelard (1079–1142), whose free-thinking opinions he relentlessly opposed and finally helped to suppress. Armstrong identified Bernard's historic defeat of Abelard in an 1141 public debate at the Council of Sens as "a symbolic moment, which marked a split between mind and heart."[8] Abelard was also famous, or rather notorious, for his illicit love affair with a Parisian student, one Héloïse, which produced a correspondence between the two lovers now considered a classic precursor of modern romantic literature.[9] Whether Chrétien was aware of these letters is uncertain, but he most likely knew of the couple, as did many others in France. The fact that these letters were written shortly before the invention of the Arthurian romance is no coincidence; both developments were part of a larger trend then playing out among educated European society. Bernard, Peter the Venerable, Peter Abelard, Héloïse, and Chrétien all belonged to the relatively small literate world of 12th-century northern France.

While Spain probably helped provide medieval French writers with a new courtly love ethos and outlook — one that Bernard surely disapproved of — in Germany another great artist was leaving her permanent mark on western culture. She too, provides a useful contrast to Bernard's then dominant worldview of clear-cut right and wrong with no grey areas in between. Saint Hildegard von Bingen (1098–1179), Abbess of Rupertsberg, sometimes known as the "Sybil of the Rhine," was renowned during her own day as a writer, musical composer, scientist, and practically every other academic discipline then known to man. Her high reputation in the 21st century continues to grow. She seems to have been an exact contemporary of Chrétien, and some features of their artistry are shared, including an unusual creative mysticism strongly eschewed by the French poet in his final work, *Perceval* (see Chapter 21). Among many accomplishments, Hildegard corresponded with Henry II and Eleanor of Aquitaine, the two monarchs who did so much to promote the early growth of the Arthurian genre. Like Bernard, she came from the aristocracy, embarked on preaching tours, and her pronouncements often enjoyed papal endorsement.[10] Unlike Bernard, she took a comparatively positive view of sex (if accompanied by love), and always demonstrated a genuine, encyclopedic curiosity towards new ideas then flowing into 12th-century Europe. Like Chrétien, she seems to have possessed a rare human ability to set aside personal prejudice whenever confronted with clear-cut empirical evidence to the contrary. In short, the dazzling range of her work speaks for itself.

While the European continent teemed with novel artistic and scientific vistas, a good argument can be made that some of the groundwork for this development had been laid in England during the previous generation, led by Saint Anselm (1033–1109), the Italian-born Archbishop of Canterbury, credited as a founder of scholasticism, the movement that would help to establish the cathedral schools in which Chrétien was most likely educated. Anselm (again, in contrast to Bernard), took a pass on endorsing the Crusades and was known to have fraternized with Muslim Saracens in southern Italy. In this sense, he had more in common with Peter the Venerable than Bernard, who enthusiastically preached holy war against the infidel. Anselm helped to propel English Catholicism to the zenith of its influence, with the first English pope, Hadrian IV, formerly known as Nicholas Brakespeare (1100?–1159), being elected during the era of Chrétien. His predecessor, Pope Eugenius III, was an intimate of Bernard who liked to keep Englishmen about him, such as his chancellor Robert Pullen. Another English papal clerk was the influential writer John of Salisbury, who later returned to England to serve under Theobald, Archbishop of Canterbury (who crowned Henry II and Eleanor), along with a newly appointed archdeacon by the name of Thomas à Becket.[11] Salisbury was the author of *Polycraticus* (1159), a landmark work in the field of scholastic, humanist education, and one that was still being used as a source during the Tudor era by Shakespeare.[12] As for Chrétien, or, for that matter, any other educated Frenchman, it would have been unlikely for him not to have been touched by these emerging trends of thought then emanating from the British Isles.

In retrospect, it is impressive that such a repressed, feudal society as 12th-century France, one so dominated by a rigid moralist like Saint Bernard, could also have produced such progressive institutions of learning. Paradoxically, it was the emergence of cathedral schools that was mainly responsible for the revival of interest in ancient pagan writers such as Ovid and Virgil. In the modern sense, it was another case of Nixon going to China. Medieval learning, which paved the way for the dawn of the Arthurian romance, had to be advanced by the most conservative quarters of society, or not at all. In a bizarre but poignant sense, the heathen sensualist Ovid came to meet the pious ascetic Bernard. Consequently, Chrétien was capable of quoting or misquoting Saint Paul while poetically meditating on the mysteries of romantic love and its potential conflicts with military and religious duty.

The architectural equivalent of these turbulent literary trends coalesced in north suburban Paris on June 11, 1144, with the dedication of the newly-constructed ambulatory to the Basilica Saint Denis. The structure is now widely recognized as the world's first fully realized gothic cathedral. Its revolutionary character also seems to have been recognized at the time, having been built under the enlightened, forward-thinking direction of Abbot Suger and financed by King Louis VII of France, then married to Eleanor of Aquitaine, his wife before she later divorced him to marry a younger Henry II.[13] Just as the temporary, sprawling unity of the Angevin kingdom in France and England assisted in the wide circulation of the Arthurian legends, the gothic cathedral style quickly proliferated across western Christendom and has never really since gone out of style. In Chrétien's own literary landmark from the 1170s, *Lancelot*, the poet makes casual reference to the popular fair at Lendit (line 1482), which would have been located in Saint Denis, probably under the shadow of the basilica itself.[14] If Chrétien was half as well-traveled as many commentators believe him to have been, he still would have witnessed these new marvels sprouting up throughout northern France and possibly England as well.

The dark side of this creative outburst found horrendous expression in the Second Crusade of 1147 to 1149, a doomed enterprise opposed by Suger, the same man who helped to invent the gothic visual esthetic at Saint Denis.[15] Prescient voices of reason such as his, however, were in short supply. More typical was the eloquent warmongering of Bernard, whose sermons, as noted by historian Christopher Tyerman, were so charismatic that no one seems to remember exactly what he said.[16] We do know, however, that his surviving sermons were popular at Troyes and could be found in the library of Chrétien's patron, Henry the Liberal.[17] Count Henry was himself knighted in 1147 at the suggestion of Bernard by the Byzantine Emperor Manuel Comnenos.[18] Henry's predecessor, Count Hugh of Champagne, had originally donated the land for Bernard's Cistercian monastery in Clairvaux and later became a Templar knight himself.[19] Lastly, it should not be forgotten that Troyes was the original home base for the Templar knights, who considered Bernard their "leading spirit" and adopted his Cistercian version of Benedictine rule for themselves.[20] Thus the poet's patronage, namesake town, Saint Bernard, the Templar knights, and the Second Crusade all came together during the late 1140s. A younger Chrétien no doubt observed the mass fiasco of the crusade from afar and may have been given pause as to the righteousness or infallibility of the then-prevailing conventional wisdom.

It would appear more than coincidental that within three years of the first gothic cathedral appearing in Europe, armies fighting in the name of that same religion during the Second Crusade would meet their first major setback in the Middle East.[21] Although the highly artificial and unstable French kingdom of Jerusalem would survive for another three decades, the debacle of 1147 to 1149 set the stage for what would follow on a larger scale, even as magnificent, technological wonders simultaneously reached for the heavens in France, England, and Germany. After centuries of absolute barbarism, Europe and particularly France, were once again becoming cultured and innovative. Another happy residual of this process included the popular advent of Arthurian romance, thanks to the genius of Chrétien and other talented writers. It is little wonder that they chose to focus their imaginations on the romantic and often morally-compromising entanglements of King Arthur's knights and their ladies. By 1170, the deteriorating position of crusader kingdoms in the Holy Land was being attributed to the deteriorating moral reputations of the knights themselves — or perhaps they had never been morally upright to begin with, except in the imaginations of poets. Regardless of whether Chrétien lived to see the final military and political meltdown of *Outremer*, he would have been, at the very least, feeling highly circumspect about the situation, like many other intelligent Europeans of that time. Perhaps it was inevitable that the culmination of his Arthurian cycle, left unfinished at the time of his death, would turn its attention away from the complexities of romantic love. Instead, the poet's last focus would be more towards the attainment of knightly virtue through one individual knight's mystic vision of a better world, symbolized in the form of the Holy Grail.

Chapter 21

Perceval Gets Religion in Spite of Himself

> *Perhaps no work of medieval literature has suffered more from learned commentary than has the* Perceval *or* Conte del Graal. *English and American scholars interested in the Celtic past have viewed it as a fragment of a lost civilization rather than as a work of art expressive of a French attitude of mind*—William Nitze.[1]

The 12th-century triumph of gothic sensibilities in the arts (along with its inherent religious fervor), combined with European paranoia towards political events unfolding in the Middle East, laid the true foundation for the birth of the Arthurian romance. The apotheosis of this trend is well represented by *Perceval*, Chrétien's last work, left unfinished at the time of his death. At 9,234 lines (Cline translation), *Perceval* is by far Chrétien's longest romance, with *Lancelot*—the poet's other incomplete opus (but completed by another hand)—coming in at a distant second with 7,112 lines total. Jean Frappier, whose dating of the romances was largely adopted from the pioneering work of Anthime Fournier (and is favored in this study as well), estimated composition between 1181 and 1183, which also postulates 1183 as the speculative date of the poet's death.[2] Issues of dating aside, all scholars agree that the final dramatic poem of Chrétien de Troyes marked a major turning point in style and began a seemingly inexhaustible literary trend, one still being embellished today in popular fiction such as *The Da Vinci Code*. As for critical commentary, it appears never-ending; this modest study represents only one in a very long line and will be surely followed by many others.

While incomplete, contradictory, and sometimes impenetrable in meaning, *Perceval* has enjoyed nearly universal admiration.[3] Most recently, Joseph Duggan forcefully proclaimed it "a masterwork of world literature."[4] Among the previous generation of scholars, the venerable Roger Sherman Loomis put Chrétien's epic poem in perspective by noting, "Though inferior in the later parts to his best work, in others it is hardly excelled in medieval fiction...."[5] Burton Raffel voiced a similar sentiment, writing, "Aged or ill, he [Chrétien] was still immensely superior, as a poet, to the 'learned cleric' who finished *Lancelot*."[6] Although a specialist himself, Urban Holmes spoke for the majority of non-specialist readers when he observed, "Even for us today who read this tale but imperfectly, the narrative has great depth and dignity."[7] Despite this indisputable greatness, Edmund Chambers reminded readers that *Perceval* will be "an enigma for ever."[8] Chambers, with his usual healthy skepticism, added that "it is doubtful whether any of Chrétien's successors knew how he meant to finish his poem, or what the significance of the Grail was. It would take me too far from my theme to discuss the conflicting theories of modern scholarship on the topic."[9] This comment was written around 1927. Since that time, "conflicting theories" on the meaning or multiple meanings of the tale have proliferated to an even greater extent.

Uncertainty in meaning, however, did not hinder a proliferation of sequels to the plot; in fact, within a generation of Chrétien's death, four continuations of *Perceval* had been written in the French language alone. Combined with Chrétien's original romance, these total more than a staggering 60,000 lines of verse.[10] In addition to the sequels, the story inspired a series of interconnected works, some representing alternative tellings of the same tale. Like the continuations, these appeared shortly after Chrétien's original and most were in written in French. Some of the more famous and influential of these included Robert de Boron's *Joseph of Arimathea* and *Merlin* (both in verse), the anonymous *Didot Perceval* (in prose), and the anonymous *Peresvaus, the High Book of the Grail*, also in prose.[11] Somewhat in a class by itself is the enormous, multi-volume Vulgate or "Lancelot-Grail" Cycle, written in French prose by an anonymous author or authors during the early 13th century.[12] Other versions of the story that were highly popular include the anonymous Welsh *Peredur*, and the German *Parzival* by Wolfram von Eschenbach, the latter going on to inspire Wagner's opera in the 19th century.[13] Detailed comparisons between these continuations and alternative versions are far beyond the scope of this study. Suffice it to say that most of them, especially the French-language variations, did more to place the story in an overtly Christian context than Chrétien ever intended. Moreover, it is difficult if not impossible to come up with a modern comparison in terms of literary popularity. It would be a fair statement to observe that the Grail theme, as first articulated by Chrétien, completely dominated serious western literature for at least half a century after his death.[14]

The very name of Chrétien's groundbreaking hero is highly suggestive of a spiritual quest or journey — one which must first pass through personal suffering and adversity in order to reach its goal. The origin of "Perceval" comes from the Old French, meaning to "pierce the valley" or "press on through the valley." The poet had earlier mentioned the hero's name in his first two Arthurian romances, *Erec and Enide* and *Cligès*, as one of King Arthur's most prominent knights. In *Perceval*, the title character does not even know his real name until guessing it in line 3574 as he is interrogated by his cousin, whom he meets by chance. Perceval does not suffer from amnesia; rather this delayed revelation serves a dual purpose. First, it follows a medieval literary convention (used by Chrétien in other works) that does not reveal important character names until the middle of the story. Second, and more crucial, this is the point in the tale that Perceval first achieves the essential spiritual quality of self-awareness; hence, he suddenly realizes his own name and speaks it out loud.[15]

This delayed self-awareness points to the main character's uniqueness as a 12th-century literary hero. Perceval is far from being a perfect individual, and this was clearly the poet's intent. Ruth Harwood Cline sums up the huge discrepancy between what we find in the romance and what we normally expect from an Arthurian knight:

> Readers who expect to find in Perceval a pure knight leading a life of fasting and prayer in hope of becoming worthy of a glimpse of the grail may be momentarily disconcerted. The original Perceval is Chrétien's clumsy adolescent hero, who spent the night with his girlfriend and never went to church. In this state of unworthiness he stumbled up on the grail, which was carried back and forth in front of him in the vain hope that he might ask about it, while he was feasting in a Welsh castle on his way home to confirm a sinking feeling that he had finally managed to break his poor mother's heart. Readers who are familiar with the successors may be surprised by Chrétien' de Troyes, but not as much as Chrétien would have been surprised by his successors.[16]

Perceval is an ignorant, graceless bumpkin, but one of noble birth and consequently, for the poet, of noble instincts and aspirations. In later, more idealized versions of the tale, Perceval, the worthy pursuer of the Holy Grail, morphs into Galahad, son of Lancelot, or, in the German version, has his own more-perfect son named Lohengrin. The implication of these embellishments is that one must be a knight absolutely pure in morals like Galahad or Lohengrin to behold the Holy Grail. On the other hand, Chrétien's Perceval is a much, much more interesting character than the Galahad or Lohengrin substituted by later storytellers. The same generally applies to all of Chrétien's characters, who are deeply flawed rather than perfect — in short, more human, like King Arthur himself. In Chrétien's version, the conventional model of perfect knighthood is Gawain, not Perceval; yet it is Perceval who is prophesized to become the greatest of all knights (line 1060). Though he did not finish the work, the poet strongly suggests that the ideal knight must always be made such through hard experience, as well as born into it. As for religious piety, Perceval seems destined to achieve this as well, although it is certainly not part of his original design.

The next major stage of self-awareness for the hero comes when he by chance encounters his pious hermit uncle (line 6342) after having ignored religion altogether for five years.[17] Perceval's uncle is, in effect, a de facto holy man who turns his nephew's spiritual life around by educating him about the church and reminding him of his ultimate duties as a knight and as a human being. In this role, Perceval's uncle plays the role of a cleric, and for the first time in Chrétien's Arthurian cycle, the church asserts its moral authority over the knightly orders, assuming supremacy over both the ideals of chivalric love and military duty. As Professor Cline writes, *Perceval* "reflects a gradual displacement of the chivalric ideal ... the inspirational force behind great deeds of chivalry became not the love of the lady but the love of God."[18] Joseph Duggan adds that, in general, "*Perceval* has a spiritual aspect that sets it apart from Chrétien's other works."[19]

One overt dimension of this spirituality is represented by the poet's repeated use of New Testament scripture in the text. Chrétien paraphrases Matthew at least three times (lines 4, 30–31, and 581), each reference criticizing, either obliquely or directly, anyone who rejects the Christian message of Jesus or pretends to follow it for mere appearance's sake.[20] The use of Matthew is interesting because this gospel is generally agreed to be the harshest of the four towards the Jews, and *Perceval* also contains one of the most notorious anti–Semitic slurs in medieval literature (see Chapter 23). More surprising is Chrétien's misquotation of Paul in line 49 (the quotation is actually from the First Letter of John). One would be tempted to say this error was caused by the great poet's declining health, except that he also misquoted Paul in a much earlier work, *Cligès* (line 5264). It could be plausibly argued that Chrétien was just being devious. Perhaps the best explanation is that the poet simply was fond of quoting Saint Paul, whether or not Paul was actually the source.

As one peruses the delightfully variant English translations of *Perceval*, it is striking how these diverse themes are cumulatively enriched and reinforced. As the young and untested hero approaches the court of King Arthur for the first time, it is readily apparent that all is not well within Camelot (Carduel), despite the presence of the supposed finest knights in the world.

With no opposition, Perceval brazenly rides his horse into the royal court only to discover the king and his knights seated, not at the Roundtable, but rather at the dinner table, with Queen Guinevere nowhere to be seen. Cline, reproducing the rhymed couplets of the French original, portrays Arthur "lost in his thoughts" as he "brooded silently withal." In contrast, his famed knights were "high-spirited" while "laughing loud and bantering."[21] Other English translators paint similar pictures. Burton Raffel has Arthur "deep in thought," as well as "lost and mute." Meanwhile, the knights are "chattering away, [l]aughing and amusing themselves."[22] William Kibler portrays Arthur "seated dejectedly ... disheartened and silent" as his knights "were eating and talking."[23] D.D.R. Owen has Arthur "deep in thought ... as he brooded in silence"; the knights are "laughing and joking."[24] David Staines has him "seated pensively ... preoccupied and silent." The knights are "engaged in conversations, amusing themselves."[25] All in all, this is not the Camelot we are used to seeing. It would appear (as indeed turns out to be the case) that Arthur is in need of a champion even greater than his near-perfect, warrior-nephew Gawain.

The theory of Perceval's ultimate moral supremacy over Gawain, had Chrétien lived to complete the work, is bolstered in the same scene by the fool's prophecy during which the hero arrives at Arthur's court. Upon beholding Perceval's uncouth, ridiculous demeanor, a maiden who had not laughed in six years bursts out in hilarity, thus fulfilling a prediction:

> because the fool was wont to say:
> "This maid won't laugh until the day
> she sees a man to whom will be
> awarded knighthood's sovereignty."[26]

In place of "knighthood's sovereignty" (Cline), Raffel uses "the knight of all knights," while Kibler opts for "all lordship of knighthood."[27] Owen preferred "supreme among knights" while Staines went even further with "supreme master of chivalry."[28] Regardless of the precise translation, the message is clear: Perceval is destined to surpass everyone as a knight, Gawain included. This is one good indicator of where Chrétien appeared to be headed with his unfinished story.

Inherited nobility is also a trait which foretells the hero's greatness, although Gawain and other successful knights share this quality as well. In fact, this is one of the most pervasive themes in all of Chrétien's works — not surprising since he was writing for the pleasure of the French nobility and most likely belonged to that caste himself. Gawain's misadventure at Escavalon provides the poet with a golden opportunity to vent his class bias with entertaining aplomb. As Gawain and the king of Escavalon's sister harmlessly make out (with the absent king's tacit approval), the castle is violently attacked by a plebeian mob enraged by the sudden revelation that Gawain had in past times killed the king's father in combat. Even with this new information, the king's sister, invoking the laws of hospitality and perhaps disguising that she is smitten with Gawain, joins him in fending off the attackers with various projectiles, as well as lots of verbal abuse. English translators have a field day with this. The royal maiden addresses her own subjects as "rabble ... mad dogs, peasants" (Cline), while bombarding them with heavy chess pieces.[29] Raffel prefers "scum ... foaming [d]ogs ... dirty rascals."[30] Others substitute various epithets such as "filthy wretches" (Kibler), "stinking menials" (Owen), and "[b]ase people ... vile serfs" (Staines).[31] All agree more or less that in between this name-calling the maid interjects her sincere hope that God or Heaven will "never grant you joy!"[32] This last bit of vitriol humorously calls to mind Chrétien's famous *Joie de la Cort* finale from his first Arthurian romance, *Erec and Enide* (see Chapter 11).

The inherited nobility of Perceval, Gawain, and their cohorts may well have a factual basis. The political background of the work, as well as perhaps the real-life individuals who served as models for the title character, appear firmly rooted in the historical French nobility of the 12th century. The dedicatee of *Perceval*, or at least the person lavishly praised in Chrétien's prologue, is the famous Philip of Alsace, Count of Flanders (1143–1190), his last patron. Chrétien's young protagonist, however, bears little direct resemblance to what we know about Count Philip. Certain aspects of Perceval's character, on the other hand, recall the man to whom Philip was godfather, teacher, and mentor—King Philip II of France (1165–1223), or Philip Augustus, as he was commonly known.[33] Philip Augustus became king in 1180 and is perhaps remembered best for his abortive participation in the Third Crusade alongside Richard I (*Coeur de Lion*) of England.[34] He is also known for initially expelling France's sizeable Jewish population from the country, only to later invite them back after realizing their indispensable role in the economic and cultural life of France (see Chapter 23).[35] Shortly after becoming king in 1180, Philip II married Isabelle of Hainaut, the niece of Count Philip.[36] Strikingly, in the story Perceval is given directions to King Arthur's court by a lowly charcoal seller in the forest. This very likely was a popular allusion to the adolescent Philip II, who in 1179 became lost in the woods en route to his own coronation before he too encountered by accident and was led to safety by a peasant charcoal seller. On the basis of this incident alone, Chrétien's Perceval has often been compared to the young king.[37]

As for Chrétien's patron, the elder (Count) Philip, his association with the great poet and his work appears to have been no accident. After the death of Chrétien's early patron, Count Henry the Liberal, in 1181, Philip lived in Troyes and until breaking off negotiations in 1183 was a suitor for Henry's widow, Marie of Champagne (the dedicatee of *Lancelot*). Philip's first wife had been Marie's first cousin. Prior to this, he had been a Crusader in the Holy Land, and a decade later would meet his fate (along with thousands of others) as a plague victim at the siege of Acre in modern-day Israel.[38] Philip was cut in the mold of his father, Count Thierry of Flanders (1099–1168), whom Crusade historian Christopher Tyerman labeled a "Holy Land addict" because of his many visits there. Interestingly, before his first journey to the Middle East, Philip consulted with the famed German mystic Hildegard von Bingen (1098–1179), who gave him somewhat less than a ringing endorsement of his Crusading enterprise.[39] While the idealistic count's immediate military objectives proved ultimately futile (see Chapter 17), it at least helped give to the world one of its greatest works of literature. Given Count Philip's lifelong devotion to France and its extended dominion in the Middle East, it may be that he gave Chrétien the source material (mentioned by the poet), for purposes of edification and entertainment to the young French king and to all of his country's young nobility in general.

More recently, in his engaging book *The Virgin and the Grail*, Professor Joseph Goering of the University of Toronto offered a new and fascinating historical candidate for the inspiration behind the character of Perceval. This personage was the famed French nobleman, Rotrou II, surnamed "the Great," count of Perche between 1099 and 1144. Apart from the obvious similarity between the names Perceval and Perche, Rotrou had a knightly résumé second to none. His father had fought on the side of the victorious Normans at the battle of Hastings in 1066. Not to be outdone, Rotrou set out as a young man with the First Crusade in 1096 and was an eyewitness to the memorable events of that expedition, including the discovery of the alleged "Holy Lance" at Antioch in 1098. After returning to France and marrying a granddaughter of William the Conqueror, the restless warrior spent a good part of the early 12th century in Spain successfully helping his cousin, King Alfonso I, in multiple campaigns against his Muslim neighbors. In his old age, Rotrou found time and energy to return to Jerusalem as a pilgrim, then back to Spain, then back to France again for the marriage of King Louis VII and Eleanor of Aquitaine at Poitiers in 1137. Finally, ironically, and much like Richard *Coeur de Lion* would a generation later (see Chapter 7), Rotrou met a violent end near his own backyard in Normandy at the siege of Rouen in 1144 — another victim of insatiable, French-Angevin political ambitions. By the time of his passing, few European knights had acquired such an impressive track record, and his heroic legacy was enduring. Moreover, Rotrou in his true-life adventures had spanned most of the western world and the places that lay claim to Chrétien's source materials. He also had ties to both of Chrétien's main patrons. Rotrou's son married the sister of Henry the Liberal, while Henry's wife Marie was a daughter of the same union (between Louis VII and Eleanor of Aquitaine) whose nuptials Rotrou had attended in 1137. To repeat, Philip of Flanders was himself married to the niece of Eleanor, and hence was the first cousin of Marie.[40] This probably was one of the bonds that eventually led to an alliance between Count Philip and the House of Blois-Champagne after Philip Augustus assumed the French throne in 1180. In any event, Rotrou the Great would likely have been revered by Chrétien's last two patrons, and consequently, made excellent (though slightly veiled and/or amalgamated) material for his last and highly influential Arthurian romance.

William Nitze's pointed comment that *Perceval* is, above all, a literary work expressing a French state of mind, cannot be repeated too often. To be more precise, it is a work forcefully expressing the attitudes, concerns, and social mores of the 12th-century French nobility. This quality is supported by the French patronage which spawned it, the French personalities obviously used as character models, and the topical allusions to French political and religious issues of the time — as well the French language in which the poem was originally written and expanded. As for the various symbols and plot devices that Chrétien appropriated for his story, these admittedly have older roots in places outside of France, as many scholars have persuasively argued. The image of the Holy Grail, which continues to dominate the western imagination, first came into sharp focus under the pens of the medieval French romancers, but even they — like most other groundbreaking artists — were in fact taking existing material and creating something totally new from it. To the background of this remarkable and lasting synthesis, we shall now turn our attention.

Chapter 22

The Grail and the Lance

The judicious scholar is driven to admit that the Grail has signified many things to many men at many times— Roger Sherman Loomis.[1]

To properly summarize the numerous theories on the intended symbolism of the Grail Procession in Chrétien's *Perceval* requires a separate book in itself. The best that we can hope to achieve in a short space is to pique the interest of the reader into further investigation, and to dispel any mistaken notions of simplicity or cut-and-dry interpretations regarding this complex subject matter. Admittedly, this writer not so long ago believed (like many others) that the Grail legend was no more than another embellished medieval tradition involving Christian religious relics, similar to the Shroud of Turin or the True Cross of Calvary. This, indeed, the legend of the Holy Grail later became; however, originally, in the hands of the poet Chrétien de Troyes it was something much more nebulous, metaphysical, and mysterious. Over the last two centuries, with a strong resurgence of interest in the King Arthur legends in general and the work of Chrétien in particular, a broad universe of interpretations has been offered by those daring to explore the sources and uses of these images before the 13th century. The going can get rough, as any unbiased scholar will quickly admit. When analyzing the historical roots of the Grail legend, figuratively speaking, one often does not know whether the tide is coming in or out; whether to shovel or to bail.

With respect to Chrétien, the great British scholar Leslie Topsfield wrote with no hyperbole that the Grail legend represented "the zenith of his literary achievement."[2] This is typical praise. Everyone seems to concur that Chrétien's creation is great and timeless, but very few can agree on exactly what it was that he created. Urban Holmes, who devoted as much energy as anyone to solving the puzzle, concluded, "This, of course, is a haunting problem," one that "still remains to be explored."³ In his last exhaustive study, Holmes gives a terrific summary of the various proposed Grail theories up to 1970, including multiple Christian, pagan, and non-religious readings.⁴ In an earlier work from 1959, Holmes and Sister M. Amelia Klenke offered up their own Judeo-Christian interpretation,⁵ but no sooner had this thesis appeared in print than it was immediately brought into question by the independent-minded criticism of Helen Adolf. Thus the debate began anew, continues to the present day, and will probably persist as long as people enjoy reading Arthurian romances for pleasure. As shall be seen presently, part of the reason for this never-ending discussion is that the symbolism of Chrétien's Grail may have been left intentionally open-ended. This in turn was the result of his source material probably coming from several directions at once (see Chapter 6), as well as his own prodigious skill as a storyteller, which invited readers and listeners to actively participate with their own imaginations.

Before plunging headlong into the various competing theories, unfamiliar readers are entitled to a brief outline of the episode in question. In *Perceval*, the young hero (still unnamed at this point in the story) serendipitously stumbles upon the Grail Castle, presided over by the lame Fisher King and his invalid father, the Grail King. The Fisher King invites Perceval to attend a banquet there.⁶ During this feast, Perceval witnesses the solemn Grail Procession, led by a youth clasping a continually-bleeding white lance, then two more youths, each carrying a brightly burning candelabra, then a maiden bearing a glowing and golden-jeweled grail, and lastly, another maiden holding a silver carving platter (lines 3191–3229). While the procession passes back and forth during the banquet, the hero refrains from asking any questions as to its meaning, for which he is later chastised. By the next morning, castle, grail, and occupants have all vanished, and the hero is left alone to wander. Thus the iconic Arthurian image of the Holy Grail makes its first appearance in world literature, courtesy of Chrétien de Troyes. Readers and critics (as well as other writers) have been discussing, debating and reinventing its meaning ever since.⁷

Any rational discussion of Chrétien's intended symbolism should begin with etymology. The Old French noun of *graal* was an unusual word at the time (circa 1180 to 1190), and was probably Provençal in origin.⁸ It signified not a chalice or a cup, but rather a deep, wide dish or bowl, often used for serving fish courses.⁹ Its most notable use in writing before *Perceval* was in the anonymous *Roman d'Alexandre*, an early 12th-century French epic poem that was surely known to Chrétien. This precedent, however, did not use *graal* in an Arthurian or even a symbolic context — it merely makes a rare appearance as a written word, albeit in a casual, offhand manner.¹⁰ In *Perceval*,

Chrétien uses the word *graal* no fewer than 25 times,[11] all in a reverential tone. Besides its shape, the adjective of "holy" applied much more loosely to Chrétien's grail than in later interpretations. Some commentators have denied that it was holy at all. At one point later in the tale, Perceval's hermit uncle refers to the grail as "such a holy thing" (line 6426), while Perceval himself merely calls it "the grail" (line 6380).[12] Later this grail is revealed to have sacramental power, keeping the Grail King alive with "one mass wafer" (line 6424). As for the other objects in the procession, the bleeding lance has generated its own fair share of debate. Typically, it is associated with the so-called lance of Longius, used on Calvary to pierce the crucified Christ.[13] The silver platter or *tailleor* has, with a few exceptions, been totally ignored. This neglect is surprising given its place at the end of the ritual and immediately behind the grail itself. Its silver composition, compared to the jewel-encrusted gold of the grail, suggests an inferior though still essential place in the overall symbolic scheme. The two candelabra, as noted by Adolf, dim in comparison to the supernatural brightness of the grail (line 3224), and their main purpose appears to be to highlight the latter, as well as to be symbols of sanctity.[14] Lastly, it should be added that Christianity, Judaism, and Islam all have used candelabra in various manners to signify holiness.[15]

Anyone attempting to glean a coherent allegory from the Grail Procession must, by necessity, examine the origins of the symbols themselves. Thanks to the intrepid 20th-century scholarship of Roger Sherman Loomis, it can now be stated with relative certainty that the physical symbols of the procession, especially those of the grail and the lance, began in Celtic pagan mythology at some very distant and indeterminate date. Loomis conclusively demonstrated that Perceval's adventures closely resemble those of pre–Christian Celtic heroes, and that there are numerous parallels with Chrétien's tale and those in older languages of the British Isles that are still preserved in writing.[16] An honorable mention in this regard should be reserved for Jessie Weston, whose "Ritualist" theory from earlier in the same century was highly influential, though also far more controversial and sometimes flawed.[17] Weston belonged to a pioneering group of scholars who traced the themes and symbols of *Perceval* even further back to various ancient sources such as the Adonis myth of the Greco–Roman world, "oriental" themes originating in Gnosticism and transmitted through Islamic Spain, or Egyptian pagan sources such as the vegetation-fertility cult of Isis and Osiris.[18]

Admittedly, by the time all of these competing sources are examined, the uninitiated head can be left spinning. If anything, combined they give new meaning and credence to the theory of historical synchronicity, or the simultaneous occurrence of similar events at different places. As for what was going on in the mind of the poet himself, perhaps Weston had the most likely explanation when she wrote: "But to Chrétien de Troyes the story was romance, pure and simple. There was still a certain element of awe connected with Grail, and Grail Feast, but of the real meaning and origin of the incidents he had, I am convinced, no idea whatever."[19] Later she adds, "[W]hile the poem of Chrétien de Troyes is our earliest surviving literary version, there is the strongest possible evidence that Chrétien, as he himself admits, was not inventing, but re-telling, an already popular tale."[20] In other words, Weston believed that Chrétien was probably not sure exactly what it was he was adapting. All he knew was that he *was* in fact adapting and what he was adapting it *for*, namely, his own artistic purposes. This included giving a Christian veneer or overlay to an established pagan story. Christians should not be shocked by this. Weston approvingly quoted her distinguished contemporary, Edmund Chambers, who noted that religious customs are often founded upon older, "heathen" mythology.[21]

Enter Christianity. Geoffrey of Monmouth and Wace had already given the Arthurian legends a Christian makeover by the time Chrétien began to compose his romances, and he followed their example of using a light touch in this regard. Christianization of pagan symbols is nothing new, having been done since ancient classical times, and Chrétien (whose writing reflects classical training) does the same in *Perceval*. One of the first articulate critics to notice this was the German scholar Stephan Hofer, who quite reasonably conjectured that had Chrétien lived to complete the work, the story would have ended with the hero restoring the Grail kingdom after he himself had achieved atonement. Reader sympathy, after all, tends to be with Perceval (as opposed to his near-faultless comrade Gawain), because Perceval has made mistakes and suffered for it.[22] Urban Holmes used Hofer as a starting point and then, in tandem with Klenke, expanded this into their own elaborate Christian interpretation. Holmes speculated that Chrétien's last patron, Philip of Flanders, when returning from the Holy Land in 1177 to 1178, may have brought with him Chrétien's alleged "sourcebook." Holmes also reminds us that Philip was the grandson of an earlier Christian king of Jerusalem (King Foulque) and was probably interested in holy relics such as the Grail and the Lance.[23] Holmes and Klenke then proposed an elaborate allegory for the conflicts between Christianity and Judaism — the Judeo-Christian theory[24] — based on multiple similarities in the symbols used by Chrétien in the Grail Procession and those found in Ecclesia-Synagoga artwork from the same period, and the reasoning that the poet was probably influenced by these (see Chapter 23). As Holmes explained, "[T]he Church, far from ignoring the Arthurian legends, deplored the superstition which it feared that they fostered and consequently strove to Christianize the old tales."[25] The appearance of Arthurian-themed artwork in churches at Modena and Otranto during the 12th century were similar examples of this same trend (see Chapter 14).

Despite the many attractions (and common sense) of this reading, it is not without inconsistencies, as critics such as Jean Frappier and Helen Adolf have pointedly asserted. A threshold objection to Judeo-Christian analysis is that Chrétien's grail was not a drinking cup (as normally portrayed being held by Ecclesia); it was more a serving bowl; in fact the very degree of the grail's "holiness" at that point in literary history is open to debate, given the poet's extremely light descriptive touch. Another problem with the Holmes-Klenke analysis is Chrétien's lance bearer is a male valet, not a female as in images of Synagoga. Furthermore, on the matter of gender, any female participation in the liturgical sacraments of the Catholic Church at that point in history was strictly forbidden. On the other hand, the objection that the Grail bearer is a young woman is surmountable because Chrétien's procession was intended to be artistic and symbolic; the very same church that forbid women as Eucharistic ministers also enthusiastically portrayed them in church artwork, such as Ecclesia holding a chalice. Holmes later called attention to Klenke's observation that Chrétien's use of the grail may have been inspired by Abbot Suger's magnificent chalice for Saint-Denis, now exhibited in the National Gallery of Art.[26] Nevertheless, Adolf effectively critiques the Judeo-Christian allegory of Holmes-Klenke as had Frappier and others before her, as simply not conforming enough to period church doctrine, liturgy, or art.[27]

Adolf then offered her own theory. In somewhat convoluted but persuasive fashion, she maintained that the strongest element of allegory present in *Perceval* was for the early Crusades. In particular, her emphasis was on the Temple of Jerusalem as a Crusader focal point, a religious landmark which later became the namesake of the Templar order of knighthood.[28] This too is a compelling proposition, but not one that is foolproof. For starters, the Holy Grail legend, as developed immediately after the lifetime of Chrétien, while certainly a transparent allegory for the Crusades (i.e., to win back the Holy Land, symbolized by the Grail), did not begin so transparently. At the time of Chrétien's death (assuming it was around 1182 or 1183), the Crusader kingdom of *Outremer* was tottering, but not yet fallen. In this specific context, *Perceval* must be viewed more as a symbolic call for all Christians to clean up their acts, and not merely as a rallying call to arms for purposes of controlling a physical place on the map. Above all, in comparing the rival "Christian" interpretations of Chrétien's grail, one is continually struck by how similar these interpretations can be, and how often so much can be read into so little.

There are hints in the text of *Perceval* that the poet, like just about everyone else at the time, had the Holy Land in the back of his mind while writing (see Chapter 17). In describing the mysterious Grail Castle, Chrétien wrote:

> as far as Beirut, they would not
> find any finer tower or spot.
> The tower was dark gray stone, and square,
> and flanked by lesser towers, a pair
> [lines 3053–3056].

There are other references to the Middle East as well, and these are best catalogued by Holmes, Adolf, and others. Moreover, and it is worth repeating, continuators who followed Chrétien picked up these hints and made them dominant themes in subsequent romances. For example, the Burgundian soldier-poet Robert de Boron, a younger contemporary of Chrétien, gives the Holy Grail an explicit though heavy-handed Christian dimension: namely, the chalice of the Last Supper.[29] This commentator would argue that by explaining such things in obvious, concrete terms, he only succeeded in taking the mystery out of the tale. Almost all of Chrétien's later imitators and adaptors were guilty of this to some degree.

Our purpose here is not to offer yet another interpretation of Chrétien's nearly inscrutable meaning. It would seem, however, that critics such as Frappier, who strenuously downplayed the Christian dimension of *Perceval*,[30] and pagan lore advocates such as Loomis and Weston, come much closer to identifying the poet's original intent than later efforts to gloss over or submerge the non–Christian elements. As William Nitze sensibly observed, "To sum up, it is clear that in Chrétien's poem the grail has two functions— pagan and Christian at the same time."[31] The physical formation of the Grail Procession suggests the shape of a cross, but the poet is (yet again) non-specific.[32] Gawain, the other hero of what appears to be a secondary plot, is later sent in search of the bleeding lance. It was probably intended that he would cross the path of Perceval at some point in the unfinished story. The lance itself is foretold as an instrument of destruction for the kingdom of Logres, or England (lines 6167–6171), while the magnificent enchanted sword given to Perceval by the Fisher King is predicted to fail him at some unspecified future date (lines 3139–3142). All of these devices have Celtic pagan origins, but are used by the poet in a vaguely Christian context. As for the relationship between the golden grail and the silver platter, that the latter is empty during the procession and composed of a baser metal would seem to suggest another one of Chrétien's dichotomies — possibly the contrast between the heavenly food of the grail's Eucharistic wafer and the sumptuous earthly food of the castle banquet.

In more recent years, one of the more intriguing theories regarding the grail's origin in *Perceval* has centered around the Pyrenees Mountains dividing Spain and France. This hypothesis was most recently articulated by Professor Joseph Goering of the University of Toronto in his 2005 book, *The Virgin and the Grail*.[33] Goering acknowledged that "for all practical purposes Chrétien de Troyes must be considered the originator of the Grail legend as we know it today."[34] He then points (with the help of lavish illustrations) to a remarkable series of mural paintings found in several ancient churches located in the Spanish Pyrenees. These depict the Virgin Mary holding an illuminated *graal*-like serving bowl, possibly a symbol of the Christian feast of Pentecost (seven Sundays after Easter), that is, the descent of the Holy Spirit upon the Apostles of Jesus after his Resurrection.[35] In *Perceval*, Chrétien seems obsessed with Pentecost to the point of mentioning it as occurring (illogically) twice within one year (lines 2785, 9192).[36] Goering goes so far as to assert that the true origin of the word is Spanish Catalan, from whence it migrated to southern France.[37] The most memorable and gripping of these paintings is still to be seen in the apse of the village church of San Clemente de Taüll (or Tahull), and shows the Virgin with "a fiery Grail" in hand; it is dated December 1123, predating Chrétien's work by some 60 years.[38]

The premise of Spanish origins for the grail of *Perceval* is buttressed by a number of collateral arguments. A growing number of literary critics believe that the origins of courtly love poetry itself came from Andalusia (see Chapter 2). In addition, and thanks to popular fictions such as *The Da Vinci Code*, there appears to be a groundswell of belief that the Cathar heresies stamped out by the orthodox church during the Albigensian Crusades of the 13th century (see Chapter 7) were somehow connected to the story of the grail. This is especially true since one of the last holdout fortresses of the Cathars (Montségur) was situated in the Pyrenees as well. Problematically, though, this particular view, like most other Judeo-Christian theories, sees the grail as a physical religious relic or historical artifact, rather than as a mystical, incorporeal symbol of the Pentecost. Goering himself acknowledges that Chrétien's creation of the grail may have been a great conjointure or convergence of cultural influences, only one of which came from Spain.[39] In doing so he summarizes the various Celtic myths, Indo-European fertility cults, Christian-Jewish-Cathar rituals, and secret, non-orthodox wisdom of the ancients.[40] The linking of the grail image to that of the Virgin Mary (and her worship) then first becoming popular, may have also represented a Christian reaction to the secular woman-worship so prominent among the French troubadours and Islamic poets. In the final analysis, to this writer at least, Chrétien's grail in *Perceval* clearly came from several directions at once. These multiple directions included, not necessarily exclusively, the Spanish Pyrenees (via the troubadours), Celtic England (via the Breton jongleurs), and, taking the poet at his word, a now lost book given to him by his patron, Philip of Flanders.

The frustration of any Arthurian scholar trying to unravel the mysteries of the Grail in Chrétien's *Perceval* were well articulated by Holmes:

> It may seem to many that there is not a great deal keeping Grail critics apart. We all accept the influence of non–Christian legends and other non–Christian source materials, and both sides agree that there was an eventual Christianization. The disagreement centers on the amount of intended symbolism found in the poem, and the suggested "message."[41]

No kidding! The staggering amount of critical disagreement in this area is fueled by the allegorical nature of the romance itself. We moderns are not used to allegory, nor do we expect and take delight in it as did medieval audiences. Alas, we are too often simply aggravated by it. Why won't poets just say what they mean? Any pleasure in ambiguity is lost on us. As Topsfield helpfully reminded us, however, "Despite the outward clarity of his narrative, Chrétien is an essentially enigmatic writer. He understates, inspires, suggests."[42] Thus, to look for cut-and-dried meanings in these romances is not only a futile exercise, but one that can take the fun out of the whole experience. An even bigger danger inherent to a blinkered interpretive approach is that we might miss suggested, intended meanings happening to go against whatever we are used to hearing, or for that matter, want to hear at all. One such omnipresent layer of influence was the extremely complex and often unpleasant relations between the French Christians and French Jews of Chrétien's own time. This topic will be explored in the next chapter. For now, with respect to the Holy Grail, perhaps it is best to remember that the Arthurian world is, ultimately, a kingdom of the mind, rather than a physical world.

Chapter 23

Ecclesia Versus Synagoga

A close look at Chrétien's symbolic use of the grail, lance, and *tailleor* in *Perceval* inevitably leads to a discussion of the Jews in 12th-century France, particularly those living in Champagne and Troyes at the time, who happened to be quite numerous. This is not necessarily to adopt or deny any particular theory of origins connecting the two, but rather to acknowledge at least the possibility of a connection. Such an acknowledgement is appropriate given the documented, intense interaction between Jews and Christians during that time and in that place, which was due in part to their close, physical proximity to one another. Such analysis is also necessary given the overtly religious overtones of Chrétien's last, great, unfinished work. Admittedly, there is no firm or conclusive evidence that *Perceval* was influenced by the Jewish community in Champagne, but sometimes that which goes unspoken during a particular literary period is also that which is on everyone's mind at the moment. Indeed, we have no concrete idea as to who exactly the poet was who created these extraordinary romances, although a handful of good surmises can be made (see Chapter 24). All that can be said with relative certainty is that Chrétien, by the time he wrote his first Arthurian romance circa 1170, would have been well aware of the prominent Jewish presence in Troyes, as would any other half-intelligent person. Whether Christians condemned the influence of the Jewish minority, embraced it, or did both at different times, would of course depend upon the individual in question. The more complex the person, then likely the more complex his or her response to this external stimuli, and we can be fairly confident that the creator of the first Arthurian romances was a relatively complicated person.

To appreciate the full magnitude of Jewish presence in Champagne, a bit of background is in order. In short, Troyes during the 12th century was ground zero for Talmudic studies worldwide. The primary reason for this local fame was the legacy of its most famous native son — not Chrétien de Troyes, but rather the man sometimes known to history as Salomon ben Isaac, or Rabbi Shlomo Yitzhaki, best known simply by the acronym of Rashi (1040–1105). Rashi was born, taught, and died at Troyes. He is most famous for being the first extensive commentator on the Torah and Talmud. His works are still printed (and read) side-by-side with sacred Hebrew (and even some Christian) texts to this day. After being educated in Germany, Rashi returned to Troyes and by 1070 (soon after the Norman conquest of England) had established his own religious school.[1] Troyes continued to have thriving rabbinic institutions right up through the time of Chrétien and beyond, until Jews were formally expelled from France by the edict of King Philip Augustus in 1182.[2]

During the lifetime of Chrétien, the most well-known Jewish educator in Troyes was Rashi's grandson, Jacob ben Meir, better known as Rabbeinu Tam (1100–1171), also a distinguished poet in his own right. Rabbeinu Tam had settled within the friendly confines of his grandfather's hometown after having barely survived the holocaust of the Second Crusade while it passed through northeastern France. There he (along with the rest of the Jewish community) enjoyed the tolerance, protection and good will of Chrétien's patron, Count Henry the Liberal, who regularly consulted Jewish scholars on Old Testament religious matters, as well as economic issues. Troyes, as a major commercial center for France at the time, owed most of its affluence to finance and trade, which in turn led to a vigorous patronage and support for the literary arts by the nobility. Taking these factors into consideration, it can be safely assumed that Count Henry was far more knowledgeable and enlightened than most of his Christian contemporaries when it came to matters of Judaism. The same could be said for almost anyone living in Troyes at that time. As Urban Holmes wrote, "It is hard to believe there was little interchange of ideas, stories, and helping hands."[3] Chrétien would have been no exception.

The Second Crusade (1147–1149), prompted by the fall of Edessa in Syria to the Turks in 1144, was personally led by King Louis VII of France, along with his then-wife Eleanor of Aquitaine, and the Holy Roman Emperor, Conrad III of Germany.[4] Though completely thwarted in its attempt to reclaim lost Christian territories, the Second Crusade did manage to brutally massacre thousands of innocent Jews who happened to cross its path. It was from this same series of atrocities that Rashi's grandson, Rabbeinu Tam, had narrowly escaped before relocating to Troyes. As religious historian Karen Armstrong ruefully noted, "The crusading anti–Semitism of the West was making life intolerable for the Jewish communities...."[5] Noting that Christian intolerance of other religions was the norm (with the exception of places like Champagne and Troyes), Armstrong added, "The situation of the Jews in the Islamic empire, where there was no anti–Semitic persecution, was far happier...."[6] One cannot help but feel that the uniquely tolerant and multi-cultural environment in Troyes also gave impetus to the dawn of the Arthurian romance during the same period. It may well be that the name "Chrétien de Troyes," if in fact a pen name (see Chapter 24), was meant to publicly convey that the author was from Troyes but not Jewish himself— Troyes being a city normally associated with Judaism by the rest of Christian Europe.

Even in Champagne, however, the taint of anti–Semitism could run high. Perhaps nowhere was this prejudice more overtly symbolized than in church art. The popular theme of Christianity triumphant over Judaism was depicted in the personification of Ecclesia and Synagoga. These representations can still be viewed in stained glass and sculpture adorning gothic cathedrals throughout France, Germany, and England. One of the earliest and most outstanding examples of this motif may be seen not far from Troyes in the cathedral of Saint-Etienne at Châlons-en-Champagne, formerly known as Châlons-sur-Marne. The site of this edifice had been formally consecrated in 1147 by Pope Eugene III and Saint Bernard, two of the main architects of the Second Crusade. Within the oldest section of church, a Romanesque tower, is a spectacular stained glass window with an upper, semi-circular panel depicting the Christian church (Ecclesia) as a crowned woman holding the banner of the cross in her right hand and a holy chalice in her left. Below her is another semi-circular panel depicting Judaism as a blindfolded woman holding tablets of the Old Testament law in her right hand and symbols of Christ's passion in her left — a broken lance with a sponge on a pole. Between the two panels is an image of Christ crucified.[7] The message speaks for itself.[8] As pointed out by Urban Holmes and Sister Klenke, it also in many respects calls to mind elements of the Grail Procession in Chrétien's *Perceval*, which includes female figures, a bleeding lance, and of course the Grail itself, although Chrétien's *graal* (see Chapter 21) was more of a deep dish or bowl, and not a chalice per se.

The window in Châlons-sur-Marne was installed only a few years after the very first gothic structure, the Basilica of Saint-Denis, had been built on the outskirts of Paris under the supervision of Abbot Suger (see Chapter 20)—also still existing. Saint-Denis contains a similar restored stained glass window, one in which Christ grabs Synagoga by the hair in admonishment while simultaneously bestowing a benediction upon Ecclesia.[9] Chrétien de Troyes (or anyone else at the time, for that matter) would have to have been deaf, dumb, and blind not to be familiar with these highly suggestive color images, which were also outstanding examples of a relatively new art form. It would not be surprising if more artwork such as this existed during Chrétien's time in the Champagne region but has since been lost to the ravages of time. As things now stand, they represent a curious chapter in the history of western art that needs to be studied (and, for that matter, acknowledged) far more than it has been in the recent past.

The uniquely vigorous Jewish presence in Troyes, particularly its groundbreaking theological schools, prompted Christian attempts at imitation, as well as artistic expression. Peter Comestor (?–1178) was perhaps the outstanding French theologian of Chrétien's day, and like Rashi before him, was born in Troyes and first began teaching there. More than one scholar has deemed it likely that Comestor knew of Rashi through his grandson, Rabbeinu Tam, and was influenced by both of their work.[10] For example, Comestor was known to have quoted Andrew of Paris, who had explicitly used Rashi's text in his own biblical studies and was subsequently accused of "judaizing" by his Christian contemporaries.[11] Comestor served as the dean of the cathedral school of Saint-Pierre in Troyes between 1147 and 1164, before spending the rest of his intellectual career in Paris.[12] Although there is no proof (and probably never will be), it is nevertheless tantalizing to think that Chrétien — especially if he was educated as a cleric — may have been one of Comestor's students in Troyes. The dates and places certainly fit as a possible scenario. Interestingly, Comestor's masterpiece, the *Historia Scholastica* (written in Paris), was dedicated to the then–Bishop of Sens, Guillaume aux Blanches Mains, brother of Chrétien's patron, Count Henry. This direct connection provides yet another good reason to believe that Chrétien probably belonged to the outstanding circle of literary activity then revolving around the ruling family of Champagne, as well as being part of its extensive kinship network within the French church hierarchy.

It would be pleasing to write that, as a likely member of this distinguished group, Chrétien too had an enlightened, benevolent attitude towards the Jewish population of his namesake town, and that the poet was way ahead of his time in this regard. Unfortunately, there is not a shred of concrete evidence to indicate such an attitude; moreover, there is stark indication showing quite the opposite to be the case. In his final, unfinished work, *Perceval*, Chrétien jars the sensibilities of modern readers with a vicious anti–Semitic outburst. As the hero of the story meets up fortuitously with his hermit uncle on Good Friday, the otherwise pious monk, while explaining the meaning of Christ's passion to his nephew, interjects (and to no particular theological purpose): "The traitor Jews, who should be slain like dogs...."[13]

The line reads like a slogan for the very worst aspects of the Second Crusade; nor can this sentiment be dismissed as out of context, since Perceval's uncle is otherwise an admirable, even exemplary individual. Clearly, the personal feelings of the poet are being expressed here. At this point, all readers are forced to contemplate whether the celebrated inventor of the Arthurian romance was himself a railing anti–Semite.

Some critic-apologists have been trying to explain away the poet's attitude for over a century, but it seems far easier to accept it for what it is, just as we would for Shakespeare or any other great writer who did not happen also to be a perfect human being. It may well be that Chrétien was allowing inner racial and religious hostilities to surface because, for one, Henry the Liberal (d. 1181) was likely dead by the time this line was written, and secondly, because he may have been pandering to popular feelings in France when the Jews were expelled by King Philip Augustus in 1182. The dedicatee of *Perceval*, Philip of Flanders, was known to have traits of a religious fanatic, and whatever his differences with the king at the time may have been, hostility towards the Jews may have been a shared sentiment. In his prologue, Chrétien flatters his new patron as one who is not a "cunning hypocrite" (line 29)—a possible veiled slur against the Jews, since the context of the entire passage is taken from Matthew.[14] A few lines later (49–50), Chrétien mistakenly attributes a quote from The First Letter of John to Saint Paul, the latter being among Christians the prototypical Jew who not only converted to the new faith but eventually became foremost among its preachers and apologists.[15] Whether or not the poet was intentionally making this misattribution, one gets the definite impression that he wanted to make a statement to the effect that true charity (as practiced by his patron, Philip) was represented by converted Jews such as Paul and Matthew rather than the unconverted.[16] The only possible excuse for this repulsive tact is that the passages in question were written and inserted by someone besides Chrétien, which is possible but nevertheless seems unlikely given the recurrent theme in the prologue.

If, on the other hand, Chrétien indeed held such an attitude, he would have been far from alone among his French contemporaries; nor would he have been the only one at the time who was tying the Arthurian legends to a specific criticism of Jewish religious beliefs. During the third quarter of the 12th century, about the same time Chrétien was creating the Arthurian romance as an art form, Gautier de Châtillon in his *Tractatus contra Judaeos* compared Jews who were still looking for the Messiah to Bretons foolishly waiting for King Arthur to return to life.[17] To repeat, this was at a time in which the new French king had officially banished the Jews from the country, so it would have been the politically correct line to take, as well as a highly popular refrain among the ignorant and the bigoted. Soon after this, as Crusader kingdoms in the Middle East began to unravel and disintegrate, the sentiment became more and more militant. The Jews made convenient scapegoats: they were at hand, defenseless, and Christians utterly depended on their commercial acumen to maintain a healthy economy. If Chrétien found himself joining in the vitriol for a few poetic lines right at this particular moment, then we should not be entirely amazed. After all, not everyone— not even a poetic genius or a king—could be as broad-minded and tolerant as Henry the Liberal or, for that matter, his countess, Marie of Champagne.

The final chapter in the bizarre relationship between the Arthurian legends and Judaism came about a century after Chrétien's death, when in 1279 there appeared a little known but endlessly fascinating Hebrew manuscript known to medieval specialists as the *Melech Artus* or "King Arthur."[18] The anonymous author of this work, one that was left unfinished like *Perceval* a century before, was probably writing in northern Italy and translated from the Italian language, but the ultimate original sources, more or less by scholarly consensus, were written in Old French like Chrétien's romances. These sources primarily included the anonymous *Mort Artu* and a later prose version of the Merlin story.[19] These in turn had been largely derived from the works of Chrétien, Wace, and Geoffrey of Monmouth.[20] In a very real sense, the appearance of the *Melech Artus* in 1279 represented the interaction between Christian and Jewish polemicists within the context of the Arthurian legends coming full circle. Close study of these works reveals that, in the end, any tradition can be glossed and appropriated for any purpose, no matter how seemingly contrary to the original author's intent. At least in the case of the *Melech Artus*, the anonymous author was not pretending to do anything but what he explicitly claimed—to offer moral edification for readers and to give himself some personal peace of mind by the act of writing it.[21]

Although there is no overt, detailed connection between the plot of the *Melech Artus* and Chrétien's earlier romances, several commonalities are discernable, which in turn become more fascinating as they are compared. As previously noted (see Chapters 1 and 22) Chrétien appears to have singlehandedly invented, or at least to have been the first to record in versions coming down to us, the popular Arthurian themes of the Grail Quest and Lancelot's adultery with Queen Guinevere. The author of *Melech Artus*, like most other medieval continuators of the legend, fully employs both of these specific themes, but also gives them a distinctively Hebrew twist. Lancelot is portrayed not as a Breton superhero-caricature of courtly love, but rather as a Jewish, Samson-like deliverer with a fatal weakness of the flesh. As for the grail, whether one views it as the "Holy Grail" favored by later French poets or as the more mysteriously original *graal* of Chrétien (but one still having latent, Christian overtones), this symbol is completely transformed as well. It becomes, in the fine, modern English translation of Curt Leviant, a "dish"; more specifically, a *tamchuy*, the mandatory charity dish of the Hebrew liturgy.[22] Particularly resonant to any reader already familiar with Chrétien's works is the close resemblance of the Jewish dish of charity to Chrétien's original vision of the *graal*, not as a cup or chalice, but rather as a large serving dish or bowl. This is not to say that Chrétien was thinking of the Jewish *tamuchy* when he introduced the Grail Procession in *Perceval*, although this may be possible. Instead, it is more likely that the anonymous author of the *Melech Artus* was utilizing a very clever (and effective) inversion of the originally Christian or pagan symbol of the grail for his own purposes within the context of Judaism. Thus it becomes an emblem of charity and selflessness, as well as the basis of an essential lesson in morality.

Leviant also perceptively notes in his commentary that the influence of Sephardic Judaism from Spain, with its more secular and less moralistic outlook, exerted a strong influence on the creation of this work. This may have been partially the result of the piece being produced in northern Italy, where many Sephardic Jews had migrated. Leviant emphasized that, "contrary to Ashkenaz, in Spain and Italy 'knowledge and religion met in peace.'"[23] This "knowledge" was represented by more than the troubadours of Aquitaine or the jongleurs of Brittany, it was primarily manifested in the scientific advances coming out of Spain. Its most outstanding embodiment was in the person of the Jewish Aristotelian philosopher, Rabbi Moses Maimonides or "Rambam" (1135–1204), one of the most brilliant minds of the age and a near-exact contemporary of Chrétien de Troyes.[24] As with Chrétien, the works of Maimonides represented a great synthesis of seemingly conflicting sources that included ancient pagan and Judeo-Christian inspiration. The same multi-cultural cross-currents and hitherto taboo influences, elements revolutionizing religious thought at the time such as the *Mishneh Torah* of Maimonides or the Christian Scholasticism of Aquinas, were also helping to crystallize the King Arthur legends in the minds of French poets.

Despite the irresistible pull of secular humanism emanating from the Iberian Peninsula and southern France, however, the main purposes of the *Melech Artus* and of most early Arthurian literature remained twofold. It edified, as well as entertained. Whichever came first depended mainly on the reader or listener. If the secular influence of Maimonides on the *Melech Artus* was pervasive, the moralistic precedent of Rashi was inescapable. This same duality of purpose is found in all of Chrétien's romances and popular

Arthurian literature. It is adaptable to almost any specific religion or creed, hence universal in its appeal. And why not? Almost by necessity, the Christianization of the King Arthur legends in the first place involved incorporation of Old Testament material. This could be employed as backdrop for Christian teachings, or for its own sake as in the *Melech Artus*. Moral lessons based on stories of King David could be readily transposed or re-filtered into morality tales about King Arthur.[25] If the inventor of the Arthurian romance was surrounded by xenophobic images of Ecclesia triumphant over Synagoga in art, such as those still to be seen at Châlons-en-Champagne and Saint-Denis, then is it so surprising that a later defender of Synagoga should call for an "Arthurian" revision? Perhaps it all boils down to the medieval debate over the true meaning of religious charity — the "cunning hypocrite" so despised by Chrétien, the "secret" almsgiver praised in Matthew, the mystical *graal* reduced to a physical holy relic, or the dish of charity as the very symbol of true religion itself. These issues finally lead us to a central and difficult question: who exactly was Chrétien de Troyes?

Chapter 24

Chrétien Who?

> *He was one of the first explorers of the human heart, and is therefore rightly to be numbered among the fathers of the novel of sentiment—* C.S. Lewis.[1]

King Arthur tends to be thought of as a historical personage (at least to varying degrees), the same way one thinks of William Shakespeare or other famous dead white men. If Arthur really existed, however, he was likely a much different person from the image most of us envision. For those who love to read (in the English language, at least), the name Arthur is typically linked to brilliant writers such as Tennyson and Twain. Those who hold graduate degrees may be a bit more sophisticated and know about the likes of Malory, Geoffrey of Monmouth, T.H. White, and yes, all those medieval French writers, including the great poet who pioneered the romance genre. Now that we know who Chrétien de Troyes was, a more troubling question arises; namely, just who *was* Chrétien de Troyes?

Lewis Thorpe, one of Geoffrey of Monmouth's English translators, made the important observation: "It frequently happens that we do not know even the name of the author of a medieval masterpiece. When we are given a name, that is often the sum of our knowledge."[2] Thorpe then went on to show that in the case of Geoffrey, we do possess additional bits and pieces about the man and his life. For example, we know with firm confidence that Geoffrey was a churchman who studied at Oxford, later became Bishop of Asaph, and died around 1155. This was a writer who lived an entire generation before Chrétien in a more remote part of the world, wrote exclusively in Latin with only two major works to his credit (as opposed to Chrétien's five), and was much less influential than Chrétien in terms of long-term literary influence. In fact, since his own time, Geoffrey has been roundly and rightfully criticized as a brazen falsifier of history (see Chapter 9). Yet we seem to know far more about Geoffrey of Monmouth than Chrétien de Troyes. How can this be? Is it because Chrétien wrote in French or (worse for Francophobes) wrote in French about "English" matters? Another possibility, currently gaining momentum in some academic circles, is that Chrétien himself wanted his identity obscured, a view which we shall examine presently. One thing is for certain: without Chrétien de Troyes, whoever he may have been, there would be no Arthurian romance as we know it today.

The assertion made from the outset in this study — that we have no way of knowing the exact details of this towering figure's life — cannot be overemphasized or repeated too often. Canadian translator David Staines summed up the mystery:

> Of almost no other major writer of the Middle Ages do we know so little. All we have are his own brief comments in his romances, and with these we have to create a portrait of the writer who is accurately called the father of Arthurian romance and who is, indeed, the creator of medieval romance.[3]

It would of course be completely unrealistic to expect biographies, memoirs, letters, original manuscripts, and the like for a medieval poet, all of which would in fact be quite unusual for any writer before the 18th century Enlightenment. Nevertheless, for a writer of Chrétien's unique stature one would at least expect to find a few more anecdotes (even critical or carping ones) by contemporaries or those who followed in his immediate wake, especially given the tens of thousands of lines added to his highly-popular romances by various continuators. As they say in courtrooms, silence is another form of testimony, and the relative silence surrounding Chrétien during and after his lifetime seems completely at odds with the sweeping international impact of his Arthurian opus. Are we dealing with another case of concealed literary identity, or instead, a historical fluke at a time when books and learning were becoming newly important to those few who had the time, wealth, and leisure to enjoy such things? The question merits brief exploration.

As noted in the previous chapter, reputable scholars such as Urban Holmes have proposed, not unreasonably, that Chrétien de Troyes was perhaps a Christianized Jew, renamed at baptism, occasionally alluding in *Perceval* to official on-going attempts by the church to convert others like himself. Part of this assertion rests on a very narrow reading of the text, just as Gaston Paris once proposed that Chrétien must have been a herald-at-arms, based on one single, ambiguous passage in *Lancelot*.[4] These speculations follow the time-honored tradition of trying to understand an author's background and attitudes through the author's writings. Another reason Holmes postulated Chrétien as a convert from Judaism was the common-sense observation that during the 12th century, Troyes was among the greatest European centers of Jewish learning and culture, as well as commerce and finance.[5] Weighed against all of these arguments are stark facts such as the poet's anti–Semitic invective in *Perceval* and his repeated misquotations of Saint Paul, both of which, however, can be explained away if one works hard enough at it.[6] All in all, while the Jewish origin of this pivotal literary figure is not out of the question — indeed, if true, he would join an already distinguished pantheon of writers with Jewish heritage — in the final analysis, the theory seems more an example of highly-trained academics reading way too much into way too little. Far more likely is the scenario that any writer of genius — Jewish or not — coming of age during the mid–12th century would have been directly or indirectly influenced by the intense foment of intellectual activity centered around the Franco–Jewish community at Troyes.

Ethnic and religious identities aside, there are many who agree that Holmes and other proponents of "Chrétien" as an adopted name may have been onto something. The name was possibly a moniker for "I am a Christian from Troyes"; that is, a Christian from a French city that during the 12th century was known primarily among literate Frenchmen as a town of Jewish learning, finance, and commerce. This mantle may have been especially necessary (as credentials) for a Catholic clergyman writing epic romantic poetry while not living in Troyes at the time, as many have suggested. Some have proposed — quite logically — that Chrétien may have been in England while producing his earlier works such as *Erec and Enide*. As Professor Cline concluded, "The possibility that Chrétien is a pseudonym or a name taken in religion cannot be excluded." It would not have been the first time that "Chrétien" — an uncommon name in Champagne — was used as an alias in France. For example, Thomas à Becket had very recently used "Chrétien" to disguise himself while hiding from King Henry II in Chartres.[7] One of the few things that most agree upon is that Chrétien had taken some degree of holy orders in the church, if for no other reason than such a step was almost always necessary to receive the higher education conspicuously displayed in his poetry. Holmes spoke for many when he wrote, "To us it seems impossible to assume that Chrétien was not a clerk."[8]

No one has more thoroughly or succinctly explored the current state of the Chrétien authorship question than Ruth Harwood Cline in her essay introduction to *Erec and Enide*, titled "The Identity of Chrétien de Troyes."[9] Appropriately enough, she begins with, "The identity of Chrétien de Troyes is a mystery,"[10] and concludes that his biography "will always remain a matter of conjecture."[11] In between, Cline declares, "Based on the internal evidence of his works, I am persuaded that Chrétien de Troyes was an aristocrat in holy orders."[12] This internal evidence includes, but is not limited to, the poet clearly demonstrating his classical education, a cosmopolitan knowledge of European geography, repeated allusions to political and current events, the moral outlook of a churchman, relative contempt for the lower social classes (especially merchants), a belief in the inherent virtue of nobility, and accurate familiarity with aristocratic court manners and customs of the times.[13] It is not our purpose here to regurgitate or critique that comprehensive overview. We would, though, like to add one additional observation, namely that the two-century-old discussion/disagreement among scholars on this topic, from a distance at least, appears to be relatively logical and restrained among the professionals engaged in it. By contrast, and during roughly the same historical period, the tumultuous and too-often acrimonious debate over the true identity of William Shakespeare the writer has been filled with bitter vituperation punctuated by outbursts of dismissive condescension or (worse) full-blown character assassination.[14] In short, all questions of literary authorship should be approached with the same comparative impartiality and disinterestedness as has the modern scholarly quest for the true identity of Chrétien de Troyes.

This is not to say that sharp disagreements never arise. For an important personage whose dates of birth and death are unknown, however, such arguments are not only natural but desirable. A competing view of Chrétien's background has not been without its supporters. Some have argued that he was of humble origin and made himself into what he later became, pulling himself up by his literary bootstraps. Professor Evelyn Birge Vitz of New York University has postulated that Chrétien was a prodigiously talented minstrel who could have acquired his education second-hand (rather than with formal schooling), thus having only a limited knowledge of Latin, not traveling beyond France, and adopting the values of his social superiors who employed him.[15] The unlikely but admittedly plausible image of Chrétien as a poor-boy-made-good may not represent the majority view among specialists, but still deserves and receives a respectful hearing from them. One day it may even be proven true. At the very least, it is essential that contrasting, speculative biographies of writers be fully presented before we can individually decide for ourselves which scenario is more likely to have occurred in actuality. At the risk of repeating the obvious, proper critical thinking demands that contradictory interpretations of an author's life and works always be given a full and impartial hearing — admittedly, a task easier said than done.

Roger Sherman Loomis, whose *Development of Arthurian Romance* was written after a lifetime of devoted study and reflection, remarked that various disagreements and schools of thought in Arthurian scholarship are similar to those found within the Shakespeare authorship question.[16] This divergence of academic opinion has been particularly applicable to interpretations over the meaning and sources for the Holy Grail legend in Chrétien's *Perceval* (see Chapter 22). Many experts, for example, would object even to my use of the adjective "Holy" or the use of capital letters for either word. And such criticism may be well-founded, since Chrétien himself never uses the exact phrase "Holy Grail." Even the most exacting critics, though, would be unlikely to question a colleague's sanity or personal values over the matter. One might be tagged ignorant, stupid, or presumptuous, but not insane or evil — at least not typically. Within the Shakespeare authorship question, by contrast, such *ad hominem* attacks are so frequent and savage as to be nearly taken for granted by partisans regularly involved in that debate. Those who continue to explore the identity and background of Chrétien de Troyes (or any other major literary figure) should rightfully be beware of this infection.

Before leaving this fascinating topic, a few general observations should be added regarding whether "Chrétien" was a penname. While it is certainly possible that Chrétien de Troyes was pseudonym for a writer who wished to disguise a (then) better-known identity, there are at least two good reasons for exercising caution before accepting this assertion as likely fact. The first is that, to date, no firm or compelling alternative candidate known at the time by another name has been put forward. In cases of contested literary identity, the best argument for replacing an old candidate is the identification of a clearly superior new one, and this has yet to transpire in Chrétien's case. A second reason for hesitation is lack of motive for concealment; indeed, this is still perhaps the most powerful argument against those who doubt the traditional Shakespeare, and the same problem, perhaps to a greater degree, applies to Chrétien. The assertion that if Chrétien had an aristocratic or military background before he became a clergyman, then the undisguised public role of *trouvère* would be too disreputable, also has limitations. For one, literary activity during the 12th century was such a relatively new phenomenon that the "stigma of authorship," as it is sometimes referred to, had really yet to fully manifest itself in western culture.

Other noblemen had by then established outstanding literary reputations despite their high social ranks. The fact is that many, if not most, of the inventors of the Arthurian literary tradition, came from some kind of aristocratic or military background, and yet they did not deem it necessary to conceal their identities. The names of Wolfram von Eschenbach, Robert de Boron, and Thomas Malory, among others, immediately come to mind.[17] Even more to the point, the very first documented, troubadour poet was Duke William IX of Aquitaine, great-grandfather to Chrétien's patron Marie, Countess of Champagne (see Chapter 4). Other great literary patrons of the era such as King Henry II of England, and Marie's husband, Henry the Liberal, Count of Champagne, were noted as being among the best educated men of their times. Whatever the faults of these individuals may have been, lack of appreciation for the humanities and, in particular, the written word, does not appear to have been among them. One is inclined to wonder if, before the 13th century, a great writer was more likely to come from the ranks of the nobility rather than the commons, simply based on the monopolistic educational advantages enjoyed by the upper classes of feudal privilege.

On the other hand, it cannot be denied that Chrétien was not nearly as political a writer as Shakespeare; nor did he become anywhere nearly as famous as Shakespeare was in later centuries. In Chrétien's romances, one gets the distinct impression that social nobility is virtuous by definition, and contemporary political events are sometimes alluded to in an obvious manner, usually flattering to the French point of view, whether this be in Champagne or on the Thames. Nowhere in Chrétien, however, do we get the constant Shakespearean thread of "Englishmen unite and do what the monarchy tells you to do," particularly overt in the Bard's history plays. In Chrétien, the focus is never far away from the never-ending conflict between romantic, courtly love and military duty as a knight, a conflict inherent in the feudal system, or at least perceived to be inherent whenever feudal ideals were strictly imposed. World politics between fledgling European nation-states, as well as their Greek, Jewish, and Muslim neighbors, is always an afterthought or ornament in Chrétien's works, and little more than that. As a clergyman, he may have needed to exercise special caution given the sensitive, volatile relations between church and state during the era of Thomas à Becket. On the balance, however, it must be admitted that any political motivation for concealment in Chrétien would seem to have been very limited, especially in comparison to the volatile, super-charged political atmosphere of Elizabethan and Jacobean England. And Shakespeare, we can be fairly confident, was not a clergyman.

Lastly, it should be acknowledged that, given a steep upward trend in interest over the last century, Chrétien may one day, like Shakespeare, become a victim of his own success, although this is unlikely to occur any time soon. It may well happen that the achievement of Chrétien de Troyes is one day celebrated outside the French-speaking world the same way a Montaigne or Molière is now honored. One explanation for the passion aroused in biographical discussions of Shakespeare is that he, unlike Chrétien, has been universally adopted as a poet in a way few (if any) others have been previously. Once large numbers of people begin to take an interest in something, especially when many of these fans consist of unprofessional, biased or uncritical advocates for pre-conceived agendas, obscure subject matter can become hazier than ever, clouded by human emotion and endlessly conflicting shades of opinion. Maybe if Chrétien had achieved a fame like Shakespeare's, then specialists would have a harder time of it. Perhaps they would not have been as restrained as they have to date because there would have been far more intellectual baggage to carry along the way. Maybe his relative obscurity in the current world at large is, in some ways, an advantage for scholarship. Should this ever change, we would all do well to learn from the example of the "Bard of Avon" and avoid at all costs trying to contort great writers into things which they never were. Very few lovers of Shakespeare have managed to avoid it; and yet, to do this goes against the very spirit of education itself.

The status quo of Chrétien's obscurity outside the world of French medieval studies may indeed one day change. In 1914, Chrétien's first widely-known English translator, W.W. Comfort, accurately wrote that "Chrétien de Troyes has had the peculiar fortune of becoming the best known of the old French poets to students of mediæval literature, and of remaining practically unknown to any one else."[18] Not much has changed in this regard since 1914, but within the world of those interested in medieval literature, there has definitely been a groundswell, particularly during the last quarter century. Multiple English translations of Chrétien are now easy to find, at least in university libraries. Interest in all forms of Arthuriana continues to grow, which has certainly helped. English speakers inclined to learn a smattering of French are now quick to encounter Chrétien's name among the great French writers. Given his apparent religious bent of thought within the realm of secular, romantic poetry, this might help to spark more interest as well. In spite of all this, however, it is still quite easy in the year 2010 to receive a master's degree without being much aware of Chrétien de Troyes. Those of us who still read for pleasure, however, definitely want to know far more about the father of the Arthurian romance than has been taught in the past.

Whether one likes to read or not, whether one is religious or not, the influence of Chrétien de Troyes on our modern mindset is inescapable. For this reason alone he should be given more priority in world literature studies than he has in the past. We suspect that many men and women who know nothing of the medieval French romancers still aspire in real life to be like the heroes and heroines of Camelot created by those same artists so long ago. The poetic, romantic creations of Chrétien de Troyes vividly live on in our imaginations, though we may try to deny his importance. We could not erase these creations from our collective memory even if we wanted to. The author of *Lancelot, Yvain*, and *Perceval* might one day be completely forgotten, but his dreams and values will still be passed down to our children's children indefinitely. Such is the power of a good story well-told.

Conclusion

Whatever we have been, in some sort we are still. Neither the form nor the sentiment of this old poetry has passed away without leaving indelible traces on our minds. —C.S. Lewis.[1]

Chrétien de Troyes is *the* pivotal figure in the development of Arthurian romance — more so than Geoffrey of Monmouth, more so than Thomas Malory, more so than Alfred Tennyson. While relatively few of the macro-details normally associated with the legend are to be found in Chrétien's five major romances, the two biggest motifs — specifically, the Holy Grail and Lancelot's liaison with Guinevere — feature prominently; moreover, he was the very first writer to introduce these themes, whether they originally came from the poet's own imagination or, more likely, were lifted from primitive oral traditions that he correctly believed could be polished and thus improved upon for a larger, more cultivated audience. While Chrétien's immediate contemporaries and continuators, along with his predecessors Geoffrey and Wace, first supplied or rendered the bulk of data that permanently manifested itself through various strands of the tradition, it was Chrétien who, nearly singlehandedly, supplied something much more crucial. It was he who first injected the spirit of courtly love and romantic chivalry into what had previously been little more than a warrior myth. In this regard, only Marie de France (see Chapter 4) possibly preceded him, and if she did, she did so on a much more modest scale.[2] In essence, Chrétien's romances introduced the heart and soul of the Arthurian genre, at least in terms of feeling and attitude. As critics have noted, Chrétien was, above all, a great love poet. These qualities have made a far greater impression on audiences than any of Arthur's alleged swordfights or mêlées. For that matter, it is nowadays difficult, if not impossible, to think of King Arthur and his Roundtable knights as anything but a unified entity, and it was also Chrétien who first raised the knights to this singular equality. Nor let us forget that he was a consummate poet and storyteller whose works can be profitably studied in depth for sheer technical virtuosity, quite apart from their immeasurable, substantive contribution to the Arthurian tradition as a whole.

Far more surprising than Chrétien's shadowiness as a historical person is the lack of familiarity with his name in the English-speaking world, even among those who still use their spare time to read for pleasure. Almost everyone has heard of King Arthur, the paragon of "English" monarchs; similarly, non–English writers distant in time such as Dante, Virgil, and Homer typically evoke some degree of familiarity from anyone possessing the slightest interest in such things. Mention of Chrétien's name, on the other hand, will more often than not draw a blank stare from anyone other than a specialist in the field of medieval literature. Admittedly, before the late 19th century, this may have been true among specialists as well. Thanks only to the surge of popular interest in King Arthur during the Victorian era did Arthur's most important inventors finally come into a long overdue spotlight. Now, Chrétien at least enjoys a high (and continually growing) reputation among students of Arthurian romance. In spite of this encouraging trend, however, one wonders why it took eight centuries to transpire. Why did Chrétien's creation, the Arthurian romance, become bigger than the creator himself, so large that the inventor was nearly forgotten? And how was he forgotten so quickly? Perhaps a more troubling question is why Chrétien's reputation as a great poet and innovator in such a wide sphere of interest is unlikely to become better known to the general reading public any time soon.

Surely part of the reason for Chrétien's relative neglect today has to do with the stubbornly irrational anti–French attitude currently making the rounds throughout English-speaking society, particularly in the United States. Anything French — including medieval Arthurian poets — cannot be good, according to current populist thought. Those clinging to such views might pause to investigate the everyday benefits given to Anglo culture by the French (beginning with our own heavily Latinized language), as well as the simple fact that France has, to varying and reasonable degrees, been a consistent U.S. ally ever since the American Revolution. It must be conceded, however, that even if our rampant Francophobia were to be magically removed from the equation, other barriers would still exist to hinder or prevent full acknowledgment of Chrétien's contributions to western literature. Foremost among these barriers is language. Chrétien versified not merely in French, but in Old French, a medieval idiom requiring careful translation by specialized academics. Fortunately, this has been accomplished by a handful of dedicated translators working with little or no financial incentive, who have made their admirable handiwork available for all. Another major obstacle is a vast cultural divide between *Le Moyen Âge* and the 21st century. Had Chrétien (hypothetically) been an American poet writing in modern English, he still would have been writing from the perspective of a long-vanished feudal society. To minimally understand and appreciate these works, a reader must possess at least a smattering of knowledge pertaining to European life during the High Middle Ages.[3] This is possibly even more crucial to an adequate comprehension of pre-modern literature than any detailed knowledge of the writer's life. Last but certainly not least, there is the formidable human problem of false preconceptions. If one firmly believes or is determined to believe that the bulk of the Arthurian myth is founded upon historical facts, or that it is a myth primarily of Celtic origins, or that modern English writers alone are worth reading, then nothing else will make much of a difference. An open-minded reader must be the first step; otherwise, all else is futility.

This brings us back to the so-called "Matter of France," "Matter of Rome," and "Matter of Britain" as competing Arthurian source materials. These phrases were all originally employed by scholars to correctly remind everyone that the Arthurian legends represent an internationalized blend of diverse cultural influences. At some point, however, this became twisted around to imply that there were various arguments in favor of or against each one, and that one and only one could be the true representative of the tradition. This, we hope one would agree by now, would be a gross distortion. In terms of overall popularity, a good case could be made that there should be a "Matter of Germany" included in this group, given that Wagnerian, operatic updates of the Arthurian legends taken straight from medieval Teutonic sources have perhaps enjoyed the widest circulation among the general public over the last two centuries. Other factors tend to render any ethnocentric debate over pure ownership of Arthur meaningless and misleading. For one, arguments against the "Matter of France" have been occasionally stacked to suggest that the category only includes early French works, such as those about Roland and Charlemagne, which, admittedly, played a secondary and preliminary role in the entire process.[4] French heavy hitters such as Chrétien, Marie, and Wace are typically excluded from their obviously rightful place while others, such as Geoffrey, are spoken of as if they were surely native Anglo-Saxons, as opposed to transplanted Bretons and Normans, a much more likely scenario (see Chapter 9). Regarding the "Matter of Rome," this should be viewed as no more than a euphemism for the ancient epic models that medieval French and Breton poets first tried to imitate. And yes, the "Matter of Britain" provided necessary material, but without learned help from the continent, it would have sunk into the same oblivion suffered by most European lore from the Dark Ages. One could say that the "Matter of Britain" and "Matter of Rome" are really incorporated within the "Matter of France," since medieval French romancers drew upon Celtic folklore and Latin classics, then combined these two with other exotic elements to create something never previously seen or heard.

In studying the ongoing enthusiasm for the Arthurian legends among modern audiences, one cannot ignore a gender gap, or more precisely, a gender schism.[5] Men tend to like war and magic; women often prefer love and romance. The tradition has always offered plenty of both, which has surely helped to maintain its wide appeal. This dichotomy in topical focus has been present from the very times during the 11th and 12th centuries in which French *troubadours*, *jongleurs*, and *trouvères* (including Chrétien) realized they could make a good living by integrating into the Arthurian mix tales of romantic love for their mostly female audiences. One could go further and say that, without this dichotomy, the legends would be less engaging. In the final analysis, however, it must be asserted that love interest triumphs over military prowess in these tales. Lancelot, Yvain, Cligès, and Erec are all great heroes and protectors of the weak, but behind every great man stands a woman, as the saying goes. It is true that Chrétien's last and incompletely sketched hero, Perceval, ultimately pursues the Holy Grail, but he first found a true sweetheart, while his chivalrous role model Gawain is arguably presented as the poet's vision of an ideal, unattached ladies' man. At the end of the day, it is the emotional vulnerability of these heroes and heroines that cause them to leap off the page and become relatable — not their physical beauty or their reliable arms, although these qualities are plentiful as well.

One final observation: Chrétien the poet allows us to glimpse a vanished world that may provide more insight into our own society than most of us might care to admit. This no longer extant world goes well beyond the generic, medieval society of Europe, which eventually gave way to the Renaissance and Reformation; it extends to former physical places and political entities once believed to be thoroughly stable and solid. The crusader kingdom of *Outremer*, the trans-channel Angevin empire of Henry and Eleanor, the affluent, powerful kingdom of Aquitaine itself, Norman Sicily and southern Italy — all had been wiped off the map within a century after Chrétien's death. Even the old French city of Troyes — known by its most famous namesake — had burned to rubble before the final decade of the 12th century. To read this poetry with any cognizance of the times in which it was written is to be highly conscious of its snapshot-like quality. It was a great landscape, but one that would not last much longer. He who helped to immortalize Camelot may have sensed this as well, adding urgency to every detail that he painted with his words. Thankfully, it is still there on the printed page for all to see.

Timeline of the High Middle Ages, 1000–1300

1000 • Beginning of the Second Millennium C.E.; Europe emerges from the Dark Ages

1020s • *The Neck-Ring of the Dove* by Ibn Hazm

1045–1099 • Life of Rodrigo Diaz ("Ed Cid")

1050–1100 • *The Song of Roland*, earliest surviving French epic

1050s • Normans conquer southern Italy

1064 • Siege of Barbastro in Spain by Normans and Duke William VIII of Aquitaine

1066 • Normans conquer England

1070s • Normans conquer Sicily

1096–1099 • First Crusade and conquest of Jerusalem

1128 • Council of Troyes; formation of the Templar Order

1136 • *History of the Kings of Britain* by Geoffrey of Monmouth

1143 • First Latin translation of the Qur'an commissioned by Peter the Venerable

1144 • First Gothic Cathedral design at Saint Denis Basilica outside of Paris

1147–1149 • Second Crusade

1150 • *Life of Merlin* by Geoffrey of Monmouth

1152 • Marriage between Louis VII of France and Eleanor of Aquitaine annulled

1153 • Death of Saint Bernard of Clairvaux

1154 • Henry II and Eleanor of Aquitaine begin Angevin rule
1155 • *Roman de Brut* by Wace
1163 • Construction begins of Notre Dame Cathedral in Paris
circa 1170 • Marie de France active as a poet
1170 • Saint Thomas à Becket murdered at Canterbury
1170s • *Roman de Rou* by Wace
1170–1180 • Chrétien de Troyes (dates of birth and death unknown) active as a poet
1180 • Louis VII of France dies and is succeeded by Philip Augustus
1180s • *The Art of Courtly Love* by Andreas Capellanus
1181 • Death of Count Henry "the Liberal" of Champagne
1187 • Crusaders defeated by Saladin at Hattin; Jerusalem falls
1187–1192 • Third Crusade
1188 • Center city of medieval Troyes destroyed by fire
1189 • Death of Henry II
1190 • Death of Count Philip of Flanders
1190–1191 • Discovery of Arthur's tomb at Glastonbury announced
1198 • Death of Marie de Champagne
1202–1204 • Fourth Crusade
1204 • Death of Eleanor of Aquitaine
1209–1229 • Albigensian Crusades
1248–1254 • Seventh Crusade
1270 • Eighth Crusade; death of Saint Louis
1271–1272 • Ninth Crusade
1295–1298 • Marco Polo returns from China and begins memoirs
1300 • Start of the 14th century C.E. (tentative beginnings of the Renaissance)

Chapter Notes

Introduction

1. Loomis, *Arthurian Romance*, p. 32.
2. These five works were *Erec and Enide, Cligès, Lancelot, Yvain,* and *Perceval.*
3. Paris, p. 66.
4. *Yvain* (Cline), p. xi.
5. *Yvain* (Cline), p. ix.
6. Topsfield, p. 16. Urban Holmes, paraphrasing Julian Harris, gives a good summary of Chrétien's remarkably brisk, unpredictable and engaging style. For example, like Shakespeare three centuries later, he loved to mix comic and tragic elements. See Holmes, pp. 25–26.
7. Hanning & Ferrante, pp. 1, 5.
8. *Yvain* (Cline), pp. vii–viii.
9. Owen, p. ix.
10. Comfort, p. xvi.
11. Duggan, p. 327.
12. Luttrell, p. 1.
13. Loomis, p. 66.
14. Chambers, p. 168.
15. Gibbon, Vol. 2, p. 1213.
16. Gibbon, Vol. 2, p. 1212.
17. Mel Ferrer plays King Arthur and a stunningly miscast Ava Gardner is Queen Guinevere.
18. Among these scholars, Loomis names W. Foerster and W. Golther in Germany, E. Faral in France, and W.W. Newell and J. Bruce in the United States. See Loomis, *Celtic Myth*, pp. 4–5.
19. Luttrell (quoting G. Jones and T. Jones) cites the Welsh *Mabinogion* and Chrétien's *Erec and Enide* as an example. See Luttrell, p. 240.
20. Luttrell, p. 253.
21. Holmes, p. 21.
22. An excellent summary of the literary and political influences shaping the poet's world can be found in Duggan, Chapter One, titled "Chrétien and His Milieu."
23. Owen, p. xviii.
24. These three operatic works are *Lohengrin, Tristan and Isolde,* and *Parsifal.*
25. Gibbon, Vol. 2, pp. 1212–1213.
26. *Erec and Enide* (Cline), p. ix.
27. Fourrier proposed the following dates: *Erec and Enide* (1170); *Cligès* (1176); *Lancelot* (1177); *Yvain* (1177–1179 or 1181); and *Perceval* (1181). See Frappier, p. 6. Contemporary American specialists such as Joseph Duggan (among others) have endorsed this dating as well. See Duggan, p. 6.

Chapter 1

1. C.S. Lewis, p. 29.
2. Lerner and Loewe's *Camelot* premiered on Broadway in 1960, featuring a stellar cast that included Goulet, Richard Burton, Julie Andrews, and Roddy McDowall. A movie version was filmed in 1967.
3. To give only one example, early in *Lancelot* (line 40) the poet has the royal court at Camelot conversing in French as a sign of refinement and culture.
4. Duggan, p. 230.
5. *Lancelot* (Cline), p. x.
6. See Holmes, p. 88. "Combined poem" refers to the fact that Chrétien's poem was completed by another acknowledged hand.
7. This perhaps reluctantly-accepted commission not only resulted in the groundbreaking *Lancelot,* it probably inspired (as an

anti-thesis) Chrétien's masterpiece *Yvain* as well (see Chapter 16).

8. Loomis, *Arthurian Romance*, p. 54.

9. Chrétien was unusual for his times in his apparent empathy for the ironic attitude in Ovid towards love. More common was the interpretation of Ovid's work with complete seriousness, or, as C.S. Lewis labeled it, "Ovid misunderstood." See Lewis, pp. 5–8.

10. In turn, French knowledge of classical authors such as Ovid may have filtered in through Spanish Andalusia. See Holmes & Klenke, p. xv.

11. It cannot be repeated too often that the Countess Marie of Champagne was the daughter of Eleanor of Aquitaine and the great-granddaughter of William IX, the acknowledged father of troubadour poetry. The medieval conventions or pretenses of courtly love could also be viewed as an anti-thesis to the Tristan legend, as least in its more primitive form. Troubadour influences on *Lancelot* such as Marcabru and Bernart de Ventadorn have been noted. See Holmes & Klenke, pp. xv–xvi. As for direct classical references, two (among many) include Virgil's *Aeneid* and Ovid's *Metamorphoses*. See *Lancelot* (Cline), p. 220, n. 3803, and p. 221, n. 4157.

12. See *Lancelot* (Cline), pp. 206–207, n. 35, and *Lancelot* (Raffel), pp. 233–234.

13. Holmes & Klenke, pp. xvi–xvii.

14. *Lancelot* (Cline), p. xiii. Saint Gildas was also closely associated with Glastonbury, one of the most popular proposed sites for the Arthurian isle of Avalon. See Holmes & Klenke, p. 15. The abduction theme appears to have been Welsh in origin. See also *Lancelot* (Raffel), p. 231. Caradoc of Llancarfan, like Geoffrey of Monmouth (see Chapter 9), was yet another writer of the period writing under Norman patronage.

15. For example, Chrétien alludes to a popular tradition that Lancelot has been raised from childhood in France by a fairy godmother (lines 2345–2353).

16. Holmes, pp. 98, 101.

17. *Erec and Enide* (Cline) p. 203, n. 5.

18. For example, there is a reference to knights crusading or taking "the cross" (line 5770), and the treachery of Gorre's citizens is compared to that of the Saracens (line 2134).

19. *Lancelot* (Raffel), p. 16. See also *Lancelot* (Cline), p. 213, n. 30.

20. *Lancelot* (Cline), p. xiv.

21. *Lancelot* (Cline), p. xxii.

22. *Lancelot* (Cline), pp. xiv-xv, 204–205, n. 27.

23. Chrétien signs off after line 6131, rather symbolically, as Lancelot is imprisoned in a tower. See *Lancelot* (Cline), pp. 207–208, n. 36.

24. *Lancelot* (Raffel), pp. 226–227.

25. Guinevere finally identifies him to a by-standing maiden, very discreetly, as "Lancelot of the Lake."

26. *Lancelot* (Cline), p. 35.

27. *Lancelot* (Raffel), p. 40.

28. *Lancelot* (Comfort), p. 286; (Owen), p. 201; (Staines), p. 185.

29. *Lancelot* (Cline), p. 124.

30. *Lancelot* (Comfort), p. 327; (Owen), p. 245; (Staines), pp. 224–225; (Raffel), p. 142.

31. *Lancelot* (Raffel), p. 142.

32. *Lancelot* (Cline), p. 87.

33. *Lancelot* (Raffel), p. 99.

34. *Lancelot* (Comfort), p. 309.

35. *Lancelot* (Owen), p. 226.

36. *Lancelot* (Staines), p. 208.

37. *Lancelot* (Raffel), p. 278.

38. *Lancelot* (Comfort), p. 329; (Raffel), p. 149; (Owen), p. 248; (Staines), p. 227; (Cline), p. 131.

39. *Lancelot* (Raffel), p. 149; (Staines), p. 227.

40. *Lancelot* (Raffel), p. 140; (Cline), p. 131; (Comfort), p. 329; (Owen), p. 248; (Staines), p. 227.

Chapter 2

1. Gibbon, Vol. 2, p. 2159.

2. The remark is often attributed to the composer Ludwig von Beethoven.

3. In contrast, Islam maintained its Iberian presence long after several major setbacks.

4. Tyerman, p. xiv.

5. Armstrong, *Gospel*, p. 79.

6. Gibbon, Vol. 2, p. 2160.

7. See *The Cabinet of Irish Literature* (Vol. IV) by Richard Francis Burton, edited by Charles Anderson Read (2007), pp. 94–95.

8. Andreas, p. 7. After citing Urban Holmes (note 30), Parry attributes all opposition of the backdoor theory to those would resist *any* outside influences to medieval love poetry beyond that of France and ancient Rome. See note 31.

9. The estimated date of composition for *The Ring of the Dove* is typically given as the 1020s, long before the Crusades or Norman expansion throughout the West (see Chapter 15). See D.L. Lewis, pp. xvi, 350.

10. Jayyusi, p. 473. See also the essays by Giffen (pp. 420–441) and Boase (pp. 457–482) contained in the 1991 Jayyusi anthology, as well as the independent 1977 work by Boase.
11. Boase, pp. 62–63, n. 43.
12. Andreas, pp. 8–12, 53–54.
13. Loomis, *Arthurian Romance*, p. 53.
14. D.L. Lewis, p. 354.
15. D.L. Lewis, p. 353.
16. Kibler, pp. 83–84.
17. Loomis also supported the theory that modern love poetry in the West began in "Moorish" Spain. See Loomis, *Arthurian Romance*, p. 53.
18. D.L. Lewis, p. 369.
19. *Erec and Enide* (Cline), p. 206, n. 30. Professor Duggan, citing Cline, specifically credits this aspect of Chrétien's romances to the transmission of new ideas to the West from Arabic literature and philosophy. See also Duggan, p. 139.
20. Armstrong, *History*, pp. 204–205.
21. Armstrong, *History*, p. 192. See also D.L. Lewis, p. 371.
22. Armstrong, *History*, p. 194. Interestingly, the work of both Averroës and Maimonides eventually became too liberal even for fundamentalist Muslims in Spain, and both were forced to flee for safety to North Africa later in life. Fittingly, Maimonides, an Aristotelian Jew, would in Egypt become court physician to Saladin — the man who probably did more than any one individual to thwart the objectives of the European Crusades. See also D.L. Lewis, p. 376.
23. D.L. Lewis, p. 376.
24. D.L. Lewis, p. 370.
25. For example, in the Staines translation see *Erec and Enide* (pp. 2, 31); *Cligès* (p. 146); *Lancelot* (pp. 190, 240, 252); *Yvain* (pp. 285, 295); and *Perceval* (p. 398).
26. Geoffrey of Monmouth, *History*, p. 236.
27. C.S. Lewis, p. 2.
28. C.S. Lewis, p. 4.

lished strong footholds in Great Britain long before these were permanently ratified by the conquest of 1066.
7. Duggan, p. 200.
8. Loomis, *Arthurian Romance*, pp. 21–22.
9. Loomis, *Arthurian Romance*, p. 32.
10. For example, in the Wace translation of Geoffrey (see Chapter 10), the occupation of the Breton *jongleur* is more or less equated with that of a professional liar. It should be added here as well that this writer is, himself, proudly of part–Irish heritage.
11. Loomis, *Celtic Myth*, p. 351.
12. For an illustration, see *Le Roi Arthur*, p. 77, figure 52.
13. Comfort, p. vii.
14. The Cimetière Montparnasse is one of the traditional, final resting spots for great poets and writers revered by the French. Some of these poets and writers (like Samuel Beckett) are not French by birth — honorary French, one might say.
15. Most scholars believe Chrétien died during the early 1180s, but a date as late as 1190 is possible.
16. This is the same Arthur later tragically portrayed in Shakespeare's history play, *King John*.
17. Chambers, pp. 108–109.
18. Chambers, pp. 110–114.
19. As students of English history know, Richard was made Henry's official successor but John ruled in Richard's absence during the Third Crusade and his subsequent captivity in Germany.
20. For an illustration, see *Le Roi Arthur*, p. 60, figure 159.
21. Strictly speaking, Queen Eleanor participated in the Second Crusade with her first husband, Louis VII of France, and her second husband, Henry II, was not a crusader. Above all, Eleanor was a great patroness of the arts. For example, the Wace translation of Geoffrey is dedicated to her.

Chapter 3

1. Loomis, *Arthurian Romance*, p. 33.
2. Some later traditions have Taliesin as the court poet of Camelot.
3. Chambers, pp. 23–24.
4. Owen, p. xiv.
5. Chambers, p. 150.
6. Loomis, *Arthurian Romance*, p. 33. The Normans and Bretons both had estab-

Chapter 4

1. C.S. Lewis, p. 11.
2. C.S. Lewis, p. 26.
3. Holmes & Klenke, pp. 25–26. In fact, this is precisely what Chrétien's hero Yvain does.
4. Mickle, p. 50.
5. Loomis, *Arthurian Romance*, p. 190.
6. Loomis, *Arthurian Romance*, p. 189.

7. Loomis, *Arthurian Romance*, p. 190.
8. Loomis, *Arthurian Romance*, p. 52.
9. C.S. Lewis, pp. 23–24.
10. C.S. Lewis, p. 24. See, for example, the prologue to *Yvain*.
11. C.S. Lewis (citing Alfred Jeanroy), p. 8.
12. Loomis, *Arthurian Romance*, p. 53.
13. Armstrong, *Gospel*, p. 81. She pointedly adds that "the Courtly Love ideal and the cult of the Virgin Mary do show some kind of rejection of the overwhelmingly masculine world of the early Middle Ages.... In Courtly love circles there was a similar rejection of the purely masculine; women were trying to refine the coarse and butch image of the knight." See p. 82.
14. As Ruth Harwood Cline wrote, "To Queen Eleanor of England and Countess Marie of Champagne, both married for dynastic reasons, and Marie to a much older man, love in marriage must have seemed a desirable but unobtainable objective." See *Erec and Enide* (Cline), p. xxi (citing June Hall McCash).
15. Given Eleanor's tremendous wealth and power, it is reasonable to speculate that almost every major literary work of that Anglo-Norman epoch owes some degree of debt to her example, if not support. These include Chrétien's important Arthurian predecessors Geoffrey and Wace. E.J. Mickle noted generally, "One cannot simply ascertain the exact relationship of these texts, except to note that they belong to the same literary milieu and derive from the same stylistic tradition." See Mickle, p. 147, n. 21.
16. *Erec and Enide* (Cline, citing Owen), p. 206, n. 31.
17. With respect to the first gothic edifice in Paris, Eleanor S. Greenhill wrote, "It would be rash indeed to deny to the Empress Eleanor a conscious role in the creation of the new visible symbol of Capetian imperial pretensions at Saint-Denis." See Kibler, p. 104.
18. Armstrong, *Gospel*, p. 83.
19. Kibler, pp. 38–39.
20. Leslie Topsfield was among several critics who noted a strong connection between the works of Chrétien and earlier troubadour poets such as Marcabru and Bernart de Ventadorn. See Topsfield, p. 8.
21. Mickle, p. 13.
22. Hanning and Ferrante, p. 1.
23. One commentator (John Fox) identifies Marie as the Abbess of Shaftsbury, the natural daughter of Geoffrey Plantagenet and thus the half-sister of King Henry II. See Mickle, pp. 20–21.
24. Chambers, pp. 142–144.
25. Béroul was a 12th-century Norman poet who produced a non-courtly version of the Tristan legend.
26. This chronology accepts the view that Chrétien died sometime during the early 1180s and that *De Amore* was written during the mid–1180s.
27. John Parry believed that *De Amore* was probably written between 1184 and 1186 for Marie at Champagne, but portrayed the court of her mother, Eleanor, at Poitiers, circa 1170 to 1174. See Andreas, p. 21. The term "courtly love" was itself coined by Gaston Paris during the 19th century. See also p. 3.
28. C.S. Lewis, p. 32.
29. Andreas, p. 4.
30. *Erec and Enide* (Raffel), p. 213. See also C.S. Lewis, p. 39.
31. For example, see Duggan, p. 325. See also *Perceval* (Cline), p. xxi.
32. *Erec and Enide* (Cline) p. 206, n. 31.
33. Armstrong, *Holy War*, p. 224.
34. Frappier, p. 168.
35. *Yvain* (Cline), pp. xiv–xv. For numerous details of the courtly love convention utilized by the poet in *Yvain*, see also p. 199, n. 1253.

Chapter 5

1. *Cligès* (Cline), p. xxii.
2. *Cligès* (Cline), p. xix.
3. *Cligès* (Cline), p. xxi.
4. "This is proof positive," wrote Urban Holmes. See Holmes, pp. 80, 83.
5. *Cligès* (Cline), p. xxiv. Though Shakespeare's fluency in French is self-evident from his works, his immediate sources were far more likely to have been other Renaissance authors published in Italy, France, and England.
6. *Cligès* (Cline), p. xxii. Shakespeare, also an aficionado of Ovid, later parodied the Pyramus-Thisbe story in *A Midsummer Night's Dream*.
7. *Cligès* (Cline), p. 206, n. 5243. These famous lovers are repeatedly mentioned in the latter books of Ovid's *Metamorphoses* as well.
8. Ovid, *Metamorphoses*, p. 363.
9. Holmes, p. 50.
10. Holmes, pp. 50–51.
11. Loomis, *Arthurian Romance*, p. 82.

12. Loomis, *Arthurian Romance*, p. 81.
13. Cline, citing Fourrier, dates the Thomas version from 1172 to 1176. See *Cligès* (Cline), pp. xvii, 201, n. 41. Holmes noted that Thomas offered the more "polite" version of the tale. See also Holmes, p. 79.
14. Professor Cline, among others, believes that Chrétien's version probably came before either of these. See *Cligès* (Cline), p. ix.
15. For example, see *Yvain* (Cline), p. 199, n. 2653 (citing Frappier).
16. *Cligès* (Cline), p. 197, n. 7. One of the *lais* written by Marie de France also mentions Tristan. This is another plausible candidate for the first recorded reference to the legend (see Chapter 4).
17. *Cligès* (Cline), p. 197, n. 7.
18. Holmes (citing Foerster), p. 19.
19. The poet neglects to mention chivalry in connection with the Islamic world, which probably helped to keep the idea alive during the European Dark Ages (see Chapter 2).
20. Holmes, p. 85.
21. *Cligès* (Cline), p. 205, n. 3821.
22. *Cligès* (Cline), p. 205, n. 2793ff. This is very similar to the device later employed by Shakespeare in his Sonnets 135 and 136.
23. *Cligès* (Raffel), p. 223. Another relationship in the romance, the one between Arthur and Alexander, is reminiscent of that found in the *Roman d'Eneas* between Nisus and Euryalus. See Holmes, p. 79.
24. *Cligès* (Raffel), p. 222.
25. *Cligès* (Raffel), p. 51 (line 1593).
26. *Cligès* (Comfort), p. 112.
27. *Cligès* (Owen), p. 114.
28. *Cligès* (Staines), p. 106.
29. *Cligès* (Raffel), p. 229.
30. *Cligès* (Cline), pp. xxiv–xxv.
31. Holmes, pp. 85–86.
32. *Cligès* (Cline), p. xvii. See also *Cligès* (Duggan), p. 13.
33. Frappier (citing Fourrier), p. 6.
34. Holmes, pp. 84–85.

Chapter 6

1. C.S. Lewis, p. 11.
2. The "matters of Britain, France, and Rome" (as these are typically categorized) are too often over-simplified and narrowly defined to the point where the story of the Arthurian legend becomes more distorted rather than clarified. The important thing to remember is that the matter of Britain, or more precisely, the matter of *Bretagne* (read: both sides of the English Channel) is key in the Arthurian tradition and overshadows the other two combined.
3. Holmes, p. 27.
4. Holmes, p. 28.
5. Holmes, p. 32.
6. Duggan, p. 17.
7. Prominent scholars in this area such as Ruth Harwood Cline have forcefully advocated the need for a greater appreciation of this international family network in studies of Chrétien's works.
8. C.S. Lewis, p. 114.
9. The question is often asked: "Why Aquitaine first?" The short answer is that it was the European province closest to Islamic Spain.
10. C.S. Lewis, p. 23.
11. C.S. Lewis, p. 113.
12. Duggan, p. 25.
13. Duggan, p. 19.
14. Book IV of *The Aeneid* deals with the ill-fated love affair between the Aeneas and Dido, Queen of Carthage. The book also exerted considerable influence on Shakespeare and many other subsequent poets.
15. The rhymed octosyllabic couplet was invented in France by the generation of poets prior to Chrétien (possibly by Benoît de Sainte-Maure), thus setting the stage for the first Arthurian romance. See Duggan, p. 33.
16. Duggan, p. 4.
17. Holmes, pp. 33–35. To this list, one may add the *Historia Scholastica* of Peter Comestor, who may have been one of Chrétien's teachers in Troyes (see Chapter 23).
18. Duggan, pp. 33–34.
19. The tale of Philomena from Book VI of Ovid's *Metamorphoses* would later inspire Shakespeare's play, *Titus Andronicus*.
20. *Cligès* (Duggan), p. 220.
21. *Yvain* (Cline, citing Jean Frappier), p. 198, n. 1076.
22. *Lancelot* (Cline, citing Foster Guyer), pp. 215–216, note 365ff (see also verse 1233ff).
23. *Lancelot* (Cline, citing Rolfe Humphries) p. 217, n. 1341.
24. *Lancelot* (Cline), p. 218, nn. 1570–1573.
25. *Lancelot* (Cline), p. 223, n. 4757ff. "Guarding a pretty girl gets you nowhere, you brute," wrote Ovid. See *Metamorphoses* [*The Art of Love*], p. 61.
26. Holmes, p. 36.
27. For example, Henry II's mother,

Queen Matilda, was one of the first identifiable patrons of literature. See Duggan, p. 10.

28. Some of these dichotomies include situations that are psychological versus allegorical in nature, or emotional sentiment versus pure adventure. See C.S. Lewis, pp. 113–114.

Chapter 7

1. Comfort, p. xi.
2. This prosperous city is mentioned by Chrétien in three of his works: *Erec and Enide* (line 33), *Lancelot* (line 240), and *Perceval* (line 377). Richard's death, it should be remembered, occurred many years after these romances were written.
3. One often hears the geographic designations of "Aquitaine," "Occitan," and "Provence" used interchangeably. All essentially refer to southern and/or southwestern France.
4. From the history of medieval Aquitaine, it is tempting to draw the conclusion that intellectual freedom and higher standards of living are causally related. Which of these two comes first in the chain will be forever debated.
5. Most sources agree that hundreds of thousands were killed.
6. Tyerman, p. 594.
7. Tyerman, p. 585.
8. Tyerman, p. 576.
9. Menocal, pp. 45–46.
10. Such "privileges" included the forgiveness of sins in return for killing heretics, "martyrdom" for those who died in the attempt, and above all, land for the victors. See Tyerman, p. 567.
11. Many detailed studies have linked the Cathars of southern France to ancient Gnostic beliefs in the Middle East. These were themselves comprised of a staggeringly diverse group of mystical creeds, many of which were often contradictory amongst themselves.
12. Tyerman, p. 577.
13. Tyerman, p. 602.
14. A more subtle link between the King Arthur legends and Catharism is the latter's close association with the developing ethos of courtly love during the same time and place. See Armstrong, *Gospel*, p. 80.
15. The statement is not footnoted or sourced in the text. See Baigent, p. 62.
16. Rahn believed that *Parzifal* by Wolfram von Eschenbach, using Chrétien as one source, was an elaborate allegory representing the Cathar heresies in southern France. In *Holy Blood, Holy Grail*, Baigent suggests that Chrétien's hero in *Perceval* is symbolic of the Holy Grail blood line. See Baigent, pp. 287–288.
17. Kienzie, pp. 179–181.
18. Kienzie (citing René Nelli), pp. 49–50.
19. *Perceval* (Cline), p. 88, n. 3220 (see also Chapter 22).
20. Goering, p. 14.
21. Holmes, pp. 33–35.

Chapter 8

1. None of these languages were modern or "Middle" English. Old English was spoken by the conquered Anglo-Saxons of southeastern England, and after the Norman conquest in 1066, the English immediately began to adopt Old French words from their new overlords.
2. Holmes, pp. 68–69.
3. The exact location is disputed among Arthurian enthusiasts, but everyone seems to agree that in was in England, Wales, or Scotland.
4. For example, Chrétien has Erec's recently deceased father presiding over Tintagel Castle in Cornwall, birthplace of Arthur according to legend (and Geoffrey of Monmouth).
5. *Erec* (Cline), p. xv. See also Duggan, p. 216.
6. Avalon as a place name first appears in Geoffrey of Monmouth's *Historia Regum Brittaniae*.
7. Geoffrey, in his *Vita Merlini*, the sequel work to the *Historia*, noted that men on Avalon are extraordinarily long-lived. See Cline, pp. 210–211, n. 1907.
8. *Cligès* (Cline), pp. 216–217.
9. *Cligès* (Cline), pp. 200, n. 32; 203, n. 1243; 204, n. 1849. See also *Erec* (Cline), p. 206, n. 32.
10. Holmes, p. 18.
11. Bullock-Davies, p. 60.
12. Bullock-Davies, p. 59.
13. *Cligès* (Raffel), p. 13.
14. *Cligès* (Raffel), p. 209.
15. Staines, p. 450.
16. Hugh was Count Henry's natural half-brother. See *Cligès* (Cline), pp. xii–xiii.
17. One of the oldest manuscripts for *Lancelot* (dating well after the lifetime of

Chrétien, however) omits any mention of Camelot and Caerleon, which naturally raises questions as to how they came to be inserted. See *Lancelot* (Cline), p. 213, notes 30a and 33a.

18. Wolfram does not use the word "Camelot," but places Arthur's court at Nantes.

19. *Lancelot* (Cline), p. 213, n. 33a (quoting Norris J. Lacy).

20. For a summary (in French), see *Bretagne Magazine*.

21. For a brief overview of the question, see *Yvain* (Cline), p. 198, n. 722. See also Duggan, p. 209.

22. This translates literally as "The Channel."

23. Ruth Harwood Cline observed, "There has been much debate about whether the Fisher King's castle is situated outside of conventional time and space and whether it disappears and reappears." For example, after their initial meeting, the lame Fisher King beats Perceval to the Grail Castle, even though Perceval goes there directly on horseback. Also, in the text, characters cannot seem to agree regarding various distances to the castle. See *Perceval* (Cline), p. 83, n. 3038.

24. The Corbenic association first appeared in the 13th-century *Lancelot-Grail* cycle.

25. Montségur also has historical connections to the Templar knights, claimed by some to have been keepers and guardians of the Holy Grail. See Goering, pp. 19–20.

26. Goering, p. 38.

27. Goering, p. 28. If in fact a literary fiction, then Wolfram's pseudo-source is reminiscent of Cervantes' humorous device of the Arab historian Sidi Hamid as a source for *Don Quixote*. As Cervantes himself wrote, "The best lies are those that most closely resemble truth" (Raffel translation, p. 326).

28. The bizarre life and death of German archeologist and adventurer Otto Rahn (1904–1939), who studied and traveled to Montségur in pursuit of Wolfram's legend, is only one example.

29. In the movie, Balian's comment is made to Queen Sibylla in reference to her esteemed and recently deceased brother, King Baldwin IV of Jerusalem.

Chapter 9

1. Gibbon, Vol. 2, p. 1212.
2. At least one and possibly two Welsh clerical works mentioning King Arthur pre-date Geoffrey's *Historia*. These are the *Life of Saint Cardoc* by Lifris of Llancarfan and the *Life of Saint Gildas* by Caradoc of Llancarfan. Neither contains material popularized by Geoffrey or normally associated with the Arthurian legends, although the latter has made an appearance in church art (see Chapter 14).

3. Geoffrey, *Historia*, p. 31, n. 1.

4. It is not widely appreciated that the King Arthur legend had severely waned in English popularity by the late Renaissance period. The re-establishment of Malory's rightful standing within the pantheon of English writers occurred during the 19th century, mainly thanks to Tennyson and the Pre-Raphaelites. As for the 1508 Paris edition of Geoffrey's *Historia*, a copy may be seen today at Chicago's Newberry Library.

5. See Geoffrey, *Historia*, p. 28.

6. For example, Geoffrey was particularly fond of giving highly-detailed descriptions of battles that never took place.

7. Wales would in fact prove far more difficult for the Normans to subdue than southeastern England. The Normans, not highly cultivated themselves, repeatedly marveled at Welsh barbarism and intransigence. This dubious Welsh image would later be immortalized in the hero of Chrétien's *Perceval*.

8. Geoffrey, *Historia*, p. 10 (quoting J.S.P. Tatlock).

9. Cline (*Erec*), p. xvi.

10. Chambers, p. 107.

11. A slightly amused Loomis added that Geoffrey "believed in making Arthur's court a mirror of the latest fashions in sport and entertainment." See Loomis, *Arthurian Romance*, pp. 36, 38.

12. Geoffrey, *Historia*, p. 17.

13. Loomis, *Arthurian Romance*, p. 38.

14. Chambers, pp. 107–108.

15. Gibbon, Vol. 2, p. 1213.

16. See, for example, Chambers (p. 31) and Loomis, *Arthurian Romance* (pp. 1212–1213).

17. The two dedicatees were Robert, Earl of Gloucester, and Waleran, Count of Mellent. See Geoffrey, *Historia*, p. 11.

18. These events are alleged by Geoffrey to have occurred in the year 542 A.D.

19. Geoffrey does introduce Morgan le Fay in the *Vita Merlini*, but not as Arthur's sister. Instead she is a benevolent healer who presides over the Isle of Avalon (see Chapter 11).

20. Geoffrey, once again displaying his ignorance of military matters, describes Frollo as being a "Tribune"—a rank much too low to be the leader of a Roman army.

21. The locale in this image is labeled "Paris" for emphasis and the combat is personally presided over by the Virgin Mary and Child Jesus.

22. Loomis, *Arthurian Romance*, p. 34. Geoffrey also signed a number of documents "Arthur," thus implying this was his surname or father's name. See Geoffrey, *Historia*, p. 13.

23. Chambers, pp. 23–24. Even those who have resisted this speculation, such as Lewis Thorpe, have at least admitted to the possibility: "Everything in his [Geoffrey's] writings and his thinly-sketched biography points to his having been a Welshman, or perhaps a Breton born in Wales." See Geoffrey, *Historia*, pp. 13, 38, n. 2. Thorpe also admitted that Geoffrey's Latin word order is nearer to modern French than classical Latin. See also Geoffrey, *Historia*, p. 24.

24. Loomis, *Celtic Myth*, pp. 9–10.

25. Geoffrey, *Historia*, p. 16.

26. Holmes & Klenke, p. 24. Henry of Blois, Bishop of Winchester, was the paternal uncle of Chrétien's patron, Henry the Liberal, Count of Champagne. For Geoffrey's surmised date of death, see Geoffrey, *Historia*, p. 13.

27. Holmes & Klenke, p. 32.

28. Modern English translations for the place sometimes read "Saussy" (from "Soesia" in the manuscripts). See Geoffrey, *Historia*, p. 247, n. 1.

29. For those unfamiliar with the French national anthem, *La Marseillaise* was a product of the French Revolution some six centuries after the times of Geoffrey and Chrétien.

Chapter 10

1. This was the 17th-century English political theorist Thomas Hobbes.

2. Perceval's mother was distraught because her husband and two other sons had been killed as knights when Perceval was young.

3. The initial point of contact for this transmittal of combined martial and courtly values would have been the Iberian Peninsula and southern France, where Muslim and Christian armies first momentously collided with each other during the 8th century (see Chapter 2).

4. The Hohenstaufen dynasty gained control of Sicily in 1194, by means of the marriage of Henry VI to the Norman heiress Constance and irresistible military intimidation.

5. The debate usually centers on to what extent the Welsh Arthurian sources of both the French and German poets were shared.

6. For example, see Baigent, p. 88.

7. Most researchers now agree that the name Robert at some point was arbitrarily assigned to Wace. See Chambers, p. 101. The name may have been yet another pseudonym.

8. Chambers, p. 103.

9. Wace, p. 63.

10. Wace, pp. 44–45.

11. Wace, p. 62.

12. Wace, p. 64.

13. A magnificent (and somewhat humorous) Renaissance-period illustration of this fanciful episode titled "Arthur à Paris" by Dans Alain Bouchart, dated 1514, can be viewed in the magnificent collection from the Bibliothèque de Rennes Métropole. In the illustration, the Parisians, including the Virgin and Child, cheer Arthur on to victory against his over-sized opponent.

14. Wace, p. 59.

15. In *Erec*, the first mention of the Roundtable ("the Table Round") is cited in conjunction with the hero's membership in that elite group; the second mention is a prelude to the cataloguing of Arthur's most famous knights.

16. Loomis, *Arthurian Romance*, p. 40.

17. Medieval feudal society was (of course) not democratic. As a practical matter, though, kings needed to prevent their equestrian orders from fighting over more trivial, symbolic matters such as priority of seating at the conference table. It was, in effect, an appeasement for over-sized egos.

18. Staines, p. xiii.

19. Others, such as this reader, believe that the poet generally felt one must first make unintentional mistakes in life and suffer the consequences before true salvation, even in symbolic form, can be achieved.

20. *Perceval* (Cline), p. 160, v. 5904.

21. Joseph Duggan highlights the many additional details that often characterized the elaborate knighting ceremonies of the period, as exemplified by Gawain's role as a dispenser of mass knighthood. See *Perceval* (Raffel), p. 313.

22. *Perceval* (Cline), pp. 47–48.

23. *Perceval* (Raffel), p. 52.

Chapter 11

1. *Erec and Enide* (Raffel), p. 232.
2. *Erec and Enide* (Cline), p. 203, n. 5.
3. C.S. Lewis, p. 26.
4. Provocatively, Chrétien begins the second half of his last, unfinished Arthurian romance, *Perceval*, by having Gawain unsuccessfully hunt a white doe (lines 5676–5684).
5. *Erec and Enide* (Cline), pp. xx, 209–210, n. 709 (citing Roger Sherman Loomis). See also Duggan, p. 204.
6. Owen, p. xiv.
7. Holmes, p. 61.
8. Holmes, p. 67.
9. Morgan is mentioned several times in *Erec and Enide*. See also lines 1907, 2358, and 4194–4195. Professor Duggan asserts, not unreasonably, that Chrétien was the first writer to make this sibling connection. See Duggan p. 202.
10. Loomis, *Celtic Myth*, p. 197. Geoffrey of Monmouth had mentioned Morgan as a sorceress and healer in his *Vita Merlini* (p. 101).
11. Guingamar, or Guigemar, is subject matter for one of Marie de France's poems (see Chapter 4).
12. Enide's name is not mentioned until line 1979, a delaying device frequently used by Chrétien for dramatic purposes. See *Erec and Enide* (Cline), p. 211, n. 1978.
13. Urban Holmes noted that these scenes more or less recite the entire story. See Holmes, pp. 66–67.
14. *Erec and Enide* (Cline), p. 212, n. 4581.
15. C.S. Lewis, p. 26. The closest overt connection between Shakespeare and the Arthurian legends (such as it is) can be found in the name of Arthur (of Brittany), the doomed Plantagenet heir from *King John*. These historical events came in the immediate aftermath of Chrétien's time, with the boy probably being named after the legendary English monarch so popular in his own day. See Duggan, pp. 11–12.
16. *Erec and Enide* (Cline), pp. xx–xxi.
17. Holmes, pp. 69–70.
18. Holmes, p. 60.
19. Holmes, pp. 70–71.
20. *Erec and Enide* (Cline), p. xxi.
21. *Erec and Enide* (Raffel), p. 81.
22. See Comfort (p. 33), Owen (p. 34), and Staines (p. 33).
23. *Erec and Enide* (Raffel), p. 79.
24. See Comfort (p. 33), Owen (p. 33), and Staines (p. 32).
25. One is reminded of the early scene in *Perceval* in which the fool, after a careless remark, is protected from Kay's wrath only by King Arthur's presence.
26. It is implied that Erec's indomitable power and strength ultimately come from God. In the story, before his very first contest — that of the sparrow-hawk in which he publicly wins acclaim for his wife to be — Erec first scrupulously hears mass (lines 700–705).
27. *Erec and Enide* (Raffel), p. 226.
28. *Erec and Enide* (Raffel), p. 227.
29. *Erec and Enide* (Cline), pp. xiv–xv. See also *Erec and Enide* (Raffel), p. 231.

Chapter 12

1. Loomis, *Arthurian Romance*, p. 185.
2. The precise title of the first printed edition was *Le Morte Darthur*, a more Anglicized version of the French original (*The Death of Arthur*), possibly attributable to the author himself.
3. The War of the Roses would eventually be immortalized in drama by Shakespeare (using a great deal of historical latitude) with his *Henry VI* trilogy and *Richard III*.
4. Loomis, *Arthurian Romance*, p. 190.
5. Warwick (1382–1439), was an older protégé of Henry V, field commander at the battle of Agincourt, and educational mentor of Henry VI. He spent much of his career in France, where he eventually died (at Rouen). His early travels took him all the way to the Holy Land and Jerusalem, as well as Eastern Europe and Constantinople. See Loomis, *Arthurian Romance*, p.168.
6. This Warwick, nicknamed the "kingmaker" because of his fluctuating support between Henry VI and Edward IV during the War of the Roses, was also a primary participant in the heaviest fighting of that conflict. If Malory did in fact belong to Warwick's contingent (which is more than likely), then he would have been a participant in these battles as well, from the first St. Albans (1455) to Barnet (1471), in which Warwick was killed.
7. Loomis, *Arthurian Romance*, pp. 168–169.
8. As Loomis perceptively wrote, "The controversy over the unity of Malory's works resembles a debate on the question: Are the United States of America separate or united? The answer is that they are both separate and

united." The same idea applies to Malory as a person, as well as a writer. See Loomis, *Arthurian Romance*, p. 173.

9. Loomis, *Arthurian Romance*, p. 172.

10. Primary among these was the early 13th-century French prose *Lancelot-Grail* cycle, which in turn was heavily indebted to Chrétien.

11. With the exception of ancillary, offshoot masterpieces in English such as the anonymous, 14th-century Middle English poem, *Sir Gawain and the Green Knight*, it is generally agreed that almost all of Malory's source material was French, with Geoffrey of Monmouth's Latin thrown in for good measure.

12. Loomis, *Arthurian Romance*, p. 174.

13. The true extent of Caxton's contribution to Malory's final work is the subject of a fascinating and ongoing academic discussion.

14. *Perceval* (Cline), p. x.

15. *Lancelot* (Cline), pp. ix–x.

16. For a good, brief description of the link between Chrétien and Malory, see the Julian Harris foreword to *Yvain* (Cline), p. vii.

17. As Professor Harris has pointed out, the French themselves were considering these tales *passé* by the time of the Renaissance. See *Yvain* (Cline), pp. vii–viii.

Chapter 13

1. Edward Gibbon made a similar remark. See Gibbon, Vol. 2, p. 1213.

2. Tyerman, p. 18.

3. Early 11th-century Europe had its own fair share of violence and rapine; however, subtracting that which was Norman-induced or strictly contained by local rulers, it was a comparatively peaceful time.

4. Southern Italy benefited from the Norman conquest in that it subsequently enjoyed more prosperity, not to mention orderly process of law.

5. The Normans first came to southern Italy as religious pilgrims. They were quickly retained by the locals as mercenaries, and after some vacillations in loyalty to each side, more or less announced to everyone that the country now belonged to them (the Normans).

6. Tyerman, p. 14.

7. The battle of Hastings was fought on October 14, 1066. It is widely (and rightfully) regarded as one of the most crucial land battles in history in terms of long-term impact on civilization.

8. William's Breton contingent was rewarded as well, receiving significant English land grants. One of the beneficiaries may have been the family of Geoffrey of Monmouth (see Chapter 9).

9. Other factors motivating the participants of the First Crusade, some of which are still being debated, included a thirst for adventure, prestige, and genuine (though often deluded) religious piety.

10. Arthur of Brittany was the son of Geoffrey, Duke of Brittany, another younger brother in the same Plantagenet royal family.

11. Mordred is first portrayed as Arthur's illegitimate and incestuous son by his sister Morgan le Fay in the Vulgate Lancelot-Grail Cycle of the early 13th century (see Chapter 21).

12. In the early 13th-century tale of *Perlesvaus* (see Chapter 21), Loholt would eventually be killed by Arthur's unsympathetic seneschal, Sir Kay. See *Erec and Enide* (Cline), p. 210, v. 1700. The source of this tradition may be Breton. See also Duggan, pp. 207–208.

13. In early tradition, Gawain (Gauvain in French) is the son of Arthur's sister and King Lot of Norway. The latter is also listed by Chrétien as a member of the Roundtable in *Erec and Enide* (line 1705).

14. "First Knight" is usually more associated with the 1995 Jerry Zucker film by that name dealing with the relationships between Arthur, Lancelot and Guinevere, played respectively by Sean Connery, Richard Gere and Julia Ormond. In Chrétien's *Erec and Enide* (Cline), Gawain is listed as first among the knights of the Roundtable (line 1672).

15. Uitti, p. 33.

16. Chrétien refers to "Excalibur" (line 5901), a more French pronunciation of the sword named by Geoffrey of Monmouth as "Caliburnus" and by Wace as "Calibore." See also Duggan, p. 201.

17. *Perceval* (Cline), p. 160, v. 5904.

18. Yet another example occurs in *Lancelot*, when the younger sister of the villain Meleagant helps the hero escape from a tower prison.

Chapter 14

1. Compare for example, the continuing British influence in India after the exit of

British government, or extensive long-term Spanish influence in the Philippine Islands.
   2. Tyerman, p. 473.
   3. Tyerman, p. 558.
   4. Tyerman, pp. 556–557.
   5. Gibbon, Vol. 3, p. 2161.
   6. See Shakespeare's *Henry IV, Part II*, Act IV, scene v.
   7. Gibbon, Vol. 3, p. 2161.
   8. Gibbon, Vol. 3, p. 2223.
   9. Loomis added, "This is the most plausible conjecture." See Loomis, *Medieval Art*, p. 31.
   10. For a good photograph of the Perros Relief, see Loomis, *Medieval Art*, Figure 3.
   11. *Lancelot* (Cline), p. xiii.
   12. Holmes & Klenke, p. 124.
   13. Holmes & Klenke, p. 15.
   14. Holmes & Klenke (citing Loomis), p. 124.
   15. It would seem that before the time of Chrétien, Gawain was the most popular and widely-known of the Arthurian knights, as evidenced by Geoffrey of Monmouth's *Historia* (see Chapter 9). As for Kay, Chrétien would cleverly and consistently portray him as an unlikable antagonist.
   16. For photographs of the Modena Archivolt, see Loomis, *Medieval Art*, Figures 4–8.
   17. See Loomis, *Medieval Art* (p. 34) and *Celtic Myth* (pp. 5–6). Loomis thought the sources of the tale were Breton *conteurs*. See also Holmes & Klenke (citing Loomis), p. 124.
   18. Work on the Modena Cathedral is believed to have begun in 1099. See Loomis, *Medieval Art*, p. 32.
   19. A black-and-white photograph of the Otranto "Rex Arturus" mosaic can be seen in Loomis, *Medieval Art*, Figure 9. An interesting, partial sketch of the same work before restoration (after an earthquake) can also be seen in Figure 9a.
   20. For a good color photographic image, see *Le Roi Arthur*, p. 6.
   21. Loomis, *Medieval Art*, p. 36. See also Holmes & Klenke (citing Loomis), pp. 140–141.
   22. Loomis, *Medieval Art*, p. 36.
   23. Holmes & Klenke, pp. 135–136.
   24. Loomis, *Arthurian Romance*, p. 186.

Chapter 15

   1. Gibbon, Vol. 3, p. 1966.
   2. In France, a similar phenomenon had occurred when the Franks, who were of Germanic origin, invaded, conquered, and assimilated into Roman Gaul. In fact, the Normans were later themselves often referred to as Franks. This was partially due to the illustrious legacy of Charlemagne, which they sought to inherit for themselves, having nothing comparable of their own.
   3. This film was based on the popular comic strip series of Hal Foster, who was more than respectably well-read and well-versed in the traditional Arthurian legends. The benefits of this comfort level were reflected in the high quality of both the comic strip and the feature film.
   4. Menocal, pp. 112, 115–125, 286.
   5. To be more precise, Scandinavian raiders had terrorized the coasts of Iberia for centuries before this but failed to permanently establish settlements there as they had in northern France.
   6. Duke William VIII of Aquitaine is not to be confused with his much more famous contemporary, Duke William of Normandy (also known as William I of England or "the Conqueror").
   7. Menocal, p. 119.
   8. Menocal, pp. 120–121.
   9. Menocal, pp. 122–123.
   10. Menocal, pp. 124–125.
   11. One of his Spanish adventures included a siege of Cordova itself.
   12. Menocal appropriately notes that the Norman experience in Islamic Spain was "something of a replay" of their recent triumphs in Islamic Sicily and southern Italy. See Menocal, p. 121.
   13. Again, this William (also known as "William the Good"), who was of the House of Hauteville, should not be confused with the conqueror of England who had lived during the previous century.
   14. Matilda II is not be confused with her mother, Matilda I. The moniker "Angevin" is derived from the House of Anjou in central France, over which the Plantagenets had previously ruled and presided.
   15. The 1987 Emmy Award-winning series *The Story of English*, produced by the BBC and PBS, effectively made this important point to a wide viewing audience.
   16. Holmes, pp. 33–34.
   17. For one, scholars note that Chrétien's Old French romances were written in a Champagnois dialect.
   18. This dynamic would not really change until the Venetians established strong com-

mercial contacts with the East during the 14th century.
    19. Gibbon, Vol. 3, p. 1999.

Chapter 16

1. *Yvain* (Raffel), p. xii.
2. *Yvain* (Cline), p. xii.
3. C.S. Lewis, p. 25.
4. Holmes, p. 102.
5. This movie in turn gave rise to its more popular spin-off, the comic musical *Spamalot* (2004).
6. Holmes, pp. 110–111. See also *Yvain* (Cline), pp. 195–196, n. 54.
7. These estimates are based on those made by Jean Frappier. See *Yvain* (Cline), p. 203, n. 5.
8. Urban Holmes thought this allusion may have referenced back to the last similar correlation in 1169. See Holmes, pp. 104–105.
9. *Yvain* (Cline) pp. 197–198, note 557 (citing Frappier). After Nureddin's death in 1173, his reputation as a formidable Crusader adversary was gradually eclipsed by his great successor, Saladin.
10. *Yvain* (Cline), pp. 195–196, notes 46, 54.
11. *Yvain* (Duggan), p. 216.
12. C.S. Lewis, p. 31.
13. *Yvain* (Cline), p. 2.
14. Owen, p. 281.
15. Professor Cline emphasized, "The lion however is far more than a helpful pet, and the role of the lion is one of the most disputed questions in the analysis of *Yvain*." See *Yvain* (Cline), p. xv.
16. *Yvain* (Cline), pp. xv–xvi (citing Jean Frappier and Julian Harris).
17. *Yvain* (Duggan), p. 209.
18. Holmes, p. 116. See also *Yvain* (Cline), p. 200, n. 3162.
19. *Yvain* (Cline), p. 201, n. 4068 (citing Arthur Brown).
20. *Yvain* (Cline), p. 79 (lines 2637–2640).
21. *Yvain* (Raffel), p. 85 (lines 2804–2807).
22. Comfort, p. 216.
23. Staines, p. 290.
24. Owen, p. 319.
25. *Yvain* (Cline), p. 98 (lines 3299–3302). The proximity of the chapel is mentioned earlier (line 363) during the tale of Calogrenant.
26. Compare with *Yvain* (Raffel), p. 105; Comfort, p. 225; Owen, p. 328; and Staines, p. 298.
27. *Yvain* (Cline), p. xxiii.
28. In reference to *The Art of Courtly Love* by Andreas Capellanus, Professor Cline observed that "the Love-Hate debate is a magnificent example of the use of dialectic reasoning in replying to the kind of question posed at the courts of love." See *Yvain* (Cline), p. 201, n. 5732. The difficult relationship between Yvain and Lunette would indeed have been a good case study for the fictional (?) love courts presided over by Eleanor of Aquitaine and Marie of Champagne (see Chapter 4).
29. *Yvain* (Cline), p. xv.
30. As the poet says at the beginning of the work: "...for words will quickly disappear, if they aren't heard in heart *and* ear" (lines 143–144).
31. As Cline puts it, Yvain and the lion's "final triumph over the demons is on a supernatural plane." See *Yvain* (Cline), p. xvi.
32. *Yvain* (Cline), p. 201, notes 4965, 5063.

Chapter 17

1. Gibbon, Vol. 3, p. 2085.
2. The Second Crusade was co-led by the German Holy Roman Emperor, Conrad III. Louis VII was the father of Chrétien's great patroness, Marie de Champagne.
3. Edward Gibbon described in graphic detail the degeneracy of *Outremer* rule by this period. See Gibbon, Vol. 3, p. 2085.
4. Adolf, pp. 13–15.
5. See, for example, Knight, p. 127.
6. Adolf, p. 11.
7. Knight, p. 127.
8. Gibbon, Vol. 3, p. 2085.
9. Tyerman, p. 369. In the semi-farcical Terry Jones documentary, *The Crusades* (1995), an excerpt from the Arab film version of the battle depicts Saladin crying out (appropriately enough, given the date of the event) "Liberty!" as his army routs the Crusaders.
10. Tyerman, p. 342.
11. Gibbon, Vol. 3, p. 2086.
12. Chrétien expounds upon the beauty and significance of the True Cross in *Erec and Enide* (lines 2321–2343), as the hero gives it as a gift to the monastery of Carnant, in the Welsh realm of King Lac, his father.
13. Curiously, the film was a financial failure in the U.S., despite being successful worldwide.

14. Tyerman gives a good analysis of the fateful decision. According to his account, the only voice of caution before the battle was Count Raymond of Tripoli, who may well have been motivated by treachery rather than patriotism. See Tyerman, pp. 368–369.
15. The Greek Christians accepted Muslim rule because, as Gibbon perceptively observed, "experience had taught [them] to prefer the Mahometan before the Latin yoke...." See Gibbon, Vol. 3, p. 2086.
16. Many casualties included fellow Christians who happened to be in the wrong place at the wrong time.
17. Gibbon, Vol. 3, p. 2088.
18. Tyerman, p. 374.
19. Tyerman, pp. 350–351.
20. *Perceval* (Raffel), p. 196 (lines 6218–6221).
21. Tyerman, p. 356.
22. Holmes & Klenke, p. 4.
23. Holmes & Klenke, p. 13.
24. King Philip Augustus expelled all Jews from France in 1182.
25. See Menocal, pp. 112–118.

Chapter 18

1. The conflict between the saint, Henry II, and Louis VII was memorably portrayed by Richard Burton, Peter O'Toole, and John Gielgud in the 1964 film, *Becket*, based largely on the 1935 play by T.S. Eliot, *Murder in the Cathedral*.
2. Duggan, p. 17.
3. Professor Cline notes that other family relatives from the court of Champagne had extensive dealings in England as well. This may have provided a source of Chrétien's geographic knowledge, assuming he did not travel there himself. See *Cligès* (Cline), p. xiii.
4. Duggan, p. 20.
5. *Erec and Enide* (Cline), pp. 204–205, n. 13.
6. Andreas, p. 21.
7. Holmes & Klenke, p. 5. Not surprisingly, scholarly opinion has been far more divided over this last item. See Holmes, p. 20.
8. Armstrong, *Gospel*, p. 38.
9. Tyerman, pp. 254–255.
10. Earlier sources for the legend, such as the 9th-century chronicler Nennius, had also made King Arthur a Christian; this aspect, however, was not emphasized until after the time of Chrétien.
11. It should be added that gorgeously vapid movies such as *Knights of the Round Table* clearly provided inspiration for the Monty Python crew in its comic work on the same thematic material.
12. Holmes, p. 19.
13. Holmes, p. 18.
14. Holmes, p. 124.
15. Staines, p. 461.
16. Holmes, pp. 119–120. See also Staines, p. 450.
17. Chrétien's poem *Philomena*, expressly attributed to him, is not considered a masterpiece either. See *Cligès* (Cline), p. x. Perhaps the poet wanted to bask in the reflected glory of the work's Ovidian source material by citing it among his credentials.
18. Staines, pp. 450, 491.
19. Professor Cline speculates that Chrétien may have been part of Henry II's entourage to England in April to May of 1170. See *Cligès* (Cline), pp. xiii–xv.
20. *Cligès* (Cline), p. 203, n. 5.
21. *Cligès* (Cline), pp. iv, 199, n. 29 (citing Lars Lindvall).
22. Staines, p. 490.
23. Staines, p. 474.
24. Staines, p. 474.
25. Staines, p. 482.
26. Staines, p. 485.
27. Staines, p. 482.
28. Staines, p. 488.
29. Staines, p. 478. Along similar lines, there is also a reference to a Castilian charger (p. 476), calling to mind the ongoing Spanish *Reconquista*.
30. Staines, p. 482.
31. Staines, p. 480.

Chapter 19

1. Loomis, *Arthurian Romance*, p. 475. The remark of Loomis applies well to Chrétien's apparent lack of interest in Merlin.
2. Loomis, *Arthurian Romance*, p. 35. These sources, the *Welsh Triads*, mention the two Myrrdins in conjunction with Taliesin, perhaps the most famous Welsh poet of them all.
3. Loomis, *Arthurian Romance*, pp. 36, 40.
4. One of Geoffrey's earliest works had been the *Prophetiae Merlini* ("Prophesies of Merlin"), an alleged Latin translation of the Welsh bard's verses, which also appears to be strictly a product of Geoffrey's vivid imagination.

5. Loomis, *Arthurian Romance*, p. 124.
6. Loomis, *Arthurian Romance*, p. 39.
7. Loomis, *Arthurian Romance*, p. 39. The wounded Arthur is escorted to Avalon by Merlin and Taliesin. Loomis, among others, praised the poetic talent of Geoffrey in the *Vita Merlini*.
8. Viviane is often equated with the Lady of the Lake, as well as the fairy stepmother of Lancelot du Lac. A striking prehistoric lake (thus associated with all of these characters) can also still be seen near Paimpont, adjacent to the Centre de l'imaginaire Arthurien.
9. *Yvain* (Cline), pp. 196–197, n. 177. This work was probably written around the approximate same time that Chrétien created his first Arthurian romance, *Erec and Enide*.
10. *Erec and Enide* (Cline), pp. 207–208, n. 42. This overlap in text between *Yvain* and *Philomena* is also a good argument in favor of the poet's authorship of the latter, which is occasionally questioned.
11. Holmes, pp. 112–113.
12. The author's wife, however, proceeded forward into the woods, took some excellent photographs, and was not bothered by the bees, whose constant humming sounded like a distant engine drone.
13. The author and his wife also witnessed a group of Breton adolescents near the forest listening intently to a docent in costume relating some of these Arthurian traditions.
14. *Yvain* (Raffel), pp. 208–209.
15. "[I]t [sterlings blanch] dated back from Merlin's role" (line 6632). See *Erec and Enide* (Cline), p. 194. Given the then-large population of Jewish merchants and financiers in Troyes, this passage almost has an anti–Semitic ring to it (see Chapter 23).
16. C.S. Lewis, p. 27.
17. In fairness, it should be added that this writer, like countless others, was first exposed to the great beauty of the imaginary Arthurian world through the incandescent artwork of the Pre-Raphaelites.

Chapter 20

1. Armstrong, *History*, p. 203.
2. Mont Saint Michel is today often cited as the leading tourist attraction in France outside of Paris.
3. *Lancelot* (Cline), p. 224, note 6074 (citing Mario Roques).
4. Armstrong, *History*, p. 203.
5. Holmes & Klenke, pp. 164–165. This noteworthy tradition, at least within a Christian context, had begun during the third century with Origen.
6. Armstrong, *History*, p. 203.
7. Uitti, p. 22.
8. Armstrong, *History*, p. 204.
9. Mark Twain, with ever a keen eye for the overblown (see Chapter 19), satirized this famous love affair in his popular novel, *Innocents Abroad* (1869).
10. In the wide range of her considerable talents, Hildegard has been compared to the great Arab intellectual of the previous century, Ibn Sina, aka Avincenna (981–1037). See Armstrong, *Gospel*, p. 255.
11. Holmes, pp. 29–30.
12. Salisbury's *Polycraticus* is often cited as a source for Shakespeare's play *Coriolanus*.
13. Marie, the daughter of Eleanor and Louis VII, would go on to patronize Chrétien as the wife of Count Henry the Liberal.
14. *Lancelot* (Cline), p. 218, note 1482 (citing Wendelin Foerster).
15. Tyerman, p. 277.
16. Tyerman, p. 279.
17. Holmes & Klenke, p. 63.
18. Holmes & Klenke, p. 14.
19. Tyerman, p. 277.
20. Holmes & Klenke, pp. 100, 158.
21. The Second Crusade was, to oversimplify somewhat, a failed European attempt to regain "lost" border territories that had been bloodily conquered during the First Crusade and then regained by the Turks after the fall of Edessa in 1145.

Chapter 21

1. Nitze, p. 281.
2. *Perceval* (Cline), p. xxiv, n. 7. See also *Erec and Enide* (Cline), p. 203, n. 5. A somewhat more romantic dating of *Perceval* places it at the beginning of the 1190s, with the poet dying alongside his patron Philip of Flanders at the siege of Acre during the Third Crusade. While not impossible, this scenario appears to place a ten-year gap between Chrétien's last work and his other four Arthurian romances. For one, it is difficult to imagine such a prolific and driven artist putting aside his pen for this length of time.
3. Among many inconsistencies in the story, one example is the time sequence of events. Perceval's adventures take five years while concurrent adventures of Gawain take one year. See *Perceval* (Cline), p. xiii. One

explanation for this problem is that the oldest manuscripts were copied from an incomplete draft. See also p. 168, v. 6221.
 4. *Perceval* (Raffel), p. 293.
 5. Loomis, *Arthurian Romance*, p. 59.
 6. Raffel reasonably questions whether Chrétien, who was at the very end of his life, was fully up to the monumental task set for him. The last 800 lines or so of the incomplete poem, notes Raffel, are not commensurate with the poet's usual high standards. See *Perceval* (Raffel), p. x.
 7. Holmes & Klenke, p. 72.
 8. Chambers, p. 140.
 9. Chambers, p. 142.
 10. Two of these continuators were anonymous. The other two identified themselves as Manessier and Gerbert de Montreuil. See *Perceval* (Raffel), pp. 300–301. See also Holmes, pp. 134–135.
 11. *Perceval* (Raffel), pp. 301–303. See also Holmes, pp. 135–136.
 12. *Perceval* (Raffel), pp. 303–304. Recent scholarly opinion has shied away from an earlier theory (based on an express attribution in the work) that the Vulgate Cycle was written by Chrétien's contemporary, the French-educated Welshman, Walter Map. See Holmes, p. 136.
 13. Both of these works are generally agreed to be later than Chrétien's *Perceval*, although they all may share older common sources. See Holmes, pp. 305–307.
 14. This may well have been because (as asserted elsewhere in this study), the western Christian Crusader kingdoms in the Middle East were at that time falling apart.
 15. *Perceval* (Cline), p. 98, n. 3575.
 16. *Perceval* (Cline), p. xxi.
 17. This is an inconsistency in the plot. See note 3.
 18. *Lancelot* (Cline), p. xvii. Cline also asserted, however, that strictly Christian or pagan interpretations of *Perceval* are oversimplified. See *Perceval* (Cline), pp. xv–xvi. The author agrees with this observation.
 19. *Perceval* (Raffel), p. 300.
 20. The context of the first two gospel references is in praise of Chrétien's patron, Philip of Flanders. The first (line 4) is also found in Luke, while the third (line 581) is echoed in Luke and John.
 21. *Perceval* (Cline), p. 29 (lines 907–911).
 22. *Perceval* (Raffel), pp. 29–30 (lines 907–911).
 23. *Perceval* (Kibler), p. 45 (887–891).
 24. *Perceval* (Owen), p. 386.
 25. *Perceval* (Staines), p. 351.
 26. *Perceval* (Cline), p. 33 (lines 1059–1060).
 27. See *Perceval* (Raffel) p. 34, and (Kibler), p. 53.
 28. See *Perceval* (Owen), p. 388, and (Staines), p. 352.
 29. *Perceval* (Cline), p. 161 (line 5955).
 30. *Perceval* (Raffel), p. 188.
 31. See *Perceval* (Kibler), p. 291, (Owen), p. 453, and (Staines), p. 411.
 32. *Perceval* (Cline), p. 161 (line 5958). See also (Raffel), p. 188, (Kibler), p. 291, (Owen), p. 453, and (Staines), p. 411.
 33. *Perceval* (Cline), pp. ix–x.
 34. Philip was the nephew of Chrétien's earlier patron, Count Henry the Liberal of Champagne. Moreover, he was crowned king by his uncle, Henry's younger brother, Bishop Guillaume aux Blanches Mains ("Whitehands"). Thus the poet would have been likely close to the family affair that was 12th-century French royal politics.
 35. *Perceval* (Cline), p. 19, v. 582.
 36. *Perceval* (Cline), p. 1, v. 13.
 37. *Perceval* (Cline), pp. xvi, 6, v. 6; 27, v. 835.
 38. *Perceval* (Cline), pp. ix-x.
 39. Tyerman, p. 341.
 40. Goering, pp. 148–157.

Chapter 22

 1. Loomis, *Celtic Myth*, p. 22.
 2. Topsfield, p. 1.
 3. Holmes, pp. 151–152.
 4. Holmes, pp. 137–152. Holmes also praised an earlier summary by I.L. Foster. See p. 151.
 5. See Holmes & Klenke, Chapter 10.
 6. Later it is revealed by the hero's hermit uncle that the Fisher King is Perceval's uncle as well, and the Grail King, his grandfather (lines 6415–6419).
 7. The only movie depiction of the Grail Procession, to the best of this writer's knowledge, was in the 1978 French film version of *Perceval* by Eric Rohmer. Though a flawed work in many ways, the moving profundity of this particular scene still shines through in its own somewhat geeky manner.
 8. *Perceval* (Cline), p. 88, n. 3220. Indeed, it has been plausibly claimed that the entire Grail legend as adapted by Chrétien is Provençal in origin. See p. xxvi, n. 19.
 9. Among English translators who do not

opt for the word "grail," David Staines uses "bowl"—appropriately reminding readers that this is not a chalice or a cup. See Staines, pp. 379, 417.

10. *Perceval* (Cline), p. 88, n. 3220. See also Goering, p. 15.

11. Goering, p. 13.

12. *Perceval* (Cline), pp. 172, 173. Burton Raffel grudgingly translates it as "holy Grail," with a small "h." See *Perceval* (Raffel), p. 201 (lines 6380–6381).

13. This relic was allegedly discovered during the First Crusade at the siege Antioch, and played a part in rallying the Crusaders to an unlikely victory. The lance was then taken back to France by Raymond of Toulouse, where it subsequently disappeared. See Adolf (citing Runciman), p. 274.

14. Adolf, p. 28.

15. Adolf, pp. 29–30. In Judaism, candelabra are distinctively seven-candled, while in *Perceval*, each one contains "at least ten" (line 3217).

16. Ruth Harwood Cline gives a good short summary of these. See *Perceval* (Cline), p. xv (citing Loomis).

17. For example, Weston influenced T.S. Eliot and his famous 1922 poem *The Waste Land* (see Chapter 21). The term is taken from the ravaged area surrounding, or adjacent to, the Grail Castle in *Perceval*. Professor Cline translates it as "wholly desolate" (line 1773). Incredibly, Weston's classic study, *From Ritual to Romance*, was first published in 1920 when she was 70 years old. See introduction to Weston, p. xxii.

18. Holmes, pp. 141–151. Still others have traced the eastern origins of the ritual through the liturgy of the Byzantine church. See *Perceval* (Cline), p. xxviii, n. 30.

19. Weston, p. 161.

20. Weston, p. 191.

21. Weston also noted that Chambers was himself influenced in this specific regard by the recent work of J.G. Frazer. See Weston, p. 66.

22. Holmes (citing Hofer), pp. 139–140.

23. Holmes, p. 139.

24. Holmes & Klenke, p. 73.

25. Holmes & Klenke, pp. 159–160.

26. Holmes, p. 166. This incredibly beautiful chalice was obtained by the National Gallery from the famous Mellon collection. It may date from the first century, A.D.

27. Adolf, pp. 39–43.

28. Adolf, pp. 140–141.

29. Robert de Boron was also responsible for various well-known innovations in Arthurian legends such as the Sword in the Stone.

30. Frappier's arguments are well-summarized by Urban Holmes. See Holmes, pp. 140–141.

31. Nitze, p. 322.

32. The lance would represent the top of the cross, while the two candelabra signify the span. The grail and the platter are at the base.

33. According to Michelle Reihert, the theory of the female grail-bearer from the churches of the Spanish Pyrenees was first advanced in a 1975 dissertation by Paulette Duval. See Reichert, p. 34.

34. Goering, p. 4.

35. Goering, p. 136. Other Pyrenees churches, besides St. Clement in Taüll, with similar mural images include Santa Eulalia d'Estaon, and Sant Pere de Burgal. A French church with a comparable mural, possibly Byzantine-inspired, has been identified at the Chapelle de Moines in Benzé-la-Ville. See also Reichert, p. 34.

36. *Perceval* (Cline), p. xxv, n. 11. In line 2785, Pentecost is referred to as Whitsuntide.

37. Goering, p. 14.

38. Goering, p. 70.

39. Using this proverbial kitchen sink approach (see Chapter 6), one can conceivably see in Chrétien's grail a diverse combination of, say, a mystic symbol of Andalusian Sufism being held by a Christian Virgin or Magdalean figure. See also Goering, pp. 4–5.

40. Goering, p. ix.

41. Holmes, p. 154.

42. Topsfield, p. 20.

Chapter 23

1. The "yeshiva" school founded by Rashi was in some ways a prototype for all that followed. See Holmes & Klenke, pp. 11–13. See also Leviant (pp. 74–75) and Duggan (p. 8).

2. Sixteen years later, Philip invited the Jews to return to France in 1198.

3. Holmes & Klenke, p. 12.

4. Louis VII, it should be remembered, was the father of Chrétien's patron, Countess Marie of Champagne, wife of Henry the Liberal.

5. Armstrong, p. 242.

6. Armstrong, p. 243. There too, how-

ever, there were exceptions such as the fundamentalist Almohades and their persecution of Jews in Spain and North Africa.

7. Holmes & Klenke, pp. 109–115.
8. For a good color reproduction and discussion, see Grodecki, Plate 8 and p. 18. Grodecki dates the window itself between 1160 and 1180, which was roughly Chrétien's most active period as a poet.
9. Like the windows in Châlons-en-Champagne, these represent some of the earliest surviving stained glass of their kind. During the mid–12th century, this art form became more distinctive and stylized, as outstandingly demonstrated by these pieces.
10. Leviant (citing Herman Hailperin), p. 76, n. 18.
11. Leviant, pp. 75–77.
12. Holmes & Klenke, p. 17. See also Duggan, p. 8.
13. *Perceval* (Cline), p. 170 (lines 6292–6293). Burton Raffel, without the constraint of rhymed octosyllabic couplets, perhaps translated the same passage even better: "They ought to be killed like dogs!" See *Perceval* (Raffel), p. 199 (line 6294).
14. See *Perceval* (Cline), p. 2, nn. 30–31. Matthew is widely considered to be the most anti–Jewish among the four gospels, even though the author of the gospel himself was probably a Christianized Jew.
15. *Perceval* (Cline), p. 3, n. 49.
16. Urban Holmes and Sister Anna Klenke advanced the controversial theory that *Perceval* was an elaborate allegory for the conversion of French Jews to Christianity, just as the poet himself may have been, according to the authors. Apart from the issue of Chrétien's personal background (see Chapter 24), there may be some validity to this interpretation, whether it was conscious or unconsciously incorporated by the poet. We are not prepared, however, to narrowly view this complex work as any particular type of brain teaser, even in an age that loved and expected allegory much more than our own.
17. Holmes & Klenke, p. 95.
18. Thanks to Jerome Bloom for first bringing this work to my attention.
19. Leviant (citing the research of M. Schuler), pp. 2–3, 108.
20. Leviant, p. 82.
21. Leviant, pp. 12–13.
22. Leviant, p. 71.
23. Leviant (quoting W. Gudemann), p. 53.
24. Maimonides was widely admired by Christian theologians such as Thomas Aquinas for his articulate incorporation of Aristotelian philosophy into traditional religious systems. See Leviant, pp. 50–51. Though born in Spain, Maimonides eventually fled to North Africa and Egypt where he produced his great philosophic masterpiece, *A Guide for the Perplexed*.
25. Leviant (citing Moses Gaster), p. 82.

Chapter 24

1. C.S. Lewis, p. 29.
2. Geoffrey, *Historia*, p. 13.
3. Staines, p. ix.
4. *Erec* (Cline), p. 204, n. 9.
5. Holmes, pp. 52–54. In one manuscript source *(Philomena)*, the poet is surnamed "li Gois," possibly meaning "the joyful." See *Erec* (Cline), p. 204, n. 11. Others have interpreted "li Gois" to mean that Chrétien was or had been an inhabitant of Gouaix, a village near Provins in Champagne, located about 40 miles from Troyes. See *Cligès* (Duggan), p. 217.
6. For example, regarding Chrétien's anti–Semitism, it might be argued that a proto-typical anti–Semite such as Adolph Hitler may himself have been of Jewish ancestry. Regarding misquotations of Saint Paul, it may be that Chrétien did not know his New Testament as well as he knew his Old Testament, or that his misquotations were intentional.
7. *Erec* (Cline), p. xi. Other professional scholars now seem to seriously consider that "Chrétien" may have been a pseudonym. See, for example, Reichert, pp. 24–26.
8. Holmes & Klenke, p. 23.
9. *Erec* (Cline), pp. x–xviii.
10. *Erec* (Cline), p. x.
11. *Erec* (Cline), p. xviii.
12. *Erec* (Cline), p. xiv.
13. *Erec* (Cline), pp. xiv–xv.
14. For example, doubters of the traditional Shakespeare are often compared by their opponents to Holocaust deniers. My first study, *DeVere as Shakespeare: An Oxfordian Reading of the Canon*, attempted to examine only one aspect of this phenomenon.
15. See Vitz, Chapter 4, "Chrétien de Troyes as A Minstrel."
16. Loomis, *Arthurian Romance*, p. 14.
17. Admittedly, the literary identities of

these authors were, for the most part, not revealed until after their deaths. Then one naturally asks, "Why not the same for Chrétien de Troyes?" Was he perhaps just *too* famous during his own day? In terms of contemporary fame, was he (figuratively speaking) in a class by himself?

18. Comfort, p. v.

Conclusion

1. C.S. Lewis, p. 1.

2. As discussed in Chapter 18, the French rendering of Geoffrey by Wace took what had originally been a mere suggestion of chivalry and tentatively expanded it, thus setting the stage for the next generation of French poets such as Marie and Chrétien.

3. Lack of such knowledge is often apparent in those who criticize Chrétien's romances as being childish or disjointed. A "mature" or "consistent" medieval artist by modern standards would never have found a livelihood.

4. Thanks to Hollywood, one could also include in this category a "Matter of Spain" with heroes such as El Cid, who were part of the same literary tradition at the beginning of the 12th century.

5. This represents a curious situation, since a closing of this gap helped to create the Arthurian romance as a genre (see chapter 4).

Bibliography

Online

Perhaps the best ongoing source for those seeking a more detailed analysis of this subject matter is the website for the International Arthurian Society (http://www.sites.univ-rennes2.fr/celam/ias/). Included are the proceedings of the 22nd triennial congress in Rennes, with numerous papers from the world's leading experts on a wide variety of Arthurian topics, including the work of Chrétien de Troyes. Many of these fascinating viewpoints will no doubt soon appear in other academic publications.

Selected English Translations of Arthurian Romances by Chrétien de Troyes

This bibliography represents a starting point for those who are curious to read more. Only one century ago it was very difficult to find any English translations whatsoever of the greatest western medieval poet before Dante. Now, fortunately, there are a number of outstanding efforts widely available to English readers that amply demonstrate Chrétien's genius, whether these translations be in prose or verse.

Although it is impossible to fully convey from Old French the power and range of Chrétien's rhymed octosyllabic couplets into English, Professor Ruth Harwood Cline of Georgetown University has come as close as anyone to date. Her series, published by the University of Georgia Press between 1975 and 2000, includes Chrétien's complete Arthurian cycle (*Erec and Enide, Cligès, Lancelot, Yvain,* and *Perceval*). These works are graced with extensive and perceptive footnote commentary, along with crystal-clear introductions by the translator herself. In addition, *Yvain* (the first in the series) features a thoughtful foreword by Professor Julian Harris of the University of Wisconsin. These are all indispensable and remain in a class by themselves.

Opting for a more free and unrhymed verse structure is Professor Burton Raffel of the University of Louisiana; this structure allows him to turn memorable phrases without resorting to prose. This complete cycle, published by Yale University Press between 1987 and 1999, makes fascinating comparison with the source above. Each volume includes a useful afterword by Professor Joseph J. Duggan of the University of California, Berkeley, who has written his own critical survey of Chrétien's works (see below).

Despite their inherent limitations, the original, classic English prose translations of Chrétien's first four Arthurian romances (not including *Perceval*) by William Wistar (W.W.) Comfort remain worthwhile reads. Originally published by J.M. Dent and Sons in 1914, they are now available as part of the Everyman Library.

In 1987, J.M. Dent and Everyman Library decided to publish an updated English prose translation of all of Chrétien's Arthurian romances (this time including *Perceval*) by Professor Douglas David Roy (D.D.R.) Owen of St. Andrews University in Scotland. The differences with the Comfort translation (published 73 years earlier) are striking and provocative. This volume also includes detailed explanatory notes, a glossary of terms, and selected bibliography.

Following hard on the heels of Owen was yet another English prose translation by Professor David Staines of the University of Ottawa, published by Indiana University Press in 1990. A close comparison between the Canadian vernacular of Staines and the formal British style of Owen will raise more than a few eyebrows. Aside from its quirkiness, another major selling point for Staines is the handy (but disputed) inclusion of *Guilluame d'Angleterre* (William of England). Also featured are extensive notes, an index of names, exhaustive bibliography, and variant Old French manuscript readings.

Last but not least, William Kibler's 1990 version of *Perceval* (edited by Rupert Pickens and published by Garland of New York) provides interesting, page-by-page comparison of the original Old French with the English translation in non-rhyming verse. This volume also includes a selected bibliography, index of proper names, notes, and exhaustive appendices on variant manuscript readings. Kibler also translated Chrétien's other Arthurian romances (with the exception of *Erec and Enide*, translated by Carleton Carroll), and all have been collected in a Penguin Books edition from 1991.

Other Primary and Secondary Sources

Adolf, Helen. *Visio Pacis: Holy City and Grail.* University Park: Pennsylvania State University Press, 1960.

Andreas Capellanus. *The Art of Courtly Love.* Translated by John Jay Parry. New York: Frederick Ungar, 1964.

Armstrong, Karen. *The Gospel According to Woman: Christianity's Creation of the Sex War in the West.* New York: Anchor Press/Doubleday, 1987.

_____. *A History of God.* New York: Ballantine, 1993.
_____. *Holy War: the Crusades and Their Impact on Today's World.* New York: Doubleday, 1988.
Baigent, Michael, Richard Leigh, and Henry Lincoln. *Holy Blood, Holy Grail.* New York: Random House, 1982.
Boase, Roger. *The Origin and Meaning of Courtly Love: A Critical Study of European Scholarship.* Manchester: Manchester University Press, 1977.
Bretagne Magazine (special issue). "La Légende du Roi Arthur," in conjunction with the exhibition "Le Roi Arthur: une légende en devenir" at Les Champs Libres, Rennes (Brittany), France. Brest: Bretagne-Publications, 2008.
Bullock-Davies, Constance. "Chrétien de Troyes and England," in *Arthurian Literature, Vol. 1.* Woodbridge, Suffolk: D.S. Brewer, 1981.
Chambers, E.K. *Arthur of Britain.* London: Sidgwick & Jackson, 1927.
Draco Normannicus. From *The Chronicles of the Reigns of Stephen, Henry II, and Richard I*, Vol. 82, No. 2, Richard Howlett, ed. London: Longman, 1884–1889.
Duggan, Joseph J. *The Romances of Chrétien de Troyes.* New Haven: Yale University Press, 2001.
Frappier, Jean. *Chrétien de Troyes, the Man and His Work.* Translated by Raymond J. Cornier. Athens: Ohio University Press, 1982.
Geoffrey of Monmouth. *The History of the Kings of Britain.* Translated and introduced by Lewis Thorpe. New York: Penguin Books, 1986.
_____. *The Vita Merlini.* Translated by John Jay Parry. Urbana: University of Illinois, 1925.
Gibbon, Edward. *The Decline and Fall of the Roman Empire* (Volumes I-III). Ed. J.B. Bury. New York: Modern Library, 1995.
Goering, Joseph. *The Virgin and the Grail.* New Haven: Yale University Press, 2005.
Grodecki, Louis. *The Stained Glass of French Churches.* Translated by Rosemary Edmunds and A.D.B. Sylvester. London: Lindsay Drummond, 1948.
Guyer, Foster Erwin. "The Influence of Ovid on Chrétien de Troyes." *Romantic Review*, Vol. 12, Nos. 2–3 (April-June and July-September, 1921).
Haskins, Charles H. *The Renaissance of the Twelfth Century.* Cleveland: World, 1965.
Holmes, Urban T. *Chrétien de Troyes.* New York: Twayne, 1970.
_____, and Sister M. Amelia Klenke. *Chrétien, Troyes, and the Grail.* Chapel Hill: University of North Carolina Press, 1959.
Jayyusi, Salma Khadra, ed. *The Legacy of Muslim Spain*, Vols. 1–2. New York: E.J. Brill, 1994.
Jung, Emma, and Marie-Louise von Franz. *The Grail Legend*, 2d ed. Translated by Andrea Dykes. Princeton: Princeton University Press, 1960/1998.
Kibler, William W., ed. *Eleanor of Aquitaine, Patron and Politician.* Austin: University of Texas Press, 1976.
Kienzie, Beverly Mayne. *Cistercians, Heresy, and Crusade in Occitania, 1145–1229: Preaching in the Lord's Vineyard.* Rochester: York Medieval Press, 2001.
Lacy, Norris J., and Joan Tasker Grimbert, eds. *A Companion to Chrétien de Troyes.* Cambridge: D.S. Brewer, 2005.
Leviant, Curt, ed., trans. *Melech Artus [King Artus]: A Hebrew Arthurian Romance of 1279.* New York: Ktav, 1969.
Lewis, C.S. *The Allegory of Love: A Study in Medieval Tradition.* London: Oxford University Press, 1936/1985.
Lewis, David Levering. *God's Crucible: Islam and the Making of Europe, 570–1215.* New York: W.W. Norton, 2008.
Loomis, Roger Sherman. *Arthurian Tradition and Chrétien de Troyes.* New York: Columbia University Press, 1961.

_____. *Celtic Myth and Arthurian Romance.* New York: Haskell House, 1967.
_____. *The Development of Arthurian Romance.* New York: Harper Torchbooks, 1963.
_____. *The Grail: From Celtic Myth to Christian Symbol.* New York: Columbia University Press, 1963.
_____, in collaboration with Laura Hibbard Loomis. *Arthurian Legends in Medieval Art.* Oxford: Oxford University Press, 1938.
Luttrell, Claude. *The Creation of the First Arthurian Romance.* Evanston: Northwestern University Press, 1974.
Marie de France. *The Lais of Marie de France.* Translated & introduced by Robert Hanning & Joan Ferrante. New York: E.P. Dutton, 1978.
Menocal, Maria Rosa. *Ornament of the World: How Muslims, Jews, and Christians Created a Culture of Tolerance in Medieval Spain.* Boston: Little, Brown, 2002.
Mickel, Emanuel J., Jr. *Marie de France.* New York: Twayne, 1974.
Nitze, William A. "Perceval and the Holy Grail: An Essay on the Romance of Chrétien de Troyes." *University of California Publications in Modern Philology*, Volume 28, No. 5, pp. viii; 281–332.
Ovid. *The Love Poems.* Translated by A.D. Melville with an introduction and notes by E.J. Kenny. Oxford: Oxford University Press, 1990.
_____. *Metamorphoses.* Translated by A.D. Melville with an introduction and notes by E.J. Kenny. Oxford: Oxford University Press, 1986.
Paris, Gaston. *Medieval French Literature.* Translated by Hannah Lynch. London: J.M. Dent, 1903.
Pickens, Rupert T., ed. *The Sower and His Seed: Essays on Chrétien de Troyes.* Lexington, KY: French Forum, 1983.
Reichert, Michelle. *Between Courtly Literature and Al-Andalus:* Matière d'Orient *and the Importance of Spain in the Romances of the Twelfth-Century Writer Chrétien de Troyes.* New York: Routledge, 2006.
"Le Roi Arthur: Une légende en devenir." Presentated at Les Champs Libres, Rennes, 15 July 2008 to 4 January 2009. Paris: Somogy editions d'art, 2008.
Setton, Kenneth M., ed. *The Age of Chivalry.* Washington, D.C.: National Geographic Society, 1969. This work provides an excellent beginner's overview of the Middle Ages supplemented by spectacular illustrations throughout, including a complete (and astonishing) color reproduction of the Bayeux Tapestry.
Sklar, Elizabeth S., and Donald Hoffman, eds. *King Arthur in Popular Culture.* Jefferson, NC: McFarland, 2002.
Topsfield, Leslie T. *Chrétien de Troyes: A Study of the Arthurian romances.* Cambridge: Cambridge University Press, 1981.
Tyerman, Christopher. *God's War: A New History of the Crusades.* Cambridge, MA: Harvard University Press, 2006.
Uitti, Karl D., with Michelle A. Freeman. *Chrétien de Troyes Revisited.* New York: Twayne, 1995.
Vitz, Evelyn Birge. *Orality and Performance in Early French Romance.* Rochester: D.S. Brewer, 1999.
Wace (Robert), and Layamon. *Arthurian Chronicles.* Translated by Eugene Mason, introduced by Gwyn Jones. New York: Everyman's Library, 1966.
Weston, Jessie L. *From Ritual to Romance,* Foreword by Robert A. Segal. Princeton: Princeton University Press, 1920/1993.
Whitaker, Muriel. *The Legends of King Arthur in Art.* Rochester: D.S. Brewer, 1990.

Index

Abelard, Peter 175
Adele (sister of Count Henry) 68
Adolf, Helen 144, 145, 186, 189, 191, 192
Alexander the Great 48, 101
Alexander III, Pope 144
Alphonso I, King 185
Andreas Capellanus see *Art of Courtly Love*
Androcles and the Lion 138
Angevin Empire 35, 53, 59, 61, 104, 105, 114, 129, 130, 177, 214, 218
Anselm, Saint 56, 65, 174, 176
Aquinas, Saint Thomas 25, 201, 235
Aristotle 25
Armstrong, Karen 21, 22, 24, 25, 39, 40, 42, 157, 171, 173–175, 191, 197, 222
Art of Courtly Love 13, 41 42, 48, 156, 218, 222, 230
Arthur, King 3, 7, 31–33, 76, 111, 120–124, 203, 218, 220
Arthur of Brittany 33, 114, 115, 227, 228
Aubert, Saint 173
Avalon, Isle of 33, 40, 69, 71, 74, 80, 96, 121, 166, 220, 224, 225, 232

Baigent, Michael 64, 224
Barbastro, Siege of 23, 128, 129, 217
Bastille Day (Rennes) 34
Beauty and the Beast (film) 73
Becket (film) 231
Becket, Saint Thomas à 149, 155–159, 176, 208, 218
Bedevere (Bedouer), Sir 81, 90, 96, 135
Benoît de Sainte-Maure 5, 6, 79, 223
Bernard of Clairvaux, Saint 25, 42, 56, 61, 65, 66, 158, 159, 173–177, 197, 217
Bernart de Ventadorn 220, 222
Béroul 41, 46, 222
Boase, Roger 22, 23, 221
Boccaccio 40, 97

Brocéliande (Paimpont) 71–73, 137, 166, 167, 232
Bulloch-Davies, Constance 70
Burton, Richard Francis 22

Caesar, Julius 101
Caesar Augustus 57
Camelot 1, 71, 74, 80, 91, 102, 104, 108, 115, 116, 155, 182, 221, 225
Camelot (film/musical) 4, 11, 166, 219
Camlann, Battle of 68, 116, 166
El Cantar de mio Cid 53, 80, 81, 88, 217, 236
Caradoc of Llancarfan 13, 121, 220, 225
Cathars 39, 63, 74, 224
Caxton, William 105, 109, 228
Le Centre de l'Imaginaire Arthurien 72, 166, 232
Cervantes, Miguel 106, 225
Chambers, E.K. 30, 33, 41, 78, 79, 82, 90, 180, 190
Le Chanson de Roland 53, 80, 81, 213, 217
Charlemagne 1, 127, 213, 229
Charles Martel 60
Chaucer 40, 97, 105
Chretien de Troyes: biography 4, 131, 205, 206; education 171, 198; geographic knowledge 67–75, 96, 177; personal attitudes 49–50, 183, 184, 198, 199
Cligès 14, 39, 43–52, 69, 70, 72, 83, 91–93, 97, 102, 134, 160–162, 181, 182, 214
Cline, Ruth Harwood 2, 6, 11, 12, 15–17, 42, 44, 45, 47–49, 70, 73, 97–99, 116, 134, 138, 139, 141, 181–184, 205, 206, 219, 221–223, 225, 230, 231, 234
Comfort, W.W. 2, 16, 17, 32, 48, 60, 66, 99, 139, 209
Conrad III 196, 230
Constance of Brittany 33
Crusade, Children's 62

Crusade, First 114, 118, 146, 185, 217, 228, 234
Crusade, Second 144, 158, 177, 178, 196, 199, 217, 230, 232
Crusade, Third 106, 114, 119, 147, 159, 218, 221, 232
Crusade, Fourth 119, 218
Crusade, Seventh 218
Crusade, Eighth 218
Crusade, Ninth 218
Crusades, Albigensian 62–66, 68, 74, 193, 218

Dante 2, 82, 148, 212
Da Vinci Code 64, 179, 193
Didot Perceval 180
Dominic, Saint 61
Draco Normannicus 32, 91
Duggan, Joseph 2, 11, 14, 42, 55, 57, 70, 95, 100, 136, 137, 167, 168, 179, 180, 182, 219, 221, 226, 227
Duval, Paulette 234

Ecclesia 190, 191, 195–202
Elaine (wife of Lancelot) 15
Eleanor of Aquitaine 14, 24, 35, 36, 39–42, 44, 53, 54, 56, 60, 61, 67–70, 90, 101, 104, 105, 114, 129, 131, 133, 161, 166, 175, 185, 186, 214, 217, 218, 220–222, 230, 232
Eliot, T.S. 105, 231, 234
Elisabeth (niece of Eleanor) 40, 186
English Channel (*La Manche*) 29, 68, 69, 72, 73, 110, 114, 130, 133, 223, 225
Erec and Enide 13, 21, 30, 32, 38, 40, 42–45, 47, 68, 69, 73, 91, 94–103, 115, 116, 123, 138, 140, 142, 160–162, 168, 177, 181, 184, 196, 206, 214, 219, 224, 226–228, 230, 232
Étienne de Rouen see *Draco Normannicus*
Eugene II, Pope 173, 197
Eustace, Saint 160
Excalibur 92, 228

Faral, E. 219
Ferrante, Joan 2, 40
First Knight (film) 228
A Fistful of Dollars (film) 112
Flagentanis 74
Foerster, Wendelin 138, 159, 219
Foster, Hal 229
Foster, I.L. 233
Foulque, King 190
Fourrier, Anthime 6, 179, 219, 223
Fox, John 222
Franklin, Benjamin 38
Frappier, Jean 6, 42, 136, 191, 219, 230

Frazer, J.G. 234
Frederick Barbarossa 51, 67

Galahad, Sir 15, 116, 135, 181
Gautier de Châtillon 199
Gawain, Sir 40, 77, 91, 92, 94, 96–98, 101, 115–117, 121, 135, 138, 140, 170, 182–184, 190, 192, 226–229, 232
Genghis Khan 119
Geoffrey, Duke of Brittany 33, 69, 101
Geoffrey of Monmouth 5, 26, 31, 32, 36, 37, 56, 58, 65, 68, 72, 75–83, 89, 90, 92, 95, 96, 116, 125, 129, 135, 136, 159, 165, 166, 173, 190, 200, 203, 204, 211, 213, 217, 220–222, 224–229, 230, 236
Geoffrey Plantagenet (father of Henry II) 130, 222
Gerbert de Montreuil 233
Gereint, Son of Erbin 30
Gibbon, Edward 3, 5, 7, 19, 22, 31, 76, 78, 79, 119, 124, 132, 143–145, 147, 228, 230, 231
Giffen, Lois A. 22, 221
Gildas, Saint 157, 220
Godefroy de Leigny 14
Godfrey of Bouillon 114
Goering, Joseph 185, 193
Grail Quest Theme 1, 2, 12, 15, 47, 55, 59, 62, 64, 65, 72–75, 91, 108, 109, 143–145, 150, 159, 178, 181, 186–194, 200, 201, 207, 211, 214, 225, 233
Graindor de Brie 123
Greenhill, Eleanor S. 222
Gregory VIII, Pope 147
Grodecki, Louis 235
Guide for the Perplexed 25, 235
Guinevere, Queen 2, 11–18, 37, 39, 40, 42, 43, 48, 80, 93, 96, 108, 115, 121, 135, 170, 183, 200, 211, 219, 228
Guingamar 40, 69, 97, 227
Guy of Lusignan 144–146

Hadrian IV, Pope 176
Hanning, Robert 2, 40
Harold of Wessex 113
Harris, Julian 2, 219, 228
Hastings, Battle of 113, 128, 228
Hattin, Battle of 106, 145–147, 149, 159, 185, 218
Hélinand of Froidmont 64
Héloïse (and Peter Abelard) 175
Henry of Blois 82, 154, 156, 226
Henry II, King 14, 32, 33, 35, 53, 59–61, 67, 69, 70, 101, 104, 105, 114, 131, 133, 149, 155, 156, 161, 173, 175, 177, 208, 214, 218, 221, 222, 231
Henry "the Liberal," Count of Champagne

13, 51, 54, 55, 67, 68, 71, 131, 136, 150, 156, 161, 174, 177, 185, 186, 196, 199, 200, 208, 218, 224, 232–234
Henry "the Lion" of Saxony 51
Herman of Carinthia 25
Hildegard von Bingen, Saint 56, 65, 66, 175, 176, 185, 232
Hobbes, Thomas 226
Hoel, King 40, 69, 81, 90
Hofer, Stephan 190
Holmes, Urban 4, 12, 37, 46, 49, 53, 54, 56, 58, 65, 96, 98, 123, 131, 134, 135, 159, 180, 187, 188, 190–192, 194, 196, 197, 204, 205, 219, 220, 223, 227, 230, 233–235
Holy Grail *see* "Grail Quest"
Homer 212
Hospitallers 87, 94, 145
Hugh of Champagne (Hugh of Troyes) 158, 177
Hugh of Lagny 54, 71, 161, 224
Hundred Years War 105–107

Ibn Hazm 22, 23, 36, 128, 150, 217
Ibn Rushd (Averroës) 25, 221
Ibn Sina (Avicenna) 232
Ider, Sir 121
Innocent III, Pope 63
International Arthurian Society 33, 63
Isabelle of Hainaut (wife of Philip II) 184
Isaiah 165

Joan of Arc 105
John, King 33, 114, 115, 221
John of Salisbury 176, 232
Jullian, Réne 121

Kay, Sir 81, 90–92, 96–98, 115, 121, 135, 136, 148, 227–229
Kibler, William 183, 184
Kingdom of Heaven (film) 75, 146, 230
Kingdom of Jerusalem (*Outremer*) 114, 118, 143, 145, 148, 150, 178, 198
Klenke, Anne 123, 188, 190, 191, 197, 235
Knight, Stephen 145
Knights of the Roundtable (film) 4, 231
Kyot, the Provençal 74

Lancelot 1, 11–20, 23, 26, 28, 37–40, 43, 47–50, 57–69, 62, 71, 72, 80, 83, 91, 97, 102, 108, 115, 116, 121, 135, 136, 148, 150, 160, 162, 170, 173, 177, 179, 180, 185, 200, 204, 210, 211, 214, 219, 220, 224, 225, 228
Lancelot-Grail (Vulgate) Cycle 12, 115, 116, 180, 225, 228, 233
Layamon 91

Lazar, Moshé 40
Leviant, Curt 201
Lewis, C.S. 11, 18, 26, 36–39, 41, 42, 52–56, 59, 94, 96, 134, 137, 138, 168, 203, 211, 220
Lewis, David Levering 22–25
Life of Saint Cardoc 225
Life of Saint Gildas 13, 121, 225
Lohengrin 116, 181
Loholt (son of Arthur) 115, 116, 228
Loomis, Roger Sherman 1, 3, 4, 12, 24, 28, 30, 31, 37–39, 46, 79, 82, 91, 103, 110, 120, 121, 123–125, 136, 164, 168, 180, 187, 189, 192, 207, 219, 221, 225, 227, 229, 231
Louis, Saint (King Louis IX) 218
Louis VII, King 51, 54, 60, 67, 155, 173, 177, 185, 186, 196, 217, 218, 221, 230, 231, 234
Luttrell, Claude 2, 4, 219

Mabinogion 30, 31, 219
Magna Carta 114, 155
Maimonides 25, 201, 221, 235
Malory, Thomas 1, 12, 71, 73, 77, 103–111, 126, 131, 135, 203, 208, 225, 227, 228
Manessier 233
Manuel Comnenus, Emperor 51, 177
Mappa Mundi 68
Marcabru 220, 222
Marco Polo 218
Marie de France 2, 13, 19, 23, 32, 40, 41, 53, 58, 127, 129, 156, 211, 213, 218, 222, 236
Marie of Champagne 4, 12–14, 24, 39, 40, 41, 43, 44, 51, 54–56, 62, 67, 90, 185, 186, 200, 209, 218, 220, 222, 223, 230, 232, 234
Matilda, Queen 130, 151
"Matter of Britain" 2, 30, 31, 53, 58, 80, 82, 83, 213, 214, 223
"Matter of France" 53, 213, 214, 223
"Matter of Rome" 53, 56, 213, 214, 223
McCash, June Hall 222
Melech Artus 200–202
Menocal, Maria Rosa 23, 63, 128, 229
Merlin 11, 80, 96, 163–170, 217, 231, 232
Merlin (TV series) 167, 200
Michael, Saint 173
Mickle, Emmanuel 37, 40, 222
Modena (Cathedral) 13, 121, 122, 124, 191, 229
Molière 208
Mont Saint Michel 72, 81, 173, 232
Montaigne 208
Montségur 74, 75, 225
Monty Python and the Holy Grail (film) 135, 159, 230

Mordred 80, 115, 116, 228
Morgan le Fay 69, 72, 80, 96, 97, 109, 135, 225, 227, 228
Le Morte d'Arthur 1, 77, 105, 108, 227

Neck-Ring of the Dove 22, 23, 128, 217, 220
Nennius 231
Nitze, William 219
Notre Dame Cathedral 218
Nureddin 136, 230

Otranto (Cathedral) 122–124, 173, 191, 229
Ovid 12, 23, 41, 45–47, 55–57, 97, 160, 176, 220, 222, 231
Owein (*The Lady of the Fountain*) 30, 136
Owen *see* Yvain
Owen, D.D.R. 2, 4, 5, 16, 17, 48, 99, 137, 139, 183, 184

Paris, Gaston 2, 70, 204, 222
Parry, John 22, 23, 156, 220, 222
Parzifal 71, 74, 88, 180
Paul, Saint 162, 177, 182, 199, 205
Perceval 1, 15, 21, 30, 42, 47, 50, 73, 74, 87, 91, 92, 94, 100, 102, 108, 116, 117, 121, 142, 143, 146–148, 150, 158, 162, 168, 175, 179–195, 197–199, 200, 204, 205, 210, 214, 219, 224, 225, 227, 232–234
Perceval (film) 233
Peredur 30, 180
Perlesvaus 180, 228
Perros Relief 120, 121
Peter Abelard 56, 174, 175
Peter Comestor 198, 223
Peter the Venerable 25, 174–176, 217
Petrarch 97
Philip of Flanders, Count 4, 74, 93, 147, 156, 184–186, 190, 199, 218, 232, 233
Philip II (Augustus), King 33, 54, 147, 184–186, 196, 199, 218, 231, 233, 234
Philomena 24, 57, 167, 223, 231, 232, 235
Placidas, Saint 160
Plato 25
Poitiers, Battle of 60–61, 106
Pre-Raphaelites 139, 169, 232
Prince Valiant (film) 127

The Qur'an 25, 175, 217

Rabbeinu Tam 196
Raffel, Burton 15–17, 48, 93, 99, 134, 138, 139, 180, 183, 184, 233–235
Rahn, Otto 64, 224, 225
Rashi 196, 234
Raymond of Toulouse 234
Reynald of Châtillon 145, 146

Richard I, King 33, 60, 114, 147–149, 184, 185, 221, 224
Robert de Boron 180, 192, 207, 208
Robert Guiscard 112, 114
Robert of Ketton 25
Robert Pullen 176
Roger I, King 112
Roger Le Cointe 161
Roman d'Alexandre 56, 188
Roman de Brut 78, 89, 218
Roman d'Enéas 24, 48, 56, 79, 223
Roman de Rou 167
Roman de Thébes 56
Roman de Troie 56
Roundtable (image) 90, 91
Routrou II 185, 186

Saint Denis Basilica 177, 191, 197, 217, 222
Saint-Etienne (Châlon-en-Champagne) 197, 198
Saladin 118, 144–148, 218, 221, 230
Shakespeare, William 2, 26, 37, 45, 49, 57, 64, 70, 77, 81, 82, 97, 103, 105, 106, 115, 119, 140, 161, 176, 199, 203, 206–209, 219, 221–223, 232, 235
Sir Gawain and the Green Knight 116, 228
Staines, David 16, 17, 48, 91, 99, 139, 183, 184, 204, 221, 234
Stephen, King 131
The Story of English (documentary) 229
Suger, Abbot 177, 191, 197
Sword and the Stone (film) 166
Synagoga 190, 195–202

Taliesin 135, 221, 231, 232
Tancred de Hauteville 112
Templars 87, 89, 94, 145, 149, 158, 177, 217, 225
Tennyson, Alfred 105, 131, 159, 203, 211, 225
Theobald, Archbishop of Canterbury 176
Theobald, Count of Blois 158
Thierry of Alsace 158
Thierry of Flanders 185
Thomas of Britain 41, 46, 47, 223
Thorpe, Lewis 78, 203, 226
Tintagel 73, 101, 224
Topsfield, Leslie 2, 187, 222
Tristan (and Isolde) legend 12, 40, 41, 43, 46, 47, 49, 96, 108, 109, 220, 222, 223
Troyes 89, 149, 150, 158, 162, 171, 195–198, 205, 214, 217, 218
Twain, Mark 70, 159, 169, 203, 232
Tyerman, Christopher 21, 63, 111, 119, 145, 147, 177, 185, 231

Uitti, Karl 116, 174
Urban III, Pope 147
Urien, King 135

Virgil 5, 48, 56, 75, 79, 97, 176, 212, 220, 223
Virgin Mary 39, 65, 193, 222, 226, 234
Vitz, Evelyn Birge 206

Wace 56, 58, 65, 73, 79, 82, 89–91, 95, 96, 129, 135, 159, 166, 190, 200, 211, 213, 218, 221, 222, 226, 228, 236
Wagner, Richard 5, 6, 74, 180, 213, 219
Walter Map 233
Walter von der Vogelweide 88, 148
War of the Roses 105
Warwick, 13th Earl (Richard de Beauchamp) 107, 227
Warwick, 16th Earl (Richard Neville) 107, 227
Welsh Triads 231
Weston, Jessie 189, 190, 192, 234

White, T.H. 76, 77, 105, 203
William II, King 124, 130, 229
William VIII, Duke 23, 128, 217, 229
William IX, Duke 24, 40, 54, 62, 129, 208, 220
William X, Duke 23
William de Hauteville ("Iron Arm") 112
William of England (*Guillaume d'Angleterre*) 50, 54, 70, 160,-162
William of Malmesbury 78
William of Newburg 79
William the Conqueror 30, 54, 67, 81, 89, 105, 113, 130–132, 185, 228, 229
William "the White Hands" (Guillaume aux Blanche Mains) 54, 156, 198
Wolfram von Eschenbach 71, 74, 75, 88, 180, 207, 224, 225, 233

Yvain 13, 29, 30, 39, 40, 42, 47, 50, 57, 72, 73, 91, 98, 102, 116, 117, 133–142, 150, 162, 167, 168, 210, 214, 219, 220, 222, 223, 225, 230, 232

www.ingramcontent.com/pod-product-compliance
Ingram Content Group UK Ltd.
Pitfield, Milton Keynes, MK11 3LW, UK
UKHW041937140426
5217IPUK00014B/529